T0118585

TRANSLATING NATIONS

THE DOLPHIN

General Editor:
Dominic Rainsford

30

TRANSLATING NATIONS

Edited by
Prem Poddar

AARHUS UNIVERSITY PRESS

AARHUS UNIVERSITY PRESS
Langelandsgade 177
DK-8200 Aarhus N, Denmark
Fax (+45) 8942 5380
URL: www.au.dk/unipress

73 Lime Walk
Headington, Oxford OX3 7AD
Fax (+44) 1865 750 079

Box 511
Oakville, Conn. 06779
Fax (+1) 860 945 9468

Editorial address:
THE DOLPHIN
Department of English
University of Aarhus
DK-8000 Aarhus C, Denmark
Fax (+45) 8942 6540

This volume is published with financial support from the Aarhus
University Research Foundation
Cover illustration by Anmole Prasad

Contents

Introduction: Violent Civilities

Prem Poddar

> Then all the nations of birds lifted together
> the huge net of the shadows of this earth
> in multitudinous dialects, twittering tongues,
> stitching and crossing it...
>
> Derek Walcott

The history of the nation as a political, conceptual and emotional entity shows it to be contradictory and internally antagonistic. The birth of the modern, liberal nation-state offered the ground for universal rights and for a radical concept of freedom, yet the social institutions which sprung from it have repeatedly been identified with new forms of inequality and coercion, both within its borders and beyond them. And while the nation promised a new form of political affiliation and emotional identification freed from the prejudices of particularity and the accidents of tradition, it has repeatedly provided the justification for prejudice and violence in the name of a privileged particularity or tradition. Indeed, this violent equivocation between the universal and the particular has come to be recognised as somehow fundamental to the nation, an insight shared by a range of critical responses which have disputed the nation's placid self-image, its understanding of itself as uniform, homogenous and at peace. Yet these critical responses have each in turn, despite their differences, been found to remain subject to the same dangerous equivocation between universality and particularity which has bedevilled the nation, a recognition that has given rise over recent years to announcements of the end not so much of the nation, but of the critical projects which hoped to move beyond it.

Translating Nations, ed. Prem Poddar, *The Dolphin* 30, pp. 7-12.
© 1999 by Aarhus University Press, Denmark.
ISBN 87 7288 381 2; ISSN 0106 4487.

The impulse behind this present collection of essays is to develop approaches which register these changes in thinking the nation, but which also resist easy pronouncements of ending, redundancy or supersession. For in recognising that this equivocation lies at the heart of both the nation and its critique, then the fate of the nation itself must be understood as equivocal, offering both the promise of violence and of different futures to come. The collection takes the return of this violent equivocation not as announcing the end of the nation and the discourses which have surrounded it, but as marking their uncanny or differential persistence within a radically new context.

Central to the different critical responses to the nation has been the awareness that the nation cannot be conceived of in isolation, and that the project of rethinking the nation cannot be conceived as the search for historical and sociological explanations of the internal coherence of national identities. Contemporary theory has developed a conceptual vocabulary which stresses the cultural formation of the nation through narratives of identity, origin and progress, and has emphasised the violent repression of difference involved in nationalist myths of pure identity and the assertion of national unity as consensual common culture.[1] Such a redescription of the nation works to acknowledge the complexities of cultural difference by raising the question of translation, a paradigm which returns anew to the equivocations that bedevil the discourses of the nation. Translation draws attention to the contortions, occlusions and distortions involved in cultural transmission—the violence within and between nations—while also raising the prospect of transnational narratives or articulations which might recognise—and even celebrate—the multiple and different voices within and across modern communities.

As a consequence, the paradigm of translation also questions the direction or ordering of cultural transmission, of the traffic between and within the nation, an impulse which has keenly marked contemporary theory. In questioning notions of identity and belonging in the recently decolonised areas of the globe, contemporary theory has also identified the need to raise similar questions in areas conventionally located at the centre. But the paradigm of translation also poses important questions for contemporary theory, since at its core lies a paradoxical conception of persistence *and* change. If translation always involves difference and misrecognition, it also involves a kind of persistence and recognition. And if contemporary theory translates the histories of the nation, and of its discourses and counter discourses, into the terrain of the present, these histories are both lost and returned, superseded and restored.

It is in this spirit that Graham MacPhee's essay identifies significant conceptual resources for approaching the difficult combination of persistence and change in the work of Walter Benjamin. The relevance of Benjamin here lies in his consideration of Enlightenment conceptions of the nation within the global transformations which mark modernity. MacPhee argues that this aspect of Benjamin's writing has not been recognised because it is often couched in terms of the aesthetic, and so before discussing Benjamin's short essay 'Theories of German Fascism' MacPhee reads Kant's account of the nation-state in 'Perpetual Peace' in some detail. In this way Benjamin's thinking is seen to identify in the aftermath of the violent release of the First World War the emergence of a new global topography which radically transforms the fate of the nation. MacPhee argues that Benjamin's thinking offers an important and neglected engagement with some of the central theoretical issues involved in the contemporary project of rethinking the nation.

Such insights into the violence of national constitution and European colonialism also inform Poddar and Mealor's analysis of Peter Høeg's novel *Miss Smilla's Feeling for Snow*. Considering Høeg's novel in terms of the spatial and temporal polarities of inside and outside, Poddar and Mealor identify a conceptual ambivalence in the text's representation of identity that can be seen to demonstrate the limits of multiculturalism. In Lars Jensen's essay, the representation of space and colonialism in contemporary Australian and Canadian writing is situated within the peculiar predicament of a national identity which, in important ways, remains trapped in the colonial shadow. While the critique of European patterns of domination has enjoyed wide-spread support in intellectual circles as well as on a more popular level, Jensen argues that the continued violence against aboriginal peoples (along with an insufficiently grounded multiculturalist sensibility) prevents a more critically aware approach to national identity formation from emerging.

The urgent need for a reassessment of traditional conceptions is underscored by Mahesh Daga's exemplary reading of vernacular archives that contain the national imaginary of the Hindi heartland. The all-too-easy assumption in political theory and historiography, however revisionist, of unruffled translatability of terms such as *jati* into 'nation' is brought into crisis by suggesting the myriad uses of local vocabulary, of the perceptibility of metonymic gaps. David Johnson's piece similarly notes the constitution of the Griqua nation by colonial voices with particular attention to the different inflections of the missionaries, the colonial officials at the Cape, and the metropolitan colonial administrators in Whitehall. The focus in re-reading these texts is on the problems colonial authorities had in deciding whether the Griqua constituted a 'tribe', a 'state', a 'captaincy', a 'horde', or a 'nation'. Another concern is to note early testimony by Griqua leaders collected in Imperial Blue Books and commissions of the colonial governments in which 'the Griqua' themselves assume the colonial definitions imposed on them. Was this a case of successful cultural imperialism, or an instance of resistant mimicry?

Where Johnson undertakes a meticulous close reading of some key colonial Griqua texts in order to disclose the violence occluded in the category of the 'nation', Hans Hauge ranges widely over many disparate contexts in his discussion of nations and literatures. He questions Johnson's thoughts on the Rainbow Nation in post-apartheid South Africa by charging postcolonial theory (as represented by Boehmer) with a (neo)Kantian epistemology.[2] For Hauge, Said's *Orientalism* then becomes 'Arab postmodern'.

In attempting to map out the cultural specificity of a particular nationalism, Neluka Silva's essay shows how overdetermined ethnic identities are pivotal to nationalist rhetoric in a post-1983 Sri Lanka which has seen civil war, terrorism and inter-communal massacres. Ideological assumptions carried over from colonialism to nationalism not only perpetuate ethnic and class inequalities, but also continue to circumscribe the subject positions of women.[3] Political violence and nationalist constructions of masculine and feminine identities are prefigured in the fiction, poetry and plays that Silva deftly examines.

Through an examination of texts written across several national languages, Caroline Bergvall argues that such texts inherently question not only the grounds of monolingualism but also the nature of the two-way traffic of conventionalised translation. The notion of translation as a productive or writerly practice forms an important aspect of her paper's argument, which explores the implications of this conception of translation for personal and cultural memory. Meena Alexander's piece is a reflection on the migrant's urgent need to articulate the 'violent edge' that marks any process of cultural translation. Crossing borders and moving between poems, autobiography, critical analysis and social commentary, she describes how a 'febrile, perilous translation' is at work in the manufacture of a self. The reality of historical experience and its inscription on the page are both filled with the divisive imagery of borderlines, which often carry over—at least to the mind—spaces where immigrant experience remains largely unwritten, even impossible to write: refugee camps, detention centres, illegal alien transports, border patrols.

This collection of essays proceeds on the assumption that there are fascinating connections, anomalies, and differences in how the nation has been translated in the different contexts discussed, and in drawing material and insights from such different contexts it is hoped that valuable and perhaps unexpected affiliations might emerge. Kosovo and East Timor make this task of remembering and re-imagining the complicated histories of such affiliations all the more pressing, and point with renewed urgency to the importance of both remembering the nation and thinking beyond it.

Notes

1. The most influential account, of course, is the volume *Nation and Narration*, ed. Homi Bhabha (London: Routledge, 1991).
2. In response to Kant's famous answer to the question 'Was ist Aufklärung', Foucault picks on the suggestion that Enlightenment holds out the possibility of 'maturity' for all 'mankind': 'A ... difficulty appears here in Kant's text, in his use of the word 'mankind', *Menschheit*. The importance of this word in the

Kantian conception of history is well known. Are we to understand that the entire human race is caught up in the process of Enlightenment? In that case, we must imagine Enlightenment as a historical change that affects the political and social existence of all people on the face of the earth. Or are we to understand that it involves a change affecting what constitutes the humanity of human beings?' ('What is Enlightenment?', *The Foucault Reader: An Introduction to Foucault's Thought*, ed. Paul Rabinow [Harmondsworth: Penguin, 1991] 35). The Kantian prescriptive conception of 'mankind' cannot contain the radical heterogeneity of human nature. The supposedly universal make-up of human existence is limited to the normative order of adult rationality. Dialogue with other ways of being human thus becomes impossible in this order of things. The non-adult becomes inhuman and then it's a short step (toddle) to the pedagogic difference between European adulthood and its childish Other. For critiques of Foucault's own eurocentrism see Gayatri Spivak, 'Can the Subaltern Speak?', *Marxism and the Interpretation of Culture*, ed. Cary Nelson and Lawrence Grossberg (Urbana: U of Illinois P, 1988); Ann Laura Stoler, *Race and the Education of Desire*, (Durham, NC: Duke UP, 1995); Homi Bhabha, *The Location of Culture* (London: Routledge, 1994). Moral agency in the Kantian sense is dependent on our detachment from the contingencies of our human-ness. Contrary to this, a postcolonial ethics has been particularly committed to a notion of morality that is predicated upon the contaminants of everyday existence, where the ethical agent is a constitutively hybrid entity—a self with all its intrasubjective complexities.

3. Partha Chatterjee's seminal work on the rupture between the 'problematic' and the 'thematic' in anti-colonial nationalisms has been productively translated by scholars to account for the once-active subordination of 'women's politics'.

An Intimate Violence:
Crossing Borders, Making Poems

Meena Alexander

Somehow there is a violent edge to the process of cultural translation I find myself involved in as a writer, the shifting worlds I inhabit, the borders I cross in my dreams. What does it mean to produce art in a condition of migrancy, I ask myself. The attempt to make up a self requires a febrile, perilous translation. And at times this species of translation sets up powerful reverberations between the activities of decolonization and the fraught world of multicultural America.

I am thinking now of questions of language and embodiment in the racialised world in which I find myself. And gender cannot be set aside. It is not something added to race—that curious, explosive social construct—nor indeed to ethnicity, rather it is an irreducible part of both. Awhile back I was giving a reading in Cambridge, Massachusetts, in a bookstore. I read prose pieces, poems, ending with the last two sections of 'San Andreas Fault'. A woman raised her hand. She picked out details from the poem: 'How can you allow these facts of the world, terrible things we would not normally want to think about, get into your poem? What does it do to your life?'

I was quiet for a bit, I took a while to respond, musing on the section of the poem she had picked out. It begins with a speaker, a woman who enters a dream state. At the end of her vision she faces her muse, a weightless creature, born of air, who has forced her to this:

> Late at night in Half Moon Bay
> hair loosed to the glow of traffic lights
> I slit the moist package of my dreams.
>
> Female still, quite metamorphic

Translating Nations, ed. Prem Poddar, *The Dolphin* 30, pp. 13-22.
© 1999 by Aarhus University Press, Denmark.
ISBN 87 7288 381 2; ISSN 0106 4487.

I flowed into Kali ivory tongued, skulls nippling my breasts
Durga lips etched with wires astride an electric tiger
Draupadi born of flame betrayed by five brothers stripped
of silks in the banquet hall of shame.

In the ghostly light of those women's eyes
I saw the death camps at our century's end

A woman in Sarajevo shot to death
as she stood pleading for a pot of milk,
a scrap of bread, her red scarf swollen
with lead hung in a cherry tree.

Turks burnt alive in the new Germany,
a grandmother and two girls
cheeks puffed with smoke
as they slept in striped blankets
bought new to keep out the cold.

A man and his wife in Omdurman
locked to a starving child, the bone's right
to have and hold never to be denied,
hunger stamping the light.

In Ayodhya, in Ram's golden name
hundreds hacked to death, the domes
of Babri Masjid quivering as massacres begin—
the rivers of India rise mountainous,
white veils of the dead, dhotis, kurtas, saris,
slippery with spray, eased from their bloodiness.

Shaking when I stopped I caught myself short
firmly faced her 'What forgiveness here?'
'None' she replied 'Every angel knows this.
The damage will not cease and this sweet gorge
by which you stand bears witness.

'Become like me a creature of this fault.' ...[1]

   She was in the back of the room, a small, neat looking woman, her brown hair drawn back and she was waiting for an answer. 'There are two things,' I began, 'and they stand apart, then come together. One is the music of poetry. Not something I am altogether conscious about, but it works with the language, and it allows the thoughts, the "facts" if you will—the terror, the violence—to be raised up, so that even as we see them imprinted in consciousness, there is a hairbreadth that allows release, allows for the transcendence poetry seeks.'

'Then my personal life.' At this I stopped, took a sip of water, looked around the small room, the faces listening intently, the windows with the white shutters letting in a pearly light. The shutters looked as if they were cut from rice paper. Outside it was spring sunshine, magnolias on the brink of bursting into light, croci prickling through the grass, spurts of people among the old parked cars, the gas station on the other side of Hampshire Road.

I took courage from all that lay around and the women and men listening in the small back room.

'I bring the intensity of my inner life, very personal emotions, into relation with these "facts" of the world. I may be standing in the kitchen looking out of the window, or washing grains of rice for dinner. Or I may be folding a pile of laundry, yet within me there is an emotion that the gesture of my hands cannot reach.

'And often there is news of the world that reaches me. And I contemplate it. So really it is by looking long and hard, allowing the intensity of that otherness to enter in, that the charged rhythm of the poem, its music comes. Breaks out onto the page.'

I may not have said all this at the time, and I wanted to speak of something that was too hard for me at the time: the migration of sense a poem requires, the way writing is tied up for me with loss, with what forces forgetfulness and yet at the very same time permits passage.

'A bridge that seizes crossing' I wrote in a poem trying to touch the edge of migrancy that underwrites the sensible world for me. The poem is called 'River and Bridge' and I wrote it at a time when I felt that I needed to begin another life, to be born again. And now I think, for me, to be born again is to pass beyond the markings of race, the violations visited on us:

River and Bridge

Trees on the other side of the river
so blue, discarding light into water, a flat

white oil tank with HESS in black, a bridge
Holzer might skim with lights—*I will take her*
down before she feels the fear—no sarcophagus here:

I have come to the Hudson's edge to begin my life
to be born again, to seep as water might
in a landscape of mist, burnished trees,
a bridge that seizes crossing.

But Homer knew it and Vyasa too, black river
and bridge summon those whose stinging eyes
crisscross red lights, metal implements,
battlefields: birth is always bloody.

But what of the ordinary self, I also want to ask, the woman who cooks, and cleans and shops, who fixes breakfast for her children in the morning? How does she enter into this complex internal transformation? Can her acts of dailiness provide the frame of the present for her poem? In the intensity of making art doesn't the common 'I' slip away? Or to put it in harsher terms, isn't the 'I' crossed out? Now one might think of this loss of self as one of the glories of writing. Yet there are grave difficulties here. Hardships of return, of figuring out home.

I was born in India and grew up both in that country and in the Sudan. Indeed for much of each year of my childhood—due to my father's work—I lived in Khartoum. That city by the Nile was where I grew up, where I learnt to read and write and savor the power of words. My earliest poems, composed when I was a teenager, were written in both English and French. I experimented with both languages. But since almost no reading public existed for literature in English, my friends translated my earliest poems into Arabic and they were published in the local newspaper in Khartoum. Now, though I used to speak Arabic quite well, I am illiterate in it. So I had the odd sensation as a young poet of being on the outside of a transparent pane of glass.

'I have seen your new poem,' someone would say to me in class, or when I was walking down the road in the university. 'What did you think of it?' I'd ask. 'I really liked it,' he would say, or sometimes: 'I wasn't so sure what to make of it.'

With the 'real poem', then, cut from me, by my own lack of access to the written language of the public world, the poem I had composed remained in my lined notebook, a secret thing, its script fluttering on the thin page. Sometimes I would wonder at the miracle of it all. At other times, I would muse on how long I could last in this fragile, translated sphere.

In 1969 I left Khartoum for ever. The civil war was raging there, and the military government that had overthrown the democracy movement was making life hard for foreigners. Many of my Sudanese friends left too, for Europe, for countries in the Gulf, some for further studies in India. In Britain where I want as a student, I found that the stickiness of my studies, doses of phenomenological theory, of early English Romanticism, as well as my own unspelt pain at dislocation, kept me from the fluidity of a world that worked so effortlessly into poems. Surrounded by British English, now a public language, I found that new poems were not coming so easily. And when they came they did not attach me to a living breathing landscape.

It was only a return to India, in my very early twenties, with the rich multiplicity of tongues that flowed all around, riots in the market place, furor in the academies, the voices of fathers, mothers and sisters, that I was able to pick up the inner history that I need in the poems I make.

As an immigrant to North America I have often felt I was living in a place where I had no history. I've had to write out my past in order to draw upon it, invent the story which made me possible. Sometimes as I worked on the memoir I was filled with nightmares, and feared that when the writing was done I too would come to a quick, even abrupt end—fall off the subway platform, be run over by a bus while crossing Broadway, dark dreams of transport and its fatal end.

I called the book *Fault Lines* as in the cracks that mark the earth after an earthquake, revealing a disturbance beneath. And for me those lines disruptive of the possibility of a clear hold of place, a single, uncomplicated geography, are also part of my ongoing story. But this image of faults in the earth would not make sense without other threads that run through the work: growing up female, and growing up in a diasporic world. And indeed my awareness on the one hand of femaleness and on the other of a colonialism that was bit by bit being dismantled, fused at times into a molten emotion that rendered coming to memory rather hard. And of course there is yet another element here, something that I need to stay with, brood on, in the months to come, for the new poems I am working on, the ways in which as a child I learnt 'race' precisely by having to travel, enter a diasporic world. And how those childhood ways of learning have marked my sense of what it means to be an Indian woman, here, now, in North America.

But to return to the memoir, while working on *Fault Lines* I had a sense that I was in the grip of two kinds of memory that seemed to have little connection with each other. This difficulty almost halted me in the autobiographical act, till I thought to myself, making a virtue of necessity, if you can't really piece them together, making them into a fluent whole, just run them into one another, let them collide and see what happens.

What follows is a piece from a chapter called 'Katha'. In Sanskrit the word very simply means story, any kind of story. And perhaps this story is about coming home and then leaving utterly:

Sometimes I am torn apart by two sorts of memory, two opposing ways of being towards the past. The first makes whorls of skin and flesh, coruscating shells glittering in moonlight. A life embedded in a life, and that in another life, another and another. Rooms within rooms, each filled with its own scent: rosehips, neem leaves, dried hibiscus leaves that hold a cure, cow dung, human excrement, dried gobs of blood.

I come from there. That conch shell, that seashore, those bellies, that dung, those dried leaves holding a cure for the aching mind, all know me. The rooms enfolded each within the other, the distant houses all have held me.

I see amma, her hands bent into brown shell shapes for the wind to whistle through. She holds up her hands in sunlight, in moonlight. She stoops to pick me up. I am two, perhaps two and a half. She lifts me high into the wind. I see appa's hands, the veins rising on them. He is almost seventy now, his hair combed back on his head, streaked with silver, that handsome face whittled from within by a blood disease, time and sickness consuming the flesh that just about sustains him. He stretches out his hands to me. I want to dissolve, become a ghost myself so I can race to my father, into his outstretched hands.

Behind him my mother stands in the doorway. She too has grown older, the laugh lines deepen on her face, the curly hair blown loose from her bun is shot through with black. Now I see her in the half darkness, the sari drawn over her head. They are utterly quiet, for there is nothing that needs to be said. They wait for me in the Tiruvella house with a sandy courtyard where the ancient mulberry tree blossoms in sunlight.

But the rooms of the house are filled with darkness. I am in that house, somewhere in between my parents, hovering as a ghost might. I cannot escape. This is the house of my blood, the whorl of flesh I am. It is all already written, already made.

Another memory invades me: flat, filled with the burning present, cut by existential choices. Composed of bits and pieces of the present it renders the past suspect, cowardly, baseless. Place names litter it: Allahabad, Tiruvella, Kozencheri, Pune, Khartoum, Cairo, Beirut, Jerusalem, Dubai, London, New York, Minneapolis, Saint Paul, New Delhi, Trivandrum. Sometimes I think I could lift these scraps of space and much as an indigent dressmaker, cut them into shape. Stitch my days into a patchwork garment fit to wear.

But when she approaches me, this Other who I am, dressed in her bits-and-pieces clothing, the scraps cobbled together to cover her nakedness, I see quite clearly what I had only guessed at earlier: she has no home, no fixed address, no shelter. Sure everything else looks fine. She has two hands, two feet, a head of long black hair, a belly, breasts. But it is clear she is a nowhere creature.

She babbles in a multitude of tongues: Malayalam, Hindi, Tamil, Arabic, English, French. Desert sands fill her eyes. Bombers spit fire down on her. She crouches right where she is, at the edge of the subway platform that runs under Broadway: uptown local, at 110th street. She listens to the youth cry out through his harmonica, lisp out of the side of his mouth for a few dimes, the odd quarter: 'She is a material girl, and she knows what she is, she is a material baby, she is an American girl, huh, huh, huh,' he cries, pitching his voice as high as he can. Now the metal body of the train grinds in, people press bellies, thighs, elbows, fists, shoving in the haste to enter. Thrust against a white ceramic pillar she crouches low witnessing it all. As the train doors smash shut, she sucks in her breath. I am here she thinks. No elsewhere. Here, now, in New York City.[2]

Pondering this piece, I feel a lack of resolution in the stuff that makes up my inner life as a writer—an unbridgeable gap between the fluid if self-enclosed memories of being housed, with so little space for a self to come into existence—'it is all already written, already made'—and that other, harsher, bleaker experience of time present, a racialised world of choices, shifting scenes, consciousness radically unhoused. Between the ghostly daughter, she who must lose body to enter the ancestral house and a babbling creature in her scraps of clothing, what bond, what hold?

How can I, a conscious, self-made woman, and I say self-made for I do not feel there is any canonical tradition into which I can enter, of which I might become an inseparable part, translate one world to the other? Or is the realm of words, a third state entirely, forged in the tension between these two contrary conditions? And where does that leave me, in terms of my personal life? Perhaps it is because I have no clear answer to these questions that I must turn to two interlinked tales to end this essay. I call them tales though both are 'real' in the sense that they happened in the shared world.

Awhile back there were a series of racial incidents in New York City. Two black children were spray painted white, a white child raped in retaliation, an Indian child stoned. Haunted by these events I wrote a poem called 'Art of Pariahs'. 'Pariah' is a word that has come from my mother tongue Malayalam into English. Perhaps one of the few benefits of colonialism is being able to infiltrate the language. I imagine Draupadi of the *Mahabharata* entering my kitchen in New York City, and the longing to be freed of the limitations of skin color and race, sing in the poem.

September 1996, I was in Delhi for an International Symposium put together by the Sahitya Akademi. Writers, artists, film makers were invited to ponder the ethnic violence that was threatening the fabric of secular India. Worn out by the flight that got me in at one in the morning I turned up a few minutes late for the start of the conference. The hall at the India International Center was packed. There were half a dozen people on the podium, dignitaries including Mulk Raj Anand, grand old man of Indian letters, the novelist who had written about the lives of untouchables. There was nowhere for me to sit. I stood uneasily at the edge casting about for a place to sit, watching as a man dressed in white khadi, looking much as I would imagine a contemporary Tagore, spoke eloquently about the destruction of Babri Masjid and the communal riots in different parts of the country. 'Our novelists will write about this,' he said, 'but it will take them several years to absorb these events.' He paused, adding, 'As the poet said,' then, after what seemed like a space for a long drawn out breath, he recited the whole of my poem 'Art of Pariahs.' He did not mention the poet's name, but anonymity made the matter more powerful as the poem, in his voice, flowed through the packed room. And listening, standing clutching my papers, I felt emotions course through me, deeper than the power of words to tell. For a brief while, a poem composed in solitude in a small New York City room, had granted me the power to return home.

Art of Pariahs

Back against the kitchen stove
Draupadi sings:

In my head Beirut still burns

The Queen of Nubia, of God's Upper Kingdom
the Rani of Jhansi, transfigured, raising her sword
are players too. They have entered with me
into North America and share these walls.

We make up an art of pariahs:

Two black children spray painted white
their eyes burning,
a white child raped in a car
for her pale skin's sake,
an Indian child stoned by a bus shelter,
they thought her white in twilight.

Someone is knocking and knocking
but Draupadi will not let him in.
She squats by the stove and sings:

The Rani shall not sheathe her sword
nor Nubia's queen restrain her elephants
till tongues of fire wrap a tender blue,
a second skin, a solace to our children.

Come walk with me towards a broken wall
—Beirut still burns—carved into its face.
Outcastes all let's conjure honey scraped from stones,
an underground railroad stacked with rainbow skin,
Manhattan's mixed rivers rising.

What might it mean for Manhattan's mixed rivers to rise? How shall we move into a truly multicultural world, reimagine ethnicities, even as we acknowledge violent edges, harsh borders? These children in Manhattan, the Muslim women raped in Surat, the Hindu women stoned in Jersey city, coexist in time. Cleft by space they forge part of the fluid diasporic world, a world in which I must live and move and have my being. I think of Derek Walcott's lines: 'that terrible vowel, / that I!'[3] And I understand that my need to enter richly into imagined worlds cannot shake free of what my woman's body brings me. I cannot escape my body and the multiple worlds of my experience.

And the sort of translation the poem requires, 'translate' in an early sense of the verb meaning to carry over, to transport—for after all what is unspoken, even unspeakable must be born into language— forces a fresh icon of the body, complicates the present till memory is written into the very texture of the senses.

Notes

In a different form some portion of these reflections were presented at Trade Routes: History, Geography and Culture: A Conference Towards the Definition of Culture in the Late Twentieth Century, Johannesburg Biennale, 15 Oct. 1997. The thoughts on *Fault Lines* first emerged as part of the closing keynote '*Fault Lines* and the Perils of Translation' at the international conference All by Myself: The Representation of Individual Identity in Autobiographical Writings, University of Groningen, 15 Nov. 1996. An earlier version of this essay appeared in *Transformations* 9.2 (1998).

1. The poems 'San Andreas Fault', 'Art of Pariahs' and 'River and Bridge' were first published in Meena Alexander, *River and Bridge* (Toronto: TSAR, 1996); the first two poems are reprinted in Meena Alexander, *The Shock of Arrival: Reflections on Postcolonial Experience* (Boston: South End, 1996).
2. Meena Alexander, *Fault Lines* (New York: Feminist, 1993) 129-30.
3. Derek Walcott, 'Names', *Collected Poems* (New York: Farrar, 1986) 306.

Europe and Violence:
Some Contemporary Reflections on Walter Benjamin's 'Theories of German Fascism'

Graham MacPhee

In recent years contemporary theory has sought to respond to a global context that exceeds the bounds of the nation-state and to develop approaches and terminologies that register the expanded coordinates of a transnational social space.[1] Given this impulse it might be thought that inquiry into the history and possibilities of the nation would be relegated to the academic past, yet this has not been the case—indeed, if anything it has become all the more urgent. However, this is not to say that such inquiries continue regardless of this new context. As a number of writers have argued, they must register the impact of the changing situation of the nation, a demand that involves a complex negotiation of persistence and change. The introduction to the influential volume *Nation and Narration*, for example, insists that long-standing questions about the articulation and constitution of the nation are not 'definitively superseded by those new realities of internationalism, multinationalism, or even "late capitalism"',[2] and implicitly this observation asks how such questions might persist or live on within a radically new context. Emerging out of the economic, social and political transformations of European modernity, the modern nation-state has its underpinnings in Enlightenment conceptions of right, freedom and violence; but now that the conditions within which the nation-state occurs are radically changed, it has to be asked how these new conditions might reformulate the very parameters of the nation, and further, whether this new situation might rearticulate its promise, its dangers, and even its 'ambivalence'.

Translating Nations, ed. Prem Poddar, *The Dolphin* 30, pp. 23-46.
© 1999 by Aarhus University Press, Denmark.
ISBN 87 7288 381 2; ISSN 0106 4487.

The work of Walter Benjamin might be expected to offer one place to begin such an assessment, given Benjamin's concern for the technological transformation of modernity and its consequences for politics and violence. In the epilogue to his essay 'The Work of Art in the Age of Mechanical Reproduction', of the mid thirties, Benjamin famously connects the persistence of older social and political forms with the technological transformation of nature on a global scale, and sees in their collision a new and expanded potential for violence or 'war'.[3] Yet the framing of this discussion, in terms of 'the work of art in the epoch of its technical reproducibility',[4] and the formulation with which the epilogue ends—that while fascism renders politics 'aesthetic', 'Communism responds by politicising art'[5]—have not been conducive for contemporary readings. The thrust of the epilogue tends to be seen as foreclosing the valuable exposition of technological change which it follows, and its final formulation is understood as illegitimately appealing to an unexplored and moralistic notion of 'politics'.[6]

Within the corpus of Benjamin's work, however, the turn taken by the epilogue is neither as abrupt nor as untheorised as such reactions may suggest, but emerges out of Benjamin's increasing concern with the transformation of experience in modernity and its consequences for the social and political forms bequeathed by the Enlightenment. The epilogue to the 'Work of Art' essay draws on a number of strands of Benjamin's thinking so as to reflect on the persistence of the European nation-state and its social and legal frameworks within conditions radically transformed since its theoretical exposition in the Enlightenment, a reflection which centres on the unacknowledged violence of its persistence. While the contexts of Benjamin's thinking may appear obscure in the 'Work of Art' essay, his short review essay of 1930, 'Theories of German Fascism', brings this larger conceptual nexus more clearly into view.[7] This essay gives access to a sustained engagement with the violent prospects of technological modernity, an engagement which reinterrogates the political inheritance of the Enlightenment by exploring the unacknowledged consequences of its figuring of space and time. However, throughout Benjamin's oeuvre this engagement is routed through a consideration of the fate of the aesthetic in technological modernity, and it is at this point that it is easy to lose sight of the range of issues at stake.

Consequently, the present study first locates its discussion of Benjamin's essay in relation to Kant's 'Perpetual Peace: A Philosophical Sketch' (1795-96), an essay which focuses on the temporal and spatial co-ordinates implied by the Enlightenment polity and its structuring of private, public and cosmopolitan right. Following recent work by Howard Caygill, Kant's exposition of the prospects of the republican nation-state is addressed here through its figuring of the negotiation of violence and civility, a context which allows the political significance of Benjamin's consideration of technology and the aesthetic to come into view. Consequently, readings which understand Benjamin as making an untheorised appeal to a moralistic notion of politics are shown to underestimate Benjamin's understanding of the aesthetic as symptomatic of the reorganisation of experience in technological modernity, and are thus understood to offer a cautionary lesson for reading Benjamin's engagement with the aesthetic. Instead, the present study stresses the need to understand Benjamin's consideration of the aesthetic as part of his examination of the consequences of technological change for the social and political forms bequeathed by the Enlightenment. Understood in these terms, Benjamin's work offers significant resources for the contemporary project of rethinking the nation through its exploration of the recognition and negotiation of violence both within and beyond the borders of the nation-state.

1. Culturing Cosmopolitanism

Kant's well known essay 'Perpetual Peace' situates the origin of the nation-state in violence, yet its main concern is to identify the nation-state's potential to supply the framework for perpetual peace in the culturing of human society towards cosmopolitanism. From this perspective, the republican nation-state is understood to supply the necessary conditions for cosmopolitan right and the achievement of perpetual peace, whose institutional expression would be the free, global federation of sovereign, republican nation-states. Yet Kant's conception of the nation-state remains troubled by violence. His natural rights theory sees the nation-state arising out of the state of nature, where violence provides the motive force for the establishment of the originary social contract which institutes the conditions for lawful freedom, a development which is characterised as a movement from a 'state of war' to a 'state of peace'.[8] And yet, violence is not so easily dispensed with. In response to the violence of the state of nature, violence is also required to institute the social contract, and an inaugural role is conceded to the heteronomy of social institutions: as the essay argues, 'the only conceivable way of executing the original idea *in practice*, and hence of inaugurating a state of right, is by *force* ', and it is upon this 'coercive authority' that 'public right will subsequently be based' (117). Further, while the nation-state is to supply the framework for the free exercise of reason by individual subjects, liberating them from subjection to the imperatives of the natural conditions within which they find themselves, the emergence of nation-states creates a new set of conditions which imposes its own particular imperatives. Understood as discrete and sovereign entities, nation-states uncannily resemble the atomised individuals of the state of nature, mutually opposed, hostile and subject to the sway of a context which lies outside their own purview. And although this external determination is most visible in cases of actual conflict and war, for Kant it is not restricted to such instances, since as long as nations exist under the threat of war they will be conditioned by this predicament, rather than by the rational ends of private and public right. As the essay observes, nation-states must 'be judged in the same way as individual men living in the state of nature' (102); that is, as existing in a state of war, even in the absence of open hostilities.

The pacified space of the nation-state is, then, acknowledged by Kant to be curiously bound up with violence: violence stands at the foundation of the nation, and returns in the form of the potential for military violence at its borders. Kant's response to this predicament is complex, and involves a particular temporal and spatial ordering through which freedom (autonomy) and necessity (heteronomy), and civility and violence are to be negotiated. If the heteronomy of the phenomenal world must be acknowledged as returning in the threat of military conflict between states, then for Kant the achievement of perpetual peace only becomes feasible if this return itself marks a progression or step towards cosmopolitanism. In these terms, the nation-state must be conceived of, first, as discrete and integral, so that an internal zone of civility can be established which is free from external determination; and second, the return of violence must also mark a stage in the incremental process of its eradication, so that the moment of violence and heteronomy involved can be conceived of as encouraging the conditions for peace while being itself progressively eliminated.

Kant secures this temporal and spatial ordering through the providential role which he ascribes to nature: 'Perpetual peace is *guaranteed* by no less an authority than the great artist *Nature* herself', the essay observes, since the 'mechanical process of nature visibly exhibits the purposive plan of producing concord among men, even against their will and indeed by means of their very discord' (108). Despite the apparent convenience of this formulation it is highly suggestive in at least one sense, in that it acknowledges that the transcendentally derived, or 'formal', practical philosophy must recognise and negotiate the claims of necessity.[9] But it also introduces some significant problems for Kant's practical philosophy, which insists on the radical separation of the autonomy of human reason and the heteronomy of the phenomenal world, a separation which underlies the political distinction between the republican nation-state—as the condition of rational freedom—and the state of nature—as the realm of natural necessity. The return of violence at the borders of the nation-state proves troubling for Kant, and what may appear as simply a convenient appeal to nature or providence involves, in fact, a complex and double response: on the one hand, it enables him to continue to insist on the transcendental separation of rational freedom and the heteronomy of the phenomenal world, while on the other, it requires that he posit their alignment in the providential teleology of nature. What becomes crucial to the essay then is the nature of this alignment, and it is possible to see two counterposed dynamics at work here. At one level, the notion of alignment allows the essay to conceive of the achievement of cosmopolitanism in terms of the reciprocal culturing of human society and the phenomenal world, or 'nature'; but at another level, the essay attempts to set limits upon this reciprocity, limits that are ordered by the linear temporality and spatial integrity of the nation-state.

The nature and limits of this reciprocal culturing become clear in the central example used in the essay to image the operation of providence, an example which significantly revolves around the impact of European social and economic development on the inhabitants of the Arctic regions on the northern fringes of Europe. The existence of human populations in the Arctic regions supplies Kant with an important example for illustrating the providential role of nature in encouraging the formation of distinct nations, and thus its role in the culturing of cosmopolitanism. This role is presented in terms of the contrary vectors of dispersion and interdependence which are continually generated by the changing disposition of nature: the configuration of nature is understood by the essay as exerting a powerful yet contradictory pressure on the configuration of human sociality, and for Kant the operation of these contradictory tendencies is nicely illustrated in this example. The impulse embodied in natural necessity towards dispersion underlies the differentiation of discrete populations, 'proto-nations' as it were, for Kant an indispensable prerequisite for the formation of nation-states. In the central example used by the essay, Kant observes that human habitation of the Arctic is only possible because of the providential supply of driftwood which originates in the temperate regions around the Ob, the Yenisei and the Lena rivers. Thus, what Kant designates as the 'provisional arrangement' (109) of nature is providential in that it encourages the dispersion of human populations across the globe, allowing the inhabitation of the most inhospitable regions and thus encouraging the formation of discrete human populations.

However, while marking a necessary step towards the conditions for rational freedom, the formation of discrete populations also threatens to bring back the war of all against all that characterised the state of nature. The essay observes that, as the social organisation of the inhabitants of the temperate regions develops, they will themselves put to productive use the timber that lines these rivers, so cutting off the supply of driftwood to the populations of the Arctic— thus, co-operation within a population gives rise to competition between populations. Yet, this rearrangement of the matter of nature is also providential according to Kant, since it encourages the inhabitants of the Arctic to recognise their dependence on human populations distant from them, and to give practical expression to this interdependence through commerce: they must now trade furs and other animal products in order to secure the vital natural resource of wood. The contrary impulse, towards interdependence, is now revealed in this new arrangement of nature, and encourages the recognition by these distinct populations of their mutual interdependence. Thus the adjusted arrangement of nature encourages mutual interchange between distinct populations alongside the impulse towards differentiation, and so, Kant observes, 'nature … compel[s]' these distinct populations 'to live in peace together' (111).

The essay's appeal to the providential role of nature can be seen to involve a particular temporal and spatial ordering of the negotiation of freedom and necessity, civility and violence. Necessity, conceived of spatially as the disposition or arrangement of the matter of nature, is qualified once conceived of temporally: in contrast to the fixity of natural law, the arrangement of nature is provisional and open to change. In these terms, Kant is able to envisage the reciprocity of human freedom and natural necessity where the claims of each would be recognised: just as the legislations of human reason dispose or form the matter of nature, so the matter of nature disposes itself in proportion to that form. Underlying what appears to be a robustly ineluctable progression towards cosmopolitanism, then, is a complex, fragile and dynamic notion of alignment or reciprocity, and it is the nature of this alignment which stands at the heart of Kant's promise of perpetual peace. For in these terms, the assertion of human autonomy in the face of the heteronomy of nature is no longer envisaged as the violent imposition of a fixed and external form on a passive and recalcitrant matter, but as the continually re-emerging moment of proportionality in which matter and form coincide freely and without violence. The harmonious and noncoercive appearance of this progression depends on the emergence of proportionality in the reciprocity of matter and form, a reciprocity that is not legislated in advance, but whose law emerges and re-emerges freely and spontaneously at each moment, again and again.

But if this is the case, then equally the example of Arctic inhabitation also serves to make clear the limits of this reciprocity, limits which are set by the temporal and spatial coordinates of the nation-state. For although the essay claims to derive the spatial integrity and progressive temporality of the nation-state from this model of reciprocity, what the example reveals is that, in fact, this model presupposes it. The progressive extension of the conditions for peace which the example is adduced to support depends on a temporal and spatial ordering that mirrors that of the nation-state and its figuring of the fate of an initial moment of violence. Just as in the case of the nation-state, where an initial moment of violence occurs in the coercive imposition of legal authority, so this example involves an initial moment of violence: the *possession* of the riverside timber by the populations of the temperate regions is also the violent *dispossession* of the inhabitants of the Arctic. And in each case, the inaugural moment of violence is understood to be left behind as a result of the new context which it has itself made possible, a new context which is designated, in the first case, as the pacified space of private and public right realised in the nation-state, and in the second, as the noncoercive trajectory towards cosmopolitan right realised in the free exchanges of commerce. But this mirroring proves troubling, since this example is supplied in order to derive the spatio-temporal framework of the nation-state, yet here we find it already in place.

Looked at more closely, this temporal sleight of hand can be seen at the very heart of the essay's conceptual vocabulary. The act of possession which generates the initial rearrangement of nature in the example itself already implies this spatio-temporal framework: possession implies an integral sphere of 'ownness', an organisation of space in terms of a discrete, inner zone of ownership, while the temporal movement from the initial moment of possession to the exchanges of commerce involves the leaving behind *without residue* of the moment of dispossession within possession. It is only in these terms that commerce becomes located as the ground on which the contrary vectors embedded in nature—differentiation and interdependence—and what the essays sees as the basic legal forms of human society—the forms of private right, namely possession, contract and the legal subject—find their alignment in a spontaneous and unconditioned proportionality. But understood in these terms, if commerce describes a linear trajectory which implies the progressive emergence of the discretely bounded and unified space of the nation-state, it also presupposes this spatio-temporal framework. It turns out, then, that commerce is not spontaneous or unconditioned at all, but presupposes the legal forms of the European nation-state—possession, contract, and the legal subject—*and* the violent histories of possession and dispossession from which they emerge. Here Kant's formulation evidences a certain forgetting, for while commerce is presented as an alignment which is supposed to emerge spontaneously, it is in fact already given by the violent acts of possession and dispossession which it claims to leave behind. Despite the gloss which the essay offers then, form and matter are not, after all, spontaneously predisposed in conformity, but rather their 'alignment' involves a moment of heteronomy, for the terms of this proportionality are already given by the histories of possession and dispossession from which the European nation-state emerges. The apparently spontaneous alignment of the autonomy of human reason and the heteronomy of natural necessity thus involves a moment of *mis*alignment, in that the apparently free exchanges of commerce remain conditioned by the contours of possession and dispossession which emerge and re-emerge in the continuing rearrangement of the phenomenal world. Although the essay recognises an inaugural violence, it looks forward to its progressive elimination in the alignment of freedom and necessity; but the identification of the moment of misalignment within this 'alignment' raises the prospect that the initial moment of violence would not be progressively eliminated once and for all, but rather would be reproduced and amplified, again and again.

The essay's presupposition of the spatio-temporal framework which it wants to derive has important consequences for its figuring of freedom and necessity and of civility and violence in the nation-state. Conceived of as a discrete and homogenous plane, the nation-state comes to imply a temporal trajectory which obscures the persistence of the violence which secures its integrity and unity. Thus, while the violence involved in the (mis)alignment of form and matter is recognised at the foundation of civility and at its frontiers, once form and matter are brought into proportion in the nation-state—the pacified space of private and public right—the history of the nation and its legal and social forms can be represented as the progressive and free development of human reason. Kant's separation and opposition of violence and civility, then, figures commerce as the noncoercive alignment of freedom and necessity by securing the temporal and spatial integrity of the nation-state, so casting the integral national polity as the basis for the uncoerced and noncoercive exercise of private, public and cosmopolitan right. But as we have seen, the noncoercive appearance of commerce is already presupposed by Kant's exposition of the nation-state, which removes violence from civil possession and exchange, and relocates it in the state of nature which precedes or exists beyond the bounds of civility defined by the nation-state. And on this point the essay is quite explicit: 'the spirit of commerce', Kant states bluntly, 'cannot exist side by side with war' (114). It is this spatio-temporal framework, and the separation and opposition of violence and civility which it implies, which allows Kant to find in the nation-state an image of the culturing of human freedom and natural necessity as the free and harmonious proportionality of matter and form. And in these terms Kant's imaging of this trajectory comes to resemble the harmonious appearance of the aesthetic, for the spontaneous alignment of matter and form which the essay sees in the emergence of the nation-state stands at the heart of the aesthetic judgement of taste.[10]

And yet, paradoxically, by positing the alignment of rational freedom and natural necessity, Kant in fact makes it much more difficult to disentangle the legislations of practical reason from the realm of necessity. In its reciprocity with the phenomenal world, the culturing of human reason is shown to rearrange the context within which its legislations are to take place, while in turn, the forms of legality which emerge through that history are themselves shown to be conditioned by the configuration of this site. Despite appearances to the contrary, the persistent complicity of the spontaneity of autonomy and the determination of heteronomy in the changing configuration of civility in fact suggests that violence still lingers there: the opposition of civility and violence, then, proves to be highly unstable and contradictory. Howard Caygill has identified this unstable opposition of violence and civility as lying at the heart of the modern discourse of right since Kant. The inability of modern political thought to pursue the complicity of violence and civility is understood by Caygill as constitutive of the modern concept of freedom, which in failing 'to achieve an internal recognition of the *violence of civility*' is limited to 'a civil freedom of possession, action and exchange'.[11] This restriction has important consequences for the constitution of the nation-state, for the appearance of the space of civility, and for the recognition of and prospects for violence. In casting violence as exceptional, whether temporally—as the temporary suspension of civility—or spatially—in the potential for military violence amassed at its borders—violence is concentrated in and monopolised by the state, lending the realm of private exchanges in civil society the appearance of a placid harmony; 'the overall effect', Caygill observes, 'is to remove violence from civil society, and to obscure its complicity with civil freedom'.[12] The separation and opposition of the freedom of practical reason and the heteronomy of the phenomenal world gives the appearance of civility as a unified and noncoercive space and so obscures the violence of civility; and because civility cannot recognise or remember its violence, it cannot take responsibility for it.

Understood in these terms, Kant's 'Perpetual Peace' provides a significant context for reading Benjamin's review essay 'Theories of German Fascism', allowing it to be understood as drawing on key elements of Benjamin's thinking during the late twenties and early thirties. First of all, it allows Benjamin's terminology to be located within a larger conceptual nexus. Kant's essay reminds us that the harmonious appearance of civility depends on the particular spatio-temporal ordering implied by the nation-state, and that it attests to the spontaneous alignment of freedom and necessity which Kant had discovered in the aesthetic judgement of taste. In this light, Benjamin's apparently untheorised leap from the aesthetic to the political begins to look quite different. Benjamin's interest in the work of art centres on its role in organising the spatio-temporal conditions of experience, its giving of the conditions of possibility for the alignment of matter and form in intuition. But in view of Kant's figuring of alignment in 'Perpetual Peace', Benjamin's stress on the historicity of aesthetic perception becomes particularly significant. Where Kant's conception of the aesthetic judgement of taste fixes the forms of intuition (space and time) in terms of uniform extension and linear progression, Benjamin's conception of the decay of aura identifies aesthetic perception as just one possible configuration of space and time; indeed, the ruined persistence of aesthetic perception is understood by Benjamin as providing an important indicator of the nature of the reconfiguration of space and time in modernity. Equally, Benjamin's complex usage of the term *Technik*—usually translated in English as 'technology'—can be understood as both registering and rearticulating Kant's attempt to align the culturing of human society and the phenomenal world: as Julian Roberts points out, for Benjamin *Technik* involves both what we might describe as 'technique'—or the organisation of experience—and 'technology'—or the disposition of the phenomenal world.[13] And crucially, this usage no longer forecloses the question of alignment, but serves rather to foreground its recurrence.

2. Landscapes of Violence

Benjamin's essay 'Theories of German Fascism' was written as a review of the collection of essays edited by Ernst Jünger, *War and Warriors (Krieg und Krieger)*, a volume which grouped together a number of writers who connected their political dissatisfaction with Weimar political culture to the shattering experience of the First World War. In one sense, Benjamin's review is concerned to offer a trenchant critique of these writers, whose glorification of the violence of trench warfare creates an intellectual context wide open to the political appeal of fascism. But the essay does much more than this: at another level, it takes the intellectual trajectory described by the volume as offering important insights into the impact of the violent experience of the First World War on German intellectual culture, and as articulating one significant—if disastrous—mode of response to that conflagration. In contrast to the perspective offered by pacifism, which is organised around the telos of the ultimate eradication of violence, this volume is understood to offer certain insights in that it places violence at the heart of contemporary experience. But if it does so, for Benjamin it fundamentally misrecognises violence, and the essay pursues this misrecognition in terms of the new spatio-temporal conditions within which the nation now finds itself.

Central to the essay's critique of Jünger's volume is its under-standing of the conflagration of the First World War as announcing the transformation of the spatio-temporal co-ordinates which underwrote the emergence of the European nation-state. For Benjamin, the war unmistakably tears apart the conceptual co-ordinates which sustained the social, political and legal ordering of European modernity in terms of the discrete borders of the nation-state and its integral self-identity over time; indeed, the 'European' conflagration of the 'Great War' refused to respect the limits of Europe itself, becoming the first modern global war. What Benjamin terms 'the new warfare of technology and material' presages a new formulation of space and time which overrides the spatial and temporal organisation of Enlightenment thought.[14] The essay cites gas warfare as one example: the gas attack along whole sectors of the front makes irrelevant the traditional geographical definition of the battlefield, and thus erases the legal and political distinction between civilian and non-combatant. As such, it abolishes the basis of the international law through which war itself was to be organised, overriding the legal framework based on nation-states and the relationships between them. Equally, the new telecommunications and transportation technologies and the new weapons delivery systems function at velocities and over ranges which shatter traditional conceptions of distance and duration, while the extended trenchlines exceed national borders and traditional conceptions of national conflict.

Benjamin's point here is not simply that the technology of warfare proved more powerful than was initially assumed, but that the First World War itself must be understood as announcing the emergence of a new structuring of the phenomenal world in modernity. As Benjamin was to write elsewhere,

> With the World War a process began to become apparent which has not halted since … For never has experience been contradicted more thoroughly than strategic experience by tactical warfare, economic experience by inflation, bodily experience by mechanical warfare, moral experience by those in power. A generation that had gone to school on the horse-drawn streetcar now stood under the open sky in a countryside in which nothing remained unchanged but the clouds, and beneath these clouds, in a field of force of destructive torrents and explosions, was the tiny, fragile human body.[15]

The ordering of experience according to the spatial and temporal purview of the individual subject—precisely what Kant had envisaged in the nation-state conceived of as the framework for the free exercise of reason by self-legislating subjects—is shown by the First World war no longer to obtain. What it reveals instead is a new spatio-temporal structuring of the phenomenal world—a new 'nature'—which is violently incompatible with traditional structures of experience. The massive and unprecedented violence of the First World War is understood by Benjamin as the violent eruption of the incompatibility or misalignment between the new spatio-temporal co-ordinates of the phenomenal world and those which structured traditional forms of social, political, legal, economic and sensory experience. But as such, what the war reveals is a transformation which is not simply 'technological' in the narrow sense of the term, but which is fundamental to the fate of European modernity.

In grasping the implications of this understanding of the war our earlier discussion of 'Perpetual Peace' becomes relevant, but equally, Benjamin's account requires that we review its claims. Kant's retrospective fixing of the spatio-temporal conditions for the emergence of the nation-state might be said already to have been out of date; that is, the fixing of the spatio-temporal conditions of the nation-state misrecognises the transformation of the phenomenal world which makes the emergence of the nation-state possible. As the essay's example reminds us, the emergence of the European nation-state depended on an expanded range of action and possession beyond the bounds of Europe, in this case with regard to the Arctic regions to the north, and this expansion already undercut its spatio-temporal co-ordinates. Paradoxically, the consolidation of the nation-state as spatially homogenous and temporally self-identical involved an expansion which brought about the coincidence of heterogeneous temporalities as European colonialism made simultaneous the experiences of different times and places, a violent rearrangement of the spatio-temporal co-ordinates of the phenomenal world. But as we have seen, Kant's essay occludes the moment of misalignment thereby generated, harmonising it in a 'commerce' which it figures as a peaceful and uncoerced exchange. This misalignment is named by Benjamin's term *Technik*: understood in the double sense identified above, the term designates the relationship between the spatio-temporal co-ordinates of this new global context and those which underlie the structuring of experience inherited from the Enlightenment, a relationship revealed by the eruption of violence in the First World War to be one of misrecognition and misalignment. And this is what Benjamin means when he argues in the review essay that we must come to understand such eruptions of violence as the 'slave revolt of technology', a formulation which consciously echoes Nietzsche's critique of Enlightenment rationality in *The Genealogy of Morals*. It is in this sense, and not as a species of 'technological determinism', that we can understand Benjamin's demand that our thinking must come to recognise 'technology's right of co-determination in the social order'.[16]

The essay's critique of Ernst Jünger's volume, then, is not based on an external antipathy but must be understood as immanent critique. In celebrating the violence of the First World War as the landscape for a reawakening of heroism and national destiny, its authors denounce what they see as the bureaucratic and despiritualised culture of the Weimar republic; but for Benjamin, their critique involves a double misrecognition. First, their conception of violence is outmoded, being based on notions of individual valour and heroism which are simply irrelevant to the experience of modern technological warfare: the individual warrior is rendered redundant by gas attack, high explosive bombardment and tank warfare. Second, their critique of the Weimar republic is based on a notion of national destiny which is equally untenable. The Weimar republic is perceived by these writers as a faceless and atomistic entity unable to bind together the national population or express its authentic spirit. In opposition to such a liberal conception of the nation-state they argue for a reaffirmation of the national destiny through the reordering of national life around the aristocratic virtues of the German warrior, virtues which they perceive as central to the experience of the front despite the incursions of technological warfare and the bureaucratisation of the military imported from civilian life. But such a critique is based on a spatio-temporal model directly countered by the experience of the war. From Benjamin's perspective, in each case these positions are predicated on the failure to recognise and come to terms with the transformation of the phenomenal world announced by the war. But further, Benjamin identifies a curious temporality at work here: it is not simply that these writers cling on to a conceptual paradigm which is now outmoded, but rather that in persisting, this paradigm is distorted and deformed and is no longer identical with itself. The appeal to the heroism of the trench soldier can be understood as the return of a model of individual action and virtue which obtained in the Enlightenment into a context which is now incompatible with it; but in its return this model is disfigured and distorted so as to resemble the premodern 'warrior'. Equally, the critique of the republican nation-state which this notion of the warrior is meant to sustain evidences a similarly inauthentic and distorted return: the national destiny invoked here at once depends on precisely the temporal and spatial integrity which the Enlightenment conception of the nation-state underwrote, while simultaneously drawing on a premodern notion of fate which the review essay describes as 'cultic'.[17]

This curious and convoluted temporality is further explored by the essay in terms of the different experience of victor and vanquished: according to Benjamin, a different temporality obtains for those who have won and those who have lost. These terms, 'to win' and 'to lose', have a double meaning, of which only the 'first, manifest meaning … refers to the outcome of the war'. The second meaning, however, 'creates that peculiar hollow space, the sounding board in these words', and 'refers to the totality of the war and … how the war's outcome also alters the enduring significance it holds for us'. The victor not only wins the war in the first sense, but also takes possession of the war, 'keeps the war in hand', 'conquers' it and 'makes it his own property'; in contrast, the loser 'no longer possesses it and must live without it'.[18] For the victor, the conflict is won in this double sense, and so it is over and can be left behind; but for the vanquished, the war lives on negatively, that is, it persists precisely in its loss, and as loss. The curious and deforming coincidence of heterogeneous temporalities which the essay observes in the volume's notion of the warrior and the destiny of the nation comes to describe a larger temporal disjunction, that of the deformed and deforming persistence of the war in German culture. Benjamin names this situation the *Nachkrieg*, which might be translated as the 'after-war' or 'post-war war'. Just as the central terms of Jünger's collection— 'warrior' and 'destiny'—return Enlightenment motifs within a context incompatible with them, so the experience of the war persists in the post-war period, generating violent distortions and deformations within a different and incompatible context. The contrast with the figuring of the temporality of possession and dispossession in Kant's conception of the progressive achievement of cosmopolitanism is striking: in 'Perpetual Peace', the harmonious alignment of matter and form supplied a linear temporality in which the moment of dispossession in possession could be progressively left behind. But Benjamin argues here that such a vision only obtains within the conditions of experience of the victor or possessor, but is unavailable within the conditions of experience of the vanquished or dispossessed.

Benjamin's charge that the contributors to the volume are warriors not of the First World War, but of the 'post-war war', carries a bitter irony that extends beyond mere name calling: his concept of the *Nachkrieg* emphasises the violence of this persistence and the persistence of violence, and so designates the prospect of future violence stored up in the present but as yet unrealised.

But equally, this different conception of persistence also implies a different conception of the conditions of appearance, and here the political dimension of Benjamin's engagement with art and the aesthetic comes more clearly into view. At one point the essay characterises the intellectual disposition of the volume through the emblematic image of the soldier's heroic stance or posture: 'Every third word in their speeches is "stance"', Benjamin notes, linking the intellectual attitude of the volume to the rigid bodily disposition inculcated in military drill.[19] Benjamin's image is not simply polemical, but draws together a complex network of conceptual motifs within a single emblem. The rigid poses of military drill freeze particular attitudes adopted on the battlefield, formalising them as fixed postures now bereft of the context to which they once offered a response. The vision offered by Jünger's volume is nicely captured in this emblem: its apprehension is structured according to conceptual paradigms ripped out of their earlier contexts and violently reimposed upon a rapidly changing set of co-ordinates, whose explosive dynamism is captured and frozen, caught as violently twisted and distorted gestures. This image concentrates a line of argument that runs through the essay: the Enlightenment's partial recognition of violence, and the rational conception of the nation-state it provides in order to overcome it, are returned in Jünger's volume, but in this return they are violently transformed to become the atemporal categories of 'eternal war' and 'the eternal Germany'.[20] The reimposition of these frozen categories deforms the appearance of modernity, rendering it inscrutable and fixed, a mysterious countenance which resembles the archaic vision of a fateful but unknowable nature.[21] But the misalignment between the forms of experience and the rapidly changing disposition of the phenomenal world is now radicalised, and presages a violent collision that can no longer be 'safely' contained at the margins, but threatens to erupt at the very centre:

Sphinx-like in appearance, the fascist's nation thus takes its place as a new economic mystery of nature alongside the old. But this old mystery of nature, far from revealing itself to their technology [*Technik*], is exposing its most threatening feature. In the parallelogram of forces formed by these two—nature and nation—war is the diagonal.[22]

It is in these terms that Benjamin's apparently extravagant claim earlier in the essay, that the vision offered by the volume 'is nothing other than an uninhibited translation of the principles of *l'art pour l'art* to war itself', becomes understandable.[23] Benjamin's point is not exhausted by noting the volume's idealising, or 'aestheticising', of the horrors of trench warfare, and indeed its force lies more squarely elsewhere, in its figuring of the fate of Enlightenment conceptions of reason, freedom and right. As we seen, Kant conceives of the republican nation-state as the harmonious alignment of natural necessity and the freedom of human reason, as the free proportionality between matter and form which he found intimated in the aesthetic judgement of taste. But Kant's notion of the reciprocal culturing of human reason and the phenomenal world might take on a different appearance if the moment of misalignment in alignment were acknowledged: instead of a proportionality that is fixed according to the spatio-temporal co-ordinates of the nation-state, the recognition of misalignment would require that their proportionality be rediscovered and reproduced at each moment of their reciprocal culturing. Seen from this perspective, the harmonious appearance of the nation-state would be understood as an illegitimate and violent petrification, and it is this petrification which Benjamin sees in the structuring of experience inherited from the Enlightenment, a structuring of experience which he sees crystallised out in aesthetic perception.

His critique of aesthetic, or 'auratic', perception in the 'Work of Art' essay and elsewhere thus extends beyond the consideration of works of art, identifying aesthetic perception as a particular organisation of experience according to the spatial and temporal co-ordinates of 'distance'; that is, a structuring of experience which depends on the integral and homogenous time and space implied by the nation-state. Benjamin's term 'auratic' emphasises what he calls the 'ritual' or 'cultic' basis of this organisation of experience, that is its resemblance to premodern structurings of experience, while conversely his frequent reference to *l'art pour l'art* emphasises the aesthetic's subsequent fate, which saw it quickly divested of the epistemological and political commitments which it was understood to involve within the Enlightenment. Understood in these terms, Benjamin's description of Jünger's volume as 'an uninhibited translation of the principles of *l'art pour l'art* to war itself' comes to describe a complex conception of persistence and transformation, one which underpins the central emblem of the essay, its imaging of the fate of German Idealism in terms of the landscape of the front:

[I]n the face of the 'landscape of total mobilisation' the German feeling for nature has had an undreamed-of upsurge. The pioneers of peace, those sensuous settlers, were evacuated from these landscapes, and as far as anyone could see over the edge of the trench, the surroundings became a problem, every wire entanglement an antinomy, every barb a definition, every explosion a thesis; and by day the sky was the cosmic interior of the steel helmet and at night the moral law above. Etching the landscape with flaming banners and trenches technology [*Technik*] wanted to recreate the heroic features of German Idealism. It went astray. What it considered heroic were the features of Hippocrates, the features of death. Deeply imbued with its own depravity, technology gave shape to the apocalyptic face of nature and reduced nature to silence—even though this technology had the power to give nature its voice.[24]

This complex formulation images the fate of German Idealism by superimposing the two different conceptions of nature which are implied by Kant's critical philosophy. The critical philosophy was, on the one hand, to secure the conditions for rational freedom by aligning it with, but keeping it distinct from, the reconfiguration of the phenomenal world. Such an alignment envisages nature as anticipating the rational forms which are to order it, rendering nature aesthetically as 'landscape'—that is, a meaningful vista which returns to the gaze of the rational subject a prospect which is already in conformity with its structuring of experience. But on the other hand, the critical philosophy was also to secure the conditions for knowledge of the sensible world, conceived in terms of discrete bodies existing in linear time and uniform space and subject to mechanical causality. In these terms, nature is rendered as an inert and passive matter awaiting the imposition of form, a violent inscription or legislation which in the terms of this image 'reduces nature to silence'. Not withstanding the claims of 'Perpetual Peace', the fate of German Idealism does not lead to the ineluctable culturing of cosmopolitanism after all, and the 'pioneers of peace' are evacuated from the landscape of modernity. But that is not to say that German Idealism is left behind; rather, it persists but in a distorted and ruined form, no longer able to sustain the appearance of harmonious proportionality. Yet if this persistence no longer sustains the aesthetic vision of harmonious nature, the organisation of experience over which it presides remains 'aesthetic' in another sense; that is, just as the Enlightenment's structuring of experience fixed the reciprocal culturing of nature and reason in terms of the spatio-temporal co-ordinates of the nation-state, so that of the *Nachkrieg* organises its experience of the technological reconfiguration of the phenomenal world according to the same rigid co-ordinates. The result, according to the essay, will be a massive and unprecedented eruption of violence: 'millions of human bodies', writes Benjamin, 'will indeed ... be chopped to pieces and chewed up by iron and gas'.[25]

Benjamin's charge against fascism in the 'Work of Art' essay, that it 'aestheticises politics', is not simply levelled at its organisation of rallies and popular mobilisations, nor its artistic policies; rather, these might be regarded as symptomatic of its structuring of experience. And indeed, Benjamin attempts to indicate this wider context at the beginning of the epilogue, noting that 'Fascism attempts to organise the newly created proletarian masses without affecting the property structure which the masses strive to eliminate'.[26] That is, fascism attempts to organise the rapidly changing configuration of the phenomenal world according to the fixed social, political and legal forms inherited from the Enlightenment nation-state. And it is in this sense that Benjamin refers to 'the aesthetics of today's war', which he describes in terms which recall the earlier 'Theories of German Fascism': 'If the natural utilisation of productive forces is impeded by the property system', writes Benjamin, 'the increases in technical devices, in speed, and in the sources of energy will press for an unnatural utilisation, and this is found in war'. The coming war is described as the 'rebellion of technology', and its violence is traced to 'the discrepancy between the tremendous means of production and their inadequate utilisation in the process of production';[27] that is, to the ossified contours of possession and dispossession which continue to set the limits of the transformation of the phenomenal world. Benjamin's response to this situation, articulated briefly at the end of the essay in terms of the 'politicisation of art', is also illuminated by the earlier essay. Far from being a simplistic demand for propagandistic art or an appeal to a moralistic notion of politics, this rather compressed formulation might better be understood in terms of the review essay's assessment of the Enlightenment's fixing of political possibility within the spatio-temporal co-ordinates of the nation-state. In these terms, the 'politicisation of art' describes a reordering of the structuring of civility which would recognise and take responsibility for its violence, and so move 'to correct the incapacity of peoples to order their relationships to one another in accord with the relationship they possess to nature through their technology'.[28] And once understood in these terms, Benjamin's account of fascism might begin to offer some kind of yield for thinking the situation of the nation within our own present.

3. Fortress Europe

It is not a straightforward process to move from Benjamin's writing of the thirties to the situation of Europe today. Clearly, Benjamin's analysis of fascism is historically specific and does not offer a generalised account of the fate of the nation-state in modernity. But it does offer a certain insight into the contemporary situation of the nation, at least in terms of the convoluted temporality or differential return which it describes. A short passage from *One Way Street*, a text published two years before the review essay, illustrates something of what this conceptual nexus might offer. The passage presents a striking and complex image of the fate of European civility:

Just as all things, in a perpetual process of mingling and contamination, are losing their intrinsic character while ambiguity displaces authenticity, so is the city. Great cities—whose incomparably sustaining and reassuring power encloses those at work within them in the peace of the fortress and lifts from them, with the view of the horizon, awareness of the ever vigilant elemental forces—are seen to be breached at all points by the invading countryside.

Not by the landscape, but by what in untrammelled nature is most bitter: ploughed land, highways, night sky that the veil of vibrant redness no longer conceals. The insecurity of the busy areas puts the city dweller in the opaque but truly dreadful situation in which he must assimilate, along with isolated monstrosities from the open country, the abortions of urban architectonics.[29]

This passage might be read in a number of different ways. It might, for example, be seen as capturing a moment in the linear temporality of decline, an inversion of the progressive culturing of cosmopolitanism, in which we observe the ineluctable collapse of the rationally ordered civil space. Alternatively, it might be read outside of any such linear trajectory, whether conceived of as progress or decline, and so be understood precisely as marking the end of such 'grand narratives'. In these terms it stands as an image of the permanent condition of European civility, where the eruption of a violent and incommensurable 'nature' within the apparently integral space of the fortress registers the unassimilability of social space to the totalising organisation of reason.

But equally, this passage might yield another interpretation when viewed in the light of our reading of 'Theories of German Fascism', one which involves a different conception of persistence. In the fortress-city we see the persistence of the structuring of the European nation-state, whose monumental architecture continues to demarcate and organise social space; but if it persists, it does so ruined and deformed. Its integrity is breached by a topography that refuses to be fixed within the temporal and spatial limits emanating from the metropolis, as 'landscape', but which instead proves violently incompatible; no longer kept at bay by the militarised exterior of civility, violence returns at its centre. But this return is quite different from those imagined above, both in terms of visibility and in terms of the direction in which it might point. If the massive curtain walls of the fortress have been breached, they still limit the visual scope and range of its inhabitants, and so must be understood to shape the prospects for action and intercourse in new and unexpected ways. It should not be assumed, therefore, that this image necessarily marks the inevitable decline of the fortress, nor that the eruption of zones of violence necessarily disrupt its fabric: it may be that the organisation of vision that emerges within its altered structure will render this situation 'opaque', and that these zones of violence would thus be regularised and fixed, and so enlisted to sustain this new configuration. This violent return is, then, neither an ineluctable decline not an atemporal condition, but occurs as a moment of persistence and change which might issue in a number of different ways. For the moments of violent eruption might also hold the possibility of transformation, and the breaches in the city walls, rather than hardening within this new configuration, might lead instead to a different conception of architecture, no longer based on the monumental self-identity and integrity of the inside. But for such a possibility to emerge, the inhabitants of the fortress must recognise and come to terms not only with the violence that occurs without, but also the violence that lies within civility.

Notes

1. See Jacques Derrida, *The Other Heading: Reflections on Today's Europe*, trans. Pascale-Anne Brault and Michael B. Naas (Bloomington: Indiana UP, 1992).
2. Homi Bhabha, ed., *Nation and Narration* (London: Routledge, 1990) 1.
3. Walter Benjamin, 'The Work of Art in the Age of Mechanical Reproduction', *Illuminations* (London: Fontana, 1973) 243.
4. This phrase is a more literal rendering of the essay's title, *Das Kunstwerk im Zeitalter seiner technischen Reproduzierbarkeit*; the significance of Benjamin's terminology is touched on below.
5. Benjamin, 'Work of Art' 244.
6. This kind of interpretation has become powerfully entrenched in readings of the essay over recent years: see for example Miriam Hansen, 'Benjamin, Cinema and Experience: "The Blue Flower in the Land of Technology"', *New German Critique* 40 (1987) and Bernd Huppauf, 'Walter Benjamin's Imaginary Landscape', *'With the Sharpened Axe of Reason': Approaches to Walter Benjamin*, ed. Gerhard Fischer (Oxford: Berg, 1996).
7. Walter Benjamin, 'Theories of German Fascism', *New German Critique* 17 (1979).
8. Immanuel Kant, 'Perpetual Peace: A Philosophical Sketch', *Political Writings*, ed. Hans Reiss (Cambridge: Cambridge UP, 1991) 98. Subsequent references to this text will be given parenthetically.
9. This recognition was seized upon and radicalised by Kant's critics, most notably by Hegel and Nietzsche; see Gillian Rose, *Hegel Contra Sociology* (London: Athlone, 1981) and Daniel Conway, 'Heidegger, Nietzsche, and the Origins of Nihilism', *Journal of Nietzsche Studies* 3 (1992), respectively.
10. See 'The Analytic of the Beautiful' in Immanuel Kant, *Critique of Judgement*, trans. W. S. Pluhar (Indianapolis: Hackett, 1987). This connection underlies the organisation of the *Critique of Judgement* into two parts, the 'Critique of Aesthetic Judgement' and the 'Critique of Teleological Judgement'.

11. Howard Caygill, *Hegel and the Speculative Community*, UEA Papers in Philosophy, New Ser. 3 (Norwich: U of East Anglia, 1994) 24 (emphasis added), 22.

12 . Caygill 23.

13. Julian Roberts, *Walter Benjamin* (London: Macmillan, 1982) 156-59.

14. Benjamin, 'Theories' 121.

15. Benjamin, 'The Storyteller', *Illuminations*, 84.

16. Benjamin, 'Theories' 120.

17. Benjamin, 'Theories' 122.

18. Benjamin, 'Theories' 123.

19. Benjamin, 'Theories' 125.

20. Benjamin, 'Theories' 125.

21. Cf. Benjamin's description of the 'quotable gesture' in 'What is Epic Theatre?', *Illuminations*, 152-53. The difference between this frozen 'stance' and Brecht's 'quotable gesture' indicates that Benjamin's approach envisages the possibility both of intervention within the structuring of appearances and of some kind of yield or return which appearances might be made to give up. In these terms it provides a contrast to the numerous accounts which see inscrutability as the inevitable condition of modernity or, subsequently, postmodernity.

22. Benjamin, 'Theories' 127.

23. Benjamin, 'Theories' 122.

24. Benjamin, 'Theories' 126.

25. Benjamin, 'Theories' 128.

26. Benjamin, 'Work of Art' 243.

27. Benjamin, 'Work of Art' 244.

28. Benjamin, 'Theories' 128.

29. Walter Benjamin, *One Way Street and Other Writings*, trans. Edmund Jephcott and Kingsley Shorter (London: Verso, 1985) 59.

'Gendering' the Nation: Literary Representations of Contemporary Sri Lankan Politics

Neluka Silva

The motif of 'woman-as-nation' is ubiquitous in the discourses of the Sri Lankan state as well as the Tamil separatists, and epitomises the kind of images which enables an exploration of the paradigms of nationalist discourse.[1] This image is predicated upon the construction of an exclusionary, discriminatory identity which, though primarily based on the concept of ethnicity, interlocks with discourses of gender, class and caste. Since 1983, Sri Lanka has endured the harrowing atrocities of terrorism, civil war and inter-communal carnage. The ongoing struggle for nationhood between the majority Sinhalese state, which is anxious to maintain its stronghold over the country, and the Tamil Tiger guerrilla force, whose demand for a separate state includes the use of terrorist activity, impacts upon every aspect of life. Effects upon human relationships and the meaning of individual and collective identity have been profound, and thus, the question of identity can be regarded as the central, most important issue in contemporary Sri Lankan society.

In this essay I intend to explore these issues in relation to nationhood. The process of 'national' fragmentation and the strategies of envisioning a new nation are negotiated through several Sri Lankan literary texts written in English. My focus is on texts written after 1983. I will demonstrate how these texts prefigure issues such as the intense suffering of the common person produced by political violence, the politics of inter-ethnic relationships, and nationalist constructions of masculine and feminine identities. Among the texts selected is Shyam Selvadurai's *Funny*

Translating Nations, ed. Prem Poddar, *The Dolphin* 30, pp. 47-87.
© 1999 by Aarhus University Press, Denmark.
ISBN 87 7288 381 2; ISSN 0106 4487.

Boy (1994), which has thus far received little critical attention. I also intend to engage with the work of Jean Arasanayagam, and two plays by Sri Lanka's most internationally recognised playwright, Ernest MacIntyre. My choice of writers and different genres are determined by the thematic relevance to the complexities of the nation and their engagement with gender.

Theatre as a Mirror of Reality: The Work of Ernest MacIntyre

The theatre is a conduit through which the encrypted codes of culture are deciphered and translated into a medium that is accessible to the public consciousness. Gilbert and Tompkins argue that, in post-colonial states, the *theatre's* capacity to intervene publicly in social organisation and to critique political structures can be more extensive than the relatively isolated circumstances of written narrative and poetry.[2] In terms of genre, the post-colonial theatre has the potential to be much more discursive than other media because of its non-verbal language, as well as providing a public forum where questions about the very nature of the post-colonial context and subject can be provoked and visualised. Moreover, it is evident that in times of social transformation or national crisis, the insecurities, anxieties and fears of a community can be either assuaged or exposed in the theatre, even when simplified and made visible through the use of ideological stereotypes. These stereotypes are deployed in an attempt to establish a sense of security and identity amidst shifting norms and realities. For instance, the prevalence of gender stereotypes of the mother, daughter, or 'whore' become symbols of identification or de-nunciation in the formation of the Nation.

In this section, two plays written after the ethnic riots of 1983 are examined as a reflection of the concerns of a nation in crisis. Until the 1980s, the English language theatre in Sri Lanka was primarily confined to continuing the theatrical tradition established during colonial rule. The prolixity of western plays increasingly came under attack by theatre critics and audiences.[3] Events of 1983 were instrumental in challenging the complacency of the English-theatre audiences (an issue which will be explored in detail later in my examination of Ernest MacIntyre's *Rasanayagam's*

Last Riot), and witnessed a change in the concerns expressed in the English theatre with playwrights engaging with themes and subjects drawn from daily realities.

More recently, in attempting to awaken audiences to the (largely uncontested) repression in Sri Lanka, playwrights such as Ernest MacIntyre are faced with the difficulties of working within a context of threats, fear and censorship.[4] In trying to overcome such constraints, they adopt an allegorical framework in which to approach the issues of contemporary political violence.

Ernest MacIntyre's reputation as Sri Lanka's most prominent playwright can be attributed to the sophisticated craftsmanship and thematic relevance of his plays. *Rasanayagam's Last Riot* (1993) is centred around the ethnic riots of 1983 while *Village in the Jungle* (1994) is a contemporary reading of Leonard Woolf's novel of the same name in the light of the 1988-89 JVP insurrection. My exploration of MacIntyre's work begins with *Rasanayagam's Last Riot* which foregrounds the ideological effects of a political crisis on its female protagonist, Sita Fernando, and her family's involvement with a Tamil friend, Rasanayagam. This is followed by a discussion of *Village in the Jungle*. I am interested in the construction of ethnic identity which is negotiated through Sita in *Rasanayagam's Last Riot* and the female figures in *Village in the Jungle*. The rising influence of the pre-Independence Ceylonese westernised elite (depicted in the characters of Wickremanayake and Ramanathan in *Village in the Jungle*) has crucial implications for contemporary politics, and these issues are conveyed through allegory. While I am aware of the danger of reducing 'third world texts' to 'national allegories', in the following section, I wish to argue that in MacIntyre's *Village in the Jungle* 'the individual experience' portrayed on stage can be read as an allegory of experiences of national conflicts.[5] MacIntyre interpolates hidden meanings into familiar experience, and in *Village in the Jungle* the allegory of colonial administration is a reminder of the perpetuation of socio-political hegemony in the post-Independence milieu.

The Angst of Identity in *Rasanayagam's Last Riot*

Rasanayagam's Last Riot takes place during the middle of the ethnic riots of 1983 and two thematic strands are interwoven. Sita, a middle-class Tamil, and her husband Philip Fernando, a Sinhalese, attempt to protect Philip's Tamil friend Rasanayagam from the anti-Tamil violence. After a few days in their house, Rasanayagam decides to go to a refugee camp because he feels that it is impor-tant to show his solidarity with the majority of the suffering Tamils. On his way there he encounters a Sinhalese mob and when he refuses to succumb to their intimidation he is killed by the mob.

The sub-plot focuses almost entirely on the effects of the ethnic crisis on Sita's sense of self. Her identity is thrown into crisis as she becomes aware of the dynamics of the ethnic struggle and its implications for her as a Tamil. In the Introduction to the play MacIntyre makes the point that

[t]his Tamil, married to a Sinhalese, gradually opens out to those around her, about her innermost thoughts and feelings on how July '83 came about. [...] For soon after the riots, Colombo's mixed society of western-ised Tamils and Sinhalese tacitly settled on an arrangement that would enable it to continue functioning. Whatever was locked in their heads or embedded in their hearts, about which organisations and people were to be held responsible, they would not utter in public.[6]

As Sita becomes increasingly conscious of her 'Tamilness', her ensuing confusion is produced from suddenly having to reconcile the meaning of her ethnic identity with her other 'selves'—her status as an English-educated woman, her position as a university lecturer in an English literature department, and her marriage to a Sinhalese man. She begins to realise that her identities have to be negotiated and redefined. This portrayal is an interesting case of the multiple (and sometimes ambivalent or interchangeable) selves that constantly work towards undermining the fixed 'I'. The complexity of identity is signalled by Daphne Marlatt when she speaks of the 'I' as being composed of 'contradictory images struggling to speak the difference we sense through rigid assump-tions of sameness and identity'.[7] For Sita, the contradictions of class, race and language force her to mediate (not always consciously or successfully) the multiplicities of the 'I'. These identities also collide with a pre-determined notion of gender which is inscribed through the variety of social practices in which she acts. As Phillipa Rothfield remarks, identities imply different subjectivities which are produced according to social context and forms of practice.[8]

For the most part of her life, Sita identifies closely with her husband's middle-class, westernised background which, conveniently, does not require her to specify her ethnic identity since it is her class identity that matters here, and it is assumed that she too is Sinhalese. One of the ambivalences that remains beyond the culture of the play is her rationale for denying her ethnicity: we do not know whether she behaves in this manner simply for convenience or as a protective device in times of communal riots. Whatever her motive though, until 1983 she regards herself only as a 'nominal Tamil'. At the outset of the play she is clearly agitated and her disquietude stems from the realisation that she can no longer evade the connotations of her ethnic background. The politicisation of being a Tamil in a majority Sinhalese community emerges gradually. She begins to unravel the complexities of her marriage and background, where her Tamil identity is blurred to such an extent that it is no longer recognisable.

In describing the effects of the East-West encounter in India, Nayantara Sahgal's observations offer an interesting commentary on Sita's predicament. Sahgal explains that '[n]ationalism produced another breed of westernised Indian for whom his plural culture meant a bewildering reckoning with himself, a balancing act, where the priorities were never in doubt, but where "Who am I?" remained the on-going search and question'.[9] Similar questions and doubts are provoked in Sita but, as she begins to understand the privileges of her position, she is also aware of how her worldview differs from the rest of her community.

The disparity between the English-educated elite and the rest of the population is clearly marked at the outset in the dialogue: 'Why such a lot of things?' (*RLR* 1). The distance between the English-educated class and the rest of population is also apparent in Sita's admission of previously having joined 'all those people in abusing the Tamils, to keep suspicion off [her] house' (*RLR* 2). This time, however, she feels that she can no longer continue the charade. Furthermore, *all* Tamils are now at risk and ethnicity is ingrained in people's notion of identity: 'the communal thing has deepened so horribly' (*RLR* 7).[10] Having denied her ethnic identity for years, Sita now finds that, 'like all [her] Colombo Tamil friends and relatives, she cannot identify with the other Tamil, because her class creates another barrier between them' (*RLR* 7). This experience unsettles her as she opens up to the possibility that interlocking structures like gender, class, religion and ethnicity often are in conflict and lead to the fragmentation of identity. Refashioning another identity is not an instant process and cannot be adapted according to circumstance. While it is provisional and has the potential to be altered, identity-formation is often traumatic.

The dilemma here is of a post-colonial subject who must come to terms with the connotations of her identity in times of nationalist struggle. As a product of a colonial education and economic system she is in a double bind because, though she occupies a privileged space, it is one which is associated with the continued injustices and exploitation wrought by colonialism. Although Sita straddles the contradictions of class, gender and ethnic distinctions/groupings, there is a way in which her predicament as a post-colonial who inhabits what she must despise, and despises what she must inhabit, allows her to confront the larger implications of her class-position. Indeed, her postcolonial identity enables her to question the existing ethnic differences and engage in a dialogue at *every* level, from the personal to the political. She adheres to the belief that 'if it can't be discussed openly, at a personal level between such old friends, in a recurring dramatic situation like this', there is little 'hope ... of a settlement at a national level' (*RLR* 6).

As a minority within a minority, that is, an English-speaking Tamil, Sita acknowledges the complicity of her class in contributing to the escalating ethnic tensions. She can recognise the chauvinist tone inscribed in nationalist identities and the need to contest and challenge it. This consciousness extends to a critique of her class. Even under crisis conditions, they are oblivious to the concerns of the masses. This is illustrated in the 'curfew parties' during national curfews, their glib ability at clothing/masking feelings in bombastic terms (as Philip frequently exemplifies), and making excuses for evading reality. When Sita voices her concern about their indifference, Philip responds with the comment: 'No individual resolution can ever have an impact on a general situ ...' (*RLR* 15). The underlying tragedy of this position is that while the elite and the intelligentsia played a crucial role in initiating the pre-Independence nationalist and political struggles, their role after Independence is one of self-seeking indifference.[11]

One of the concerns of the play is the Sinhala/Tamil ethnic and ideological divide, and Rasanayagam's first-hand experience of ethnic violence and his knowledge of the cultural nuances of his ethnic group make him a representative of the 'nationalist' voice of the Tamils. Rasanayagam's refusal to be identified as a Sinhalese conveys his ideological affiliation with the Tamil population: 'every grievance and discrimination that the Tamils are claiming I subscribe to' (*RLR* 34). Towards the culmination of the play it is this ideological affiliation that prompts Rasanayagam to align himself with the suffering Tamils and decide to move into a refugee camp. When he meets the mob this time he realises that the Sinhala/Tamil distinction is so strong and the differences are so clearly defined that he can no longer betray his ethnic identity and he meets the demands of the mob with silence.

The final scene of the play uses the form of an Epilogue and depicts the Fernandos at Singapore airport waiting to board their plane to Australia. A recent massacre of a Sinhalese village by the Tamil militants is shown in a BBC World Service report on television in the airport lounge. This scene may be construed as MacIntyre's endeavour to present the atrocities committed by the Tamil militants. Hearing the news, the play culminates with Philip and Sita's conciliatory remark that 'at least between [sic] the two of us there must be something called Sri Lankan' (*RLR* 50). Such a position is facile because, although MacIntyre strives to explore the complexities of ethnic politics, regrettably, the Epilogue simplifies issues: the solution does not lie in *equating* the atrocities committed by the two sides. It is unfortunate that MacIntyre falls prey to this kind of strategy because, the rest of the play's radical content exceeds this conservative denouement.

The playwright's ambivalence emerges from these two scenes, the disinclination to take risks, to make choices and stand by them while not having a watertight theory-as-dogma to rely on for support. Nonetheless, despite the conservative ending, *Rasanayagam's Last Riot* launches an assault on the English-educated elite. In trying to be 'objective' MacIntyre reveals the risks he faces in transporting 'traumatic' issues onto a public forum: of criticism from his audience, state censorship and political intervention.

Village in the Jungle as Political Commentary

After the escalation of armed conflict and civil war in 1983, any form of political dissent was suppressed, and oppositional representation of the Sri Lankan nation became more oblique. For the playwrights, allegory offers a useful way of representing state and anti-state interventions. *Village in the Jungle* takes Leonard Woolf's novel *The Village in the Jungle* as its point of reference in allegorising contemporary politics and exploiting the semantic indeterminacy of allegory. Allegory depends on the socio-historical, temporal, political and cultural context that it endeavours to portray. Signifiers from the 'world out there' are semantically fixed to a culturally positioned and historically grounded 'master code'.[12] The 'master code' here relates to the management of a political crisis that resembles another historical period: colonialism.

Like Leonard Woolf's novel, the play ostensibly maintains the vision of colonial Ceylon. However, reworkings, significant elisions and points of departure from the former text accentuate the contemporary setting, making it possible for the audience to assume that such conflicts persist in the modern era.

An obvious similarity between the novel and MacIntyre's play is the economic exploitation of the villagers by the forces of power. Silindu and his family are entrapped within, and impoverished by, a corrupt socio-economic system. When he can no longer evade the harsh taxation scheme, Silindu murders the corrupt local government representative, Babehami and his business ally, Fernando. The device of critiquing the 'establishment' is worked through by setting up a polarity of the exploiters and exploited in a western-ised/rural dichotomy. This is remarkably similar to the pre-Independence nationalists who constructed the Imperialists as privileged and evil exploiters, and the indigenous as the 'authen-tic' oppressed.[13] This kind of romantic construction is problematic for it does not adequately explore the mechanisms of power, and avoids an engagement with the complex web of relations in a neo-colonial setting.

In MacIntyre's version, Silindu's act of personal survival is reinvented to give it a contemporary, political reading. It is interpreted by the Ceylonese as an act of subversion, even though it is not so. Silindu is taken into police custody and ruthlessly tortured by a Ceylonese policeman, Ramanathan. He subsequently dies in prison. In Woolf's novel a substantial section is devoted to Silindu's court case, whereas in the play MacIntyre does not repeat this scene. It is, instead, replaced by the torture scene. In doing so MacIntyre evokes the political climate of the 1980s in Sri Lanka.[14] Uneasy links are forged between colonial and neo-colonial re-pression in such a portrayal reminding the audience that these practices continue to be a part of the political character of the post-Independence state.

The taxation system is devised in such a manner that it ensures the villagers' permanent state of poverty. Babehami acts as the middle-man between the power-brokers and the populace. His use of terror-tactics (in his dealings with the villagers) recalls the coercion of both the state and counter-state forces during the last decade in Sri Lanka. The web of exploitation is implemented from above.

> **Silindu**: Ralahami, I am a poor man. How can I pay four
> shillings or even three? There is not a fanam in the house.
> [...] You are my father and my mother.[15]

Silindu's lamentation epitomises the predicament of the villagers. The dialogue is supported by a visualisation of the extreme poverty of the villagers through a variety of theatrical devices such as the costumes and sparse sets. MacIntyre's sensitive portrayal of this oppression and poverty reflects the basis of the recent socio-political tensions. The corruption of the elite and the rigid class structure give rise to economic inequalities by exploiting the nation's economic resources and neglecting the poor. These conditions, combined with political repression and violence, provide the optimal conditions for anarchy. In such a fraught climate, Silindu's 'survival' tactic against the forces of power, that is, his murder of Babehami and Fernando, is assigned a political significance. Classifying Silindu as a political prisoner blurs the distinction between personal and political resistance. Hence Silindu is denied a trial and his death in custody is uncontested.

MacIntyre is also aware of mechanisms to counteract the structures of dominance institutionalised by the westernised elite. Emphasis on indigenisation by the Sinhala nationalist ideologues is a powerful strategy which finds a place in the play. The reference to Sri Lankan food, especially Fernando's description of rice and curry, as well as certain linguistic devices, intrinsically re-create a rural ethos. For instance, Silindu's speech patterns are characterised by the repetition of 'aiyo', a typical Sinhala utterance which captures a gamut of emotional states from sadness to frustration. The rehabilitation of an indigenous, cultural identity, in this case Sinhala Buddhist, is frequently pitted against the 'western' corruption of Wickremanayake and may be a deliberate attempt on the part of the playwright to draw attention to the mobilising strategy of the Marxist Sinhala resistance group, the JVP. Against the corrupt, westernised elite, MacIntyre constructs an authentic, Sinhala nationalist identity which he projects onto the rural woman women characters. Indeed, as I argue in the next section, these women become the locus of national identity. However, while setting up the rural/urban dichotomy, MacIntyre also subverts it in crucial ways.

A further point of departure between Woolf's novel and the play occurs in the representation of the women characters. In the former, Silindu's daughters inhabit a peripheral social position in the village and their way of life is regarded as aberrant by the rest of the villagers. A distinction is made between Silindu's daughters and the 'Colombo' women (the European and the westernised Ceylonese) as well as the village women. In the play, on the other hand, MacIntyre polarises the women according to locale and class, that is, urban rich or rural poor. The only portrayals of village women are of Silindu's daughters, Punchi Menike and Hinnihami. Of the two the former is extensively 'fleshed out' and, in many respects, she becomes the sole representative of the village women. She stands for dignity through hardship, close contact with her roots, and resistance to materialism. The virtue and victimisation of the village woman is counterposed to the commodified and sexually exploited western, or westernised woman.[16] Her everyday life is circumscribed by a triple bind: the complex relations of race, class and gender.

Punchi Menike's plight is textually rendered in Fernando's attempts to seduce her. His economic power grants him the right to have sexual relations with her even though she is married to Babun, a villager. He tries to entice her by flaunting his experiences of the 'city' women: the European women and the westernised Ceylonese women. Part of his braggadocio involves describing their past times: 'And I remembered how the white *mahathmayas* [gentlemen] took their white ladies close to their stomachs like this, with their bodies pressed' (*VIJ* 29) .

He compares the westernised Ceylonese women to the European women—'Oh! what a town is Colombo! And there the rich Sinhalese ladies have learnt to enjoy life, from looking at how the white ladies enjoy life'—and assumes that activities like dancing signify sexual licentiousness (*VIJ* 38). Hence his confident assertion, 'When I get back to the town there will be plenty of women' (*VIJ* 30).

On one level, Fernando's narrative blatantly exposes the mechanics of male dominance by defining women along a narrow spectrum of behavioural codes. It is not just the ideological formations of western and 'traditional' that are applied as the yardsticks for constructing the codes of 'appropriate' and 'inappropriate' female behaviour, but, in stressing the sexual element of the 'city' women's behaviour, sexuality becomes instrumental in inscribing a virgin/whore paradigm. Fernando relies on familiar metaphors to reinforce this paradigm. In his description of the urban character's seduction techniques, with its Sri Lankan nuances of eating a meal, sensuality is evoked through olfactory, visual, and tactile senses. The heat of the chillies and the smell and taste of the curries underscore the impact of the sexual experience for both Punchi Menike and the audience (*VIJ* 39). The metaphor derives its efficacy from contextual appropriateness. Both character and audience can identify with it. As the metaphor develops, it is accompanied by a gradual shift in emotion from mere boasting to menace, and the inescapable unease that Punchi Menike experiences is profoundly transmitted to the audience through the subtext of Fernando's speech.

Despite his boastfulness, Fernando does not valorise the behaviour of the city woman because such excessive codes of behaviour are an outright threat to her indigenous roots. Their perceived absence of 'morality', registered here by the physical closeness to men is appropriated to determine the standards for women in general. It is an instance where, as Lynda Nead argues, 'the moral behaviour of women has to be regulated because it is a part of a wider formation of class, identity and nation'.[17] In the same way that 'clothing becomes emblematic of a cultural or racial group', the female body enters an 'unstable arena of scrutiny and meaning'.[18] A parallel trend in nationalist ideology in India is recognised by R. Radhakrishnan when she states that 'questions of change and progress posed in Western attire were conceived as an outer and epiphenomenal aspect of [Indian] identity, whereas the inner and inviolable sanctum of identity had to do with home, spirituality, and the figure of Woman as representative of the true self'.[19]

The identification of women as privileged bearers of corporate identities and boundary markers of their communities can be read into Punchi Menike's role in the play. Her identity is inextricably linked to her husband. Fernando refers to her as 'the woman of Babun' (*VIJ* 41). Just as she sees men as the arbiters of female (im)morality, so she is content to leave all the negotiations that involve her fate to be performed by men, whether it is her father or her husband. Although in one way her portrayal seems to veer towards a romantic construction of the *daughter of the nation,* to dismiss MacIntyre's portrayal of Punchi Menike as mere gender stereotyping overlooks the subversive potential of the text.

One such aspect is prompted in questions about the construction of 'appropriate' female behaviour. Both Punchi Menike and Hinnihami help their father by working in the fields 'like men' (*VIJ* 8). The older village women, Nonchahami in particular, are quick to denigrate this involvement because it violates the boundaries of the home, 'the archetype of privacy'.[20] What is most interesting here is MacIntyre's consciousness of the paradox faced by Sri Lankan women. Women, especially rural women, make a significant input to the agrarian economy and, as Phillipa Rothfield has suggested, '*vis-à-vis* women's association with the private sphere, women have not universally and transhistorically lived and worked only within the home'.[21] Furthermore, Punchi Menike's consciousness of the repressive mechanisms within her social ambit emblematises the question of how women in Sri Lanka (both from the urban and rural sectors) are often highly politicised and are increasingly agitating for social change. In this regard, the stereotyping of women in nationalist discourses relates to an atavistic or constructed myth. For both men and women this position feeds into a wish-fulfilment of their socially-programmed outlook.

Village in the Jungle complicates and challenges the use of these popular stereotypes. As we have seen in the figure of Punchi Menike, equating the 'land' with the passive mother/daughter image fails to account for the empowering possibilities that arise when individuals grapple for meaning between their personal and political worlds. Deniz Kandiyoti's argument is applicable to understanding the 'hidden agenda' of such imaging. She notes that '[t]he association of women with the private domain reinforces the merging of the nation/community with the selfless mother/devout wife; the obvious response of coming to her defence and even dying for her is automatically triggered'.[22]

MacIntyre's reputation as Sri Lanka's most sophisticated playwright derives from his radical thematic concerns and technical creativity. His innovative dramatic technique and experimentation with form have contributed to the wide appeal of his work. His sure grasp of language, dramatic tension, comedy and subject matter have made an impact on the English language

theatre in Sri Lanka. His achievement as a playwright is also
marked by a sensitive portrayal of gender relations. The kind of
assumptions made about women, whether it concerns taking a
husband's surname or working in the fields, are contextualised
and problematised within the nationalist conflict. The contradictions, provisionality, and wide-ranging complexity of female
identity finds a voice in his plays. The co-option of the 'pure'
woman into the symbolic repertoire of the nation and the burden
of it is seen in different manifestations.

Negotiating Identity: The Poetry of Jean Arasanayagam

While images of women have continuously emblazoned nationalist
propaganda in Sri Lanka, their effects in the imaginative consciousness have rarely received public attention in either literature
or the media by women themselves. Jean Arasanayagam's constructions of women are grounded in the shifting historical and
socio-political circumstances of contemporary Sri Lanka. The
thematic content of her work is located within the intricacies of
female identity and its fragmentation, negotiation and reinvention.
    Arasanayagam (*née* Solomons) is a Burgher, that is, a descen-
dant of the Europeans. After her marriage to Thiagarajah Arasanayagam, a Tamil, she identified herself with the Tamil community. Part of her rationale for doing so was to gain acceptance into
her in-laws' family. She claims that she was also attracted to the
religious and social rituals of Tamil culture.[23] She captures the
stages of this procedure with forceful clarity in the poems from the
sequence 'Thirtham is Bitter' in *A Colonial Inheritance and Other
Poems* (1985). The implications of being identified with two
minority cultures in an era of ethnic chauvinism have been the
source of inspiration for a large body of poetry.
    The daily realities of political violence, ethnic chauvinism and
patriarchal pressures are reflected in her work in a wide range of
tones and emotions, from urgency and anger to confusion and
helplessness. She does not confine herself to the present-day ethnic
crisis but traces its roots to the violence of colonialism. The
exploration of the diverse identities that women inhabit in a
nationalist context is mapped by transporting the experiences from

the personal to the political realm. The imperatives determining the construction of identity are emphatically foregrounded in her poems. The different periods of her poetic development illustrate the process of arriving at a notion of 'self'. Starting with an interrogation of the self in her earliest poems in *Kindura and Other Poems* (1973), I will demonstrate that this collection marks the beginning of her politicisation, which is more clearly registered in later works such as *A Colonial Inheritance* (1985), *Apocalypse '83* (1987), *Reddened Water Flows Clear* (1991) and *Shooting the Floricans* (1993). Her experiences during the ethnic crisis and the politics of post-1983 Sri Lanka have provided a point of reference for articulating the concerns faced by women in conflict. The poems written immediately after 1983 signify a deeply personal response to the crisis, graphically documenting the violent potential of nationalism and the contradictions between the ethnic violence and the symbolic configuration of woman-as-national icon.

In her earliest collection, *Kindura and Other Poems*, an introspective quest for the meaning of 'self' is prominent. There is an awareness of the ambivalence of identities, that is, her own gender and ethnicity, as she strives to overcome the unease associated with it. The emotional states depicted are intensely personal, framed within and against natural landscapes. The strongest image in these poems is of isolation.[24] In 'Narcissus', the lonely self is positioned against nature.

> [...] all nature
> was his glassy pool, even the water breathed
> and pulsed at wink of eyelid and of lash,
> the ripple gazed, took shimmer from the dazzle [...][25]

The deep involvement with the landscape is created through the visual and tactile splendour of the flora and fauna. What is prominent here is the search of a lone individual, struggling to find a meaning in nature for a condition relating to and engendered by human realities. The underlying strain of isolation can be explained with reference to the complexities of her socio-political milieu more satisfactorily. These poems were written soon after the 1970 general election. To present the background: the platform of the elected party, the Sri Lanka Freedom Party, reinstituted Sinhala Buddhism, and their victory was a testimony to Mrs Sirimavo Bandaranaike's endorsement of the hegemony of the Sinhala Buddhist ethos created by her late husband in *his* election victory in 1956, which marginalised the Burghers and the English-educated elite.[26] Although Arasanayagam chose to live in Sri Lanka, rather than joining the exodus of these groups to the west, she, like most people of her class, felt the tensions of this climate. The poems evoke the beginnings of recognising the ramifications of her ethnic and class background, but they are limited by a narrow focus and only rarely go beyond the sense impressions to a larger political vision.

The human contact that was lacking in the earlier poems was redressed later in the political crucible of 1983, the ethnic riots. The change was generated, according to Regi Siriwardene, by the fact that, 'like so many women of her class, she found herself under-going the hitherto inconceivable as violence overwhelmed her and her family, and she was compelled to share the anguish and terror of a community to whose fate she was bound not by birth but by marriage'.[27] Her Burgher lineage was of no consequence to the Sinhalese majority who targeted her family. In order to develop as a poet she had to progress beyond the reactions of shock or empathy with the victims of 1983. Nonetheless, this was a vital stage as it was a necessary emotional catharsis for her, and an act of atonement for the collective guilt of her community. The aftermath of the ethnic riots provoked her to strive for a more meaningful identity, all the more intense, the more wide-ranging because the suffering she had undergone made clear the horror of ethnocentric divisions.

The most evocative poems in *Apocalypse '83* derive their impact from the immediacy of the subject matter. Through sensory images she describes the relentless pain, brutality and death of the carnage of 1983. One of the most evocative poems from this collection is 'Nallur'. The poetic impact of 'Nallur' emerges from the forceful fusion of religion and political violence. The description of religious sacrifice in Nallur, one of the most renowned Hindu temples in the Jaffna peninsula, the stronghold of the Tamils, underlines the close association of death with religious rites and political acts.

    it's there
          death,
          smell it in the air [...]
    it's there
    amid the clangour of
the temple bells, the clapping hands,
the brassy clash of cymbals.
               the zing of bullets
               the cries of death
               drowned in the roar
               of voices calling Skanda
               by his thousand names
               Murugan, Kartikkeya
               Arumugam [...]
'We pray, we cry, we clamour
oh Sri Kumaran, be not like the god
who does not hear, deaf Sandesvaran.'[28]

A close reading of the above section of the poem exposes some of the underlying complexities of the contemporary political scenario in Sri Lanka. On a thematic level, the subject of death alludes to the violence of protracted and prolonged conflict in which over fifty thousand people have been killed to date. The language of the poem contributes to its impact. For example, the evocative onomatopoeic 'zing of bullets' connotes the swiftness with which death strikes its innocent victims. Likewise, 'smell' takes on a double meaning. On a literal level it applies to the odour of dead bodies that are often allowed to rot on the streets during a time of war. In its metaphoric guise, the word plays on the idiomatic use of 'smell', which is linked to the proximity of danger. The physical and psychological confusion wreaked by conflict is conveyed through the confusion within the Hindu temple. In contrast to Christian places of worship, Hindu rituals are accompanied by a profusion of sounds, from the 'clapping hands' to the alliterative 'clash of cymbals'. The blurring of sounds mirrors the blurring of rational thinking, of individuality, in the realm of armed conflict.

Interestingly, the poet draws on her Christian background and interweaves Hindu and Christian symbols in an attempt to find a meaning to the wanton destruction incurred in the process of

nationalist struggles. The plethora of religious symbols in the
passage serves an ideological function in establishing a nexus
between religious discourses and concepts of 'patriotism', 'nation'
and 'sacrifice'. 'Nallur' underscores the increasing co-option of
religion into the nationalist cause.

Bringing the violence to a place of worship serves another
function. It refers to the violent practice of inter-communal
conflicts and is reminiscent of one of the LTTE's most prominent
strategies since 1983, of targeting Buddhist temples.[29] The underlying tone of hopelessness, registered in the people's appeal to the
gods is made more poignant when framed against this backdrop.
The poetic devices such as a lack of punctuation, short, discontinu-
ous phrases, accentuate the desperation, and the invocation to the
Hindu gods re-enact the incantatory effect of religious chants. The
note of breathlessness is achieved through the poetic form, the
enjambed lines, half-lines and staccato rhythm, all of which make
the devotees' appeal seem all the more urgent. Yet the relentless
cries of the people are undercut by the 'deafness' of the god
'Sandesveran'. While Sri Kumaran is implored to hear, the lack of
punctuation can suggest that the final invocation is not made to Sri
Kumaran but to 'deaf' Sandesveran who will not hear their cries
anyway, connoting the futility of the final invocation. It is an
assault on the irrelevance of religion.

The graphic representation of religious ritual is juxtaposed
against the omnipresence of death. These images speak of the
grandeur of religious and cultural rituals of an elite community
under the threat of violent separatism. The landscape is divested of
its people and only the 'charred stones' of the temple are left
standing. The façades are the only reminders of a lost splendour.
In situating the rituals precisely in their cultural context, Arasanayagam also makes a comment about the exclusionary paradigms of Hindu society where non-Hindus are not granted access
to the socio-cultural and religious life.

Even as Arasanayagam grapples with such political themes,
her negotiation is framed in relation to her preoccupation with a
definitive sense of identity. The pathos in the reference to the
'nameless dead' and their 'lost identities' is unmistakable. The
anonymity of being buried in mass graves or dumped into rivers

or seas, enables her to search for her identity even more vehe-mently. Her own search for identity is contrasted with the way in which the victims of war are denied even the fundamental claim to an identity, their name. This position is counterposed against an admission of her own privileged position: 'I had my identity / safe from marauders.' An ambivalence in her subjectivity is that, despite the privileges of class and culture, as a victim of ethnic violence, these privileges no longer shield her and expose the brutal actuality that, 'now I'm in it [...] at last history has mean-ing'.[30]

Paradoxically, a disabling condition—incomprehension—is here enabling, ultimately leading to the realisation that identity is perpetually in a state of flux. The dilemma captured in the poem can be understood in relation to Homi Bhabha's assertion that 'identity is never an *a priori*, nor a finished product; it is only ever the problematic process of access to an image of totality'.[31] In Arasanayagam's case the 'image of totality' entails recognising that identity is constitutive of 'difference'. Both her 'identities', as a Burgher and later a Tamil, are differentiated from the dominant Sinhalese.

The pivotal line 'at last history has meaning' can be read as an epigraph for her next collection *A Colonial Inheritance and Other Poems*.[32] It is in this collection that she extensively explores the implications of her dual identities, the Burgher woman who married a Tamil and acquired a Tamil surname. *A Colonial Inheri-tance and Other Poems* is almost entirely devoted to Arasanaya-gam's Burgher ancestry. It is a portrayal of privilege and genteel-ness: 'blue glass, painted roses and ebony', 'Edwardian collars, aunts in / Brussels lace'.[33] This nostalgic vein is carried through in other poems and is designed to highlight the positive aspects of her inheritance.[34] The cultural sophistication forms an integral part of Arasanayagam's ethno-historic background. Erasure or efface-ment of this heritage would be an indicator of Arasanayagam's inability to reconcile herself to her past. On the contrary, her celebration of this heritage is progressive in a nation where colonialism is still a contentious issue. On another level, her

portrayal of her past contributes towards rehabilitating an empowering image of the Burgher woman.

   Her work is underpinned by the specific dilemma of locating
this lineage within a colonial praxis that included untrammelled
violence. The recurring reminders of colonialism work to situate
the present destruction in a broader historical context and gesture
towards the mutually reinforcing relation between ethnic violence
and neo-colonialism. This 'cultural identity' is also the source of
her alienation as a Burgher from the mainstream because the
outcome of colonial intervention is the fissures and rupture of
identity. The metaphors of colonialism unveil its disruptive effects.
In 'Genealogies', for instance, 'blood' has multiple connotations. It
is a metaphor for 'blood line' or 'heritage', a direct marker of her
lineage, but can also refer to the 'blood' split during the violent
transactions of colonisation.

> Have I no shame or guilt
> That my inheritance came
> With sword and gun
> Storming the land,
> Crushing the wind,
> Sowing with dragon teeth
> The golden strand?[35]

   Two interrelated interpretations of the above excerpt provide a
point of access to the different dimensions of colonialism. One
reading applies to colonial violence. The brute force of her ancestors' arrival on the Island is captured here. 'Storming' and
'crushing' are bolstered by the metaphor of 'dragon teeth'. The
latter is a play on the physical outline of the ships which, in the
distance, recalls the stock image of a monster looming through the
sea. One can imagine the terror of an indigenous people who are
unable to rationalise or explain these strange shapes in the sea.
'Dragon teeth' blends with 'crushing' to reveal the material reality
of colonialism, that is, the subordination of the indigenous inhabitants of these territories. The stress on their power is achieved
in the poem through the repetition of 'storming', with 'sword' and
'gun'.

In her consideration of the past, Arasanayagam is extremely mindful of the sexual implications and consequences of the colonialist enterprise. In the above excerpt the sexual metaphor in the last two lines, the 'dragon teeth', has an evocative reference, echoing the *dragoon* of soldiers raping or sexually exploiting the indigenous women and thereby 'sowing their seed'. 'Dragoon' appropriately captures the coercion that may have been applied to seduce the women with their 'golden strand'. 'Golden strand' similarly has a metaphoric application as sperm or, on a more literal level, the colour of the invaders' hair, both of which play a part in sexual intercourse: one as a component of it, and the other as a physical trait that is transmitted through it. Arasanayagam's interest in this dimension of colonial relations can be seen in terms of her personal involvement. Her identity is intricately bound to the diverse levels of colonial exploitation, including sexual exploitation.

Here is evidence of the complexity of her heritage. The atrocities of colonial intermixing result in the contemporary anxiety over miscegenation. If she tries to convince herself that she was the result of a union of 'love' she is also faced with the reality of colonial relations and hence the comment that 'consummation' was *'perhaps* of their lust'.[36] This ambivalence emerges from the double bind of, on the one hand, denying their 'blood', her heritage, where the consequences would leave her a 'beggar, intestate', while on the other hand, accepting her 'blood' would mean bearing the guilt of almost three hundred years of oppression. The self-questioning tone is symptomatic of the psychological burden. At the same time, however, it denotes the psychological state of people like Arasanayagam as offering 'possibilities of (individual and communal) psychic regeneration' and her poetry is the vehicle for achieving this.[37]

For Arasanayagam personally, the security of the past is undermined by nationalistic forces. It emphasises a lack of roots in a nation where every person's identity is determined by and dependent upon 'connections'. These connections are appropriated to become the defining markers of an 'authentic', 'pristine' identity. These aspects of identity are lamented in poems like 'Ancestors' and 'Roots'. Roots' evokes the need for personal stability.

> I learn how important it is to have roots
> just when it is too late [...].
> My eyes looking into yours tell me that I
> *cannot* belong, even the buffaloes wallowing and the snakes
> gliding through silver mounds[38]

'Cannot belong' strategically conveys a yearning as she compares her state of physical and psychological unrest with the stability of the animals and nature, which is lacking in her life. The sensual language and imagery strongly resemble the sentiments expressed in her earliest work. The anxieties borne through cross-cultural mixing are articulated through the natural phenomena. The permutations and combinations of colonial miscegenation are so far removed from their European original that, in Arasanayagam's case, she can no longer be recognised as a European, but then she is neither Sinhala nor Tamil. Experiences of split identity and miscegenation are made visible by her presence in Sri Lanka.

The section entitled 'The Thirtham is Bitter' in *A Colonial Inheritance* is devoted to charting the dialectic of intermarriage. Many of the poems interrogate the rituals and social practices of her husband's conservative Tamil family and culture. Prejudice is evidenced by the attitude of Arasanayagam's mother-in-law towards her Burgher daughter-in-law. The older woman's attitude, combined with the family's deep-rooted cultural mores, exacerbates the poet's need for roots. While wrestling with the bewilderment of occupying neither the Tamil nor the Burgher space, she maintains a complexity of judgement and a subtly-poised ambivalence of feeling. She is able to use, with the inwardness of sympathy, the language of Hindu belief and ritual, simultaneously unveiling the clannishness, the authoritarianism, the attachment to property of a conservative society.[39]

The most forceful poem in this section, 'My Mother-in-Law', embodies the most prominent facets of the Tamil elite. The overriding impression is of a matriarchal figure who is steeped in religious superstition and pride of her noble heritage. The mutual hostility and contempt between the two women are transmitted through a skilful use of tone. The graphic detail of the older woman's antagonism towards a 'foreign' daughter-in-law exposes the potency of deep-rooted ethnic prejudices:

> She *chose* not to know me
> or my family, perhaps she remembers
> My name so foreign on her tongue
> So alien, but vaguely[40]

Two dominant images are juxtaposed in the poem. The first one: of treating her daughter-in-law like a social pariah (I have emphasised 'chose' not to know me, a refrain which unmasks it as a voluntary act) is matched by the older woman's adherence to all the religious rituals and prayers 'for long hours'. This ironic contrast exposes the hypocrisy and meaninglessness of religion. The rigidity of such religious ideology does not accommodate religious, cultural or racial difference. The mother/whore dichotomy within the Hindu discourses which I have discussed earlier underlines the mother-in-law's rationale. The older woman's compliance in perpetuating patriarchal practices, such as the asceticism expected of a widow, affirms her ideological commitment to this value-system which, through the explicit details of the Hindu traditions, becomes the marker of discrimination.

In the Hindu social structure, the mother/whore dichotomy is reconfigured as a mother/whore/partner-in-ritual trichotomy because woman is invested with the role of *partner in ritual*. She supports her husband in performing the prescribed sacrifices to ancestors and gods. In his absence she takes on the complete responsibility of this role. Hence her socio-religious position is held in high esteem. These terms of reference provide the principal reason for the mother-in-law's contempt towards her Burgher daughter-in-law. It is based on the younger woman's inability to participate in the *Tamil* socio-cultural and religious rituals. The 'alien' race and religion invalidate her position as the wife of a Tamil man. She is thus relegated to a status that is, at best, equivalent to an outsider, at worst a 'whore'. In her analysis of gender and nationalism in colonial Bengal, Samita Sen makes a point which is relevant to understanding of the dynamics in the relationship between Arasanayagam and her mother-in-law. The culturally ignorant wife becomes a variant of the *immoral* woman who holds the stage in the drama of moral doom and chaos.[41]

On another level, the older woman's underlying resentment can be traced to the knowledge that her daughter-in-law cannot produce pure *Tamil* sons.[42] 'Purity' here can be applied as a metaphor for the mother's brave, warrior sons. This ideological position is the outcome of years of conditioning, encoded within a masculinist discourse of the brave, male warrior safeguarding their community and, by extension, their mothers.

From a nationalist perspective, the older woman's anxiety about producing pure blood corresponds to the Nation's valorisation of a mother's capacity to continue the Sinhala and Tamil races, more importantly, the procreation of warrior *sons*. The 'warrior' mentality is important for a community's self-image. Arasanayagam's mother-in-law displays familial and social pride and cultural exclusivity based on a notion of ethnic superiority. The solidity of Tamil culture captures the central irony within Arasanayagam's poems where, despite being excluded from this clan she is continually attracted to it. The line, 'I tried to learn all I could [...] about [...] her all consuming rituals' is a mechanism for coping with her in-laws' hostility.[43] However, embracing another culture creates other problems. It makes it more difficult to maintain a completely distinct identity. The subliminal pressure to assimilate and embrace her husband's culture and identity is depicted with sensitivity. The poems carry a cautionary note, reminding the reader of the tensions and unease of confronting the internalisation of marginalisation which women also perpetuate. Socially-ascribed conventions leave a woman with little room to assert her own individual identity.

While in Arasanayagam's work 'feminine' and 'female' experiences are negotiated through a poetic form, these negotiations are framed against the backdrop of socio-political struggle and raise fundamental questions about patriarchy and the deployment of women for political gains.[44] Indeed, the stability of the nation-state is predicated upon the central image of the female body. The female body, either in the form of writing on the body or about the body, is not one wracked by war and its attendant torment, pain and brutality but also contains an emancipatory potential. It appears as a construct shaped by socio-political forces that stipulate specific strategic interests.

In this section I intend to decode the diverse meanings inscribed within the female body as it appears in Arasanayagam's poems. Using this metaphor as a starting point, I will map out the way it speaks of Arasanayagam's personal dilemma of reconciling her 'plural' selves with the monolithic identity thrust upon her by external forces. I will also consider how mothering is perceived and exploited in the service of nationalism. In the poetry, the female body and its gendered markers enable us to interrogate assumptions of ethnic 'purity' and recognise the need for more inclusive, empowering paradigms.

As a woman poet speaking within a post-colonial context, Arasanayagam expresses the prescriptions of biological difference, of female biology and female culture, through her particular ethnic contours. In her case the female body is marked by the configurations of cross-cultural interventions, nationalist anxieties and female and feminine determinisms. In her most recent collections of poems, *Reddened Water Flows Clear* (1991) and *Shooting the Floricans* (1993) the female body is a trope for contesting, challenging and reinforcing personal and political aims. Biological specificities, like childbirth, puberty rites and breast-feeding, carry political overtones, 'the very body of Sri Lanka seems often to be a female torso tattooed by the pen of politics and strife'.[45] The metaphor of the female body is not merely inscribed to depict the *anxieties* of the nation, but is cast in such a way to construct national and personal identities and to foist discriminatory paradigms upon the woman of mixed ancestry.

The poetic analysis of the female body's socio-cultural and biological inscriptions begins with puberty. Specific cultural codes pertaining to feminine attributes are made visible in poems like 'Puberty Rites' and 'Mothers, Goddesses and Mythologies'. In the former, the young woman in the puberty rituals, or the washerwoman who bathes her, speak of a multiplicity of possibilities that transcend the realms of the domestic, or the national icon, and register a discontinuity in the limited matrix of female images.

In Sri Lanka, celebrations of puberty traverse ethnic, class and regional parameters. Although the rituals are not strictly adhered to within the middle- and upper-class urban milieu, most families register a girl's entry into womanhood. At the end of her first period, the young woman is bathed by the washerwoman from the community. The choice of the washerwoman is significant. She is a central participant in the social fabric, and although her function is indirectly linked to the anticipated mothering of the young woman, in performing the rituals, it is the washerwoman's occupation that is foregrounded.

Cleansing emblematises a certain type of purity. The symbolic function of the 'bath' is to divest the body of the impurities of menstruation and prepare it for its socially-prescribed role of reproduction. 'Puberty Rites' evocatively maps this process. The metaphors underpin the Sinhalese ritualistic discourse. For instance, the line, '*reddi nanda* [washerwoman] who brought carved brass *bandesi* [vessels] / of *rasa kevili* [sweet meats] for the *aluth avurudu* [New Year]' weaves the rich tapestry of indigenous ritual.[46] The deliberate refusal to translate these terms or explain through a glossary reinforces the indigenous ethos and exhibits the speaker's intimate knowledge of the Sinhalese cultural rituals. On a positive level, the poem is an reinvestment of the dignity and individuality of woman. The onset of puberty or 'coming of age' symbolises a new beginning and the hope for 'love and pro-creation'. The celebratory tone is forestalled by another vision carried through the prophetic codings of the physical pain and suffering of puberty. The recurrence of blood inscribes a cluster of meanings.

> The water flowed away
> From the body like cut vein
> Red the drooping cockscombs [...]
> Red the blood of my new wounds.[47]

While signalling the pain of motherhood, 'blood of my new wounds' figuratively captures the incipient signs of female victimisation. The female body is invested with the totality of identity. Specific codes of cultural coherence, as we have seen in Arasanayagam's poem, are embedded in the body through 'markings' or practices. Social values, limits, postures, and modes of exchange define 'what it is that constitutes bodies'.[48] This poem unveils the coercive mechanisms of 'traditional' cultural practices. Traditions, whether they are related to the feminine or not, perpetuate patriarchal hegemony. The absence of unqualified enthusiasm for these 'female' rituals on the part of the poet is a candid appraisal of her cultural landscape.

The poem is significant for an understanding of Arasanayagam's search for identity because her display of the intimate knowledge of the cultural context makes a plea for the legitimacy of birth right. Although her mixed ancestry precludes her from gaining social acceptance within the dominant culture, she is as much a part of her cultural milieu as any other 'pure' Sinhalese or Tamil. The 'I' in this case testifies to the plurality of selves. The speaking voice in the poem is, to use Daphne Marlatt's phrase, a complex of fractured identities.[49] The poetic voice is both of a victim and an agent. When the rituals are performed *for* her, she is a victim; but later when she is a mother, her role shifts and she becomes the agent.

However, the complexities do not end here for, in the process of these ritualistic acts, her identity changes from a Burgher girl to a Tamil wife who still embraces her Burgher roots but performs Sinhalese rituals. This moment testifies to a larger reality that the Sinhala and Tamil nationalists are perpetually trying to suppress in official discourses: the interstices of overlapping and disconnecting ethno-religious and cultural strands. While cultural syncretism is an actuality, the vein of bitterness underlying Arasanayagam's poem demonstrates the disjuncture between lived experience and representation. By representation I mean, nationalism's representation of ethnic identity.

In 'Mother-in-law' the disruption of the claim of ethnic 'purity' is further developed. The poem successfully maps the relationship between the two women. A controlled tone conveys patriarchal anxieties, for instance, a son's 'duty to look after his mother'.[50] The older woman's attitudes also typify the ambivalences within nationalist discourse. The mother-in-law describes how a *Sinhala* wet nurse fed her.

> 'Achchi you have Sinhala blood,
> You drank milk of a Sinhala woman'
> 'Who told you that? A Sinhala nona
> Gave me milk. They were all
> Respectable Sinhala nonas.'[51]

The irony here is unmistakable. The older woman fails to grasp her granddaughter's horror at drinking the milk of a Sinhalese woman and she retaliates by invoking class rather than race. Likewise the older woman is fiercely proud of her son's marriage to an English woman but she cannot reconcile herself to her Burgher daughter-in-law. It is clear that for the other communities the Burghers carry a special threat. This situation metonymically captures the condition of the nation at large. It is, on one level, evidence of the close alliance between the races, where the 'milk' of one race literally and metaphorically nourishes the other. It is not simply the presence of the Burghers that transmogrifies the ethnic character of the peoples of Sri Lanka.

For Arasanayagam, the exploitation of land and the female body are conjoined and it is a part of a larger 'feminist' project. The impulse to revert to a 'maternal' relationship with a coherent politico/cultural entity such as the 'nation' or 'motherland' is reflected in many poems, and the *inability* to form such a link because of her 'alien' heritage is one of the primary sources of discontent.

Besides the link between the female body and the land, as a *Burgher*, there is another more fraught relationship which she must come to terms with: of the association between the land and colonial power relations. The poetic representation of the 'motherland' for Arasanayagam coexists with other feminised concepts such as the *violation* of the female body through the intervention of 'alien' forces. Colonialist exploitation is coded through the motif of rape.

> To leave your name implanted
> With some compliant virgin
> As you caroused
> Raping the land.[52]

Here, the rhetorical force of rape is impeded by its metaphori-sation. Rape is not just about economic exploitation wreaked by colonialism but refers literally to sexual violation. In the context of colonialism the rape motif does not exonerate or efface colonial violence and destruction. The above revelation, for instance, provides an explanation for the speaker's tenuous position within a nation that still carries the scars of colonialism and victimises the reminders of that colonial past, the Burghers. Hence her admission:

> We share the same guilt
> We were once invaders
> We bear branded the mark of Cain[53]

The mediation between past and present allows the speaker to work out an identity that is a consummation of the coloniser and colonised. This identity still seems to be underlined by anxiety and yearning as she discovers a plethora of *selves* that are caught in a flux of desire, frustration, insecurity and alienation. It encompasses a notion of hybridity that has a significance beyond the personal realm. Her strength is the 'I' that weaves in and out of her poetry. The controlling 'I' moves from line to line, 'caressing the luxurious landscape, comforting the suffering victims, despising the acts of violence, neglect, despair'.[54]

In Arasanayagam's writing, alliteration, assonance and rhythmic pattern are utilised to convey unspeakable personal suffering and human exploitation, from the familial to the national; that is, domestic violence within family structures and ethnic violence at a national level. According to Simms, 'the body of suffering is the body of the poet's writing' and her poetic devices

give expression to the truths of private suffering.[55] Through
subtlety and nuance she reveals the ways in which women's
identity is effaced. The image of a pen cutting into the flesh of the
woman's body mirrors the larger image of a nation destroying
itself.

Arasanayagam's poetry details an in-depth and painful
searching for the meaning of a self that is circumscribed by
discourses of hybridity. The confessional tone of her poetry is the
result of being forced to confront and witness violent events. After
years of searching, in her most recent collection of poems she
seems to have finally assuaged this feeling of angst. In the poem
'Mother' she appears to reconcile herself to the identity she
acquires through birth.

> She gave me this history
> Now I am proud of it.[56]

Nationalism and Sexuality: Shyam Selvadurai's *Funny Boy*

When Selvadurai's *Funny Boy* was published in 1994, it was hailed
as one of the most powerful renditions of the trauma of the
prevailing ethnic tensions in contemporary Sri Lanka. In his novel,
Selvadurai brings together the struggles of class, ethnicity and
sexuality. All these differentials impinge upon the development of
personality, as depicted in the struggles of the protagonist, Arjie.
Arjie's affluent family life is framed against their resistance to his
awareness of his homosexuality, and the escalating political
conflict resulting in racial riots, thereby directly forging a nexus
between sexuality and nationalism.

Gender roles are demarcated from childhood. The distinction
between girls' and boys' activities are clearly and overtly positioned in the novel's opening chapter, 'Pigs Can't Fly'. In the
realm of play, the boys indulge in the outdoor, physically strenu-
ous game of cricket, whereas the girls confine themselves to the
domestic imaginary of 'bride-bride': 'Territorially, the area around
my grandparents' house was divided into two'.[57] The different
types of play carefully construct the gender spaces and these
spaces preclude the slippages of boundaries. Tragically, there is no

space for a child like Arjie, who is not attracted to the 'macho' sport and is 'caught between the boys' and girls' worlds' (*FB* 39). Masculinity and femininity are determined along these contours. As his mother says, 'big boys must play with other boys' (*FB* 20). The sensitivity of a child like Arjie, whose interest is fantasy, is a point of derision. He is the 'funny boy' who is the lampooned by his family (*FB* 17).

Selvadurai juxtaposes these attitudes to gender roles against the trajectories of Sri Lankan politics and these roles have implications on a larger level. To be 'proper' men and women, citizens of the nation, or maintain the boundaries of the ethnic group, it is essential that anomalies, in whatever form, be suppressed. Hence, any threat to the group's sanctity, whether it be from Arjie's sexuality, or his aunt 'Radha aunty''s relationship with a Sinhalese man, has to be contained. In both cases, there is a polarity between agent and victim. Although victimisation takes many forms, the goal of inculcating and protecting the socially-ascribed values is constant. Similarly, the agents are the same figure: it is the mother who is the functionary of transmitting the norms of good citizenship. Arjie's father indictment against his wife for not fulfilling her role is couched thus: '[I]f he turns out to be the laughing stock of Colombo, it'll be your fault. ... You always spoil him and encourage all his nonsense' (*FB* 14). Radha's mother is also the chief instigator in suppressing her daughter's clandestine affair. Ammachi virulently stands against it, and goes to the extent of using physical force to exhibit her outrage.

From a nationalist perspective, the mother's role corresponds with the ways in which Nira Yuval-Davis and Floya Anthias have recognised as participating in the ethnic and national processes. They argue that '[t]he role of women as ideological reproducers is very often related to women being seen as the 'cultural carriers' of the ethnic group. Women are the main socialisers and ... they may be required to transmit the rich heritage of ethnic symbols and ways of life to the other members of the ethnic group.' In addition to transmitting the values of the community, part of these women's agenda involves vilifying the other communities. This is to achieve a sense of ethnic superiority. In the novel, Ammachi's assault against her daughter invokes racial stereotypes: 'Only a Sinhalese would be impertinent enough to offer an unmarried girl a lift' (FB 58). Tapping into the morals of a particular group is also an important facet of identity-formation. Self-definition entails not only making oneself feel superior in terms of race, religion, language and culture but also in terms of sexual behaviour and morality. Nation and sexuality converge in moments like this, and ultimately, in the novel, 'Radha aunty' submits to the dominant ideology and marries within her community after she appraises the situation within mixed marriages.

One of the most poignant moments in the novel is enacted in the plight of Doris. Her marriage to a Tamil leads to estrangement from her family. Finally, she is left on her own. Her loneliness is a testimony to the reality of ethnic intermixing. Neither community accepts the individual and the process of ostracism is forcefully played out in personal relationships. The interplay of money and ethnic status are the mitigating factors in drawing the boundaries. Radha herself anticipates the complexities of being married to a Sinhalese when she becomes the target of ethnic violence.

In his depiction of ethnic violence, Selvadurai centralises the human and material costs. Textually, the impact of the 1983 riot is derived from the effects on the protagonists' lives. Not only is Arjie's home destroyed, but his grandmother and grandfather are burnt to death in their car. Seen through the eyes of a young boy, these events are cast as the long-term ramifications of political machinations. Crucially, blame is imputed upon the politicians: 'The president expressed no sympathy for what we Tamils have suffered, nor did he condemn the actions of the thugs' (FB 303). To a large extent the state is linked in the process of fuelling the underlying tensions. Electoral lists are freely available and become the tools for identifying the victims (FB 289). Hence mob violence is highly organised and its force is constantly reinforced through Arjie's sense of bewilderment and wonder.

Here the writer reveals a perceptive analysis of the psychology of a riot. Firstly, what Veena Das persuasively describes as '[a]lternate interpretations constitut[ing] the meaning of violence for people located in different social positions' are evident in the reactions of 'Chithra aunty' and Arjie's mother.[58] The former, who is a Sinhalese, cries when she sees her friends' charred home, and it is the 'victim' who comforts her. From Arjie's perspective it is explained as 'Chithra aunty was free to cry' (FB 298). Secondly, political parties and the state collude in fuelling the tensions, which simultaneously involve not only two communities, but the community versus the state. Das notes that a sizeable proportion of killings during riots have been perpetrated by professional soldiers and police against protesters rather than simply those engaged in popular protest. In turn, although the State has at its disposal a well-developed repertoire for the management of collective episodes of violence, including the use of curfews, deployment of limited force and preventive arrests, in the implementation of these measures, the police are partisan and in the case of ethnic or communal tension, the police are biased towards members of the majority community.[59]

While much of the narrative energy is devoted to the actual ethnic riot, a gradual build-up of violence in the text reaches a crescendo here. Police brutality occurs in other incidents. The disappearance of the journalist Daryl in Jaffna and the reaction of the police frame the political climate of the time. Here Selvadurai telescopes incidents from a later era, recalling the disappearance of the journalist, Richard de Zoysa in 1990 during the height of the Marxist insurrection.

An interleaving of gender and class with political violence is enacted in the police officer's reaction to Arjie's mother. He treats her in a patronising manner, dismissing her fears as the ranting of an irrational, upper-class woman. The responses to her questions are couched in a sexism that is symptomatic of the way in which patriarchy tackles women who enter the public space. Although it is not verbalised, underlying his concern is a castigation of the impropriety of a middle-class woman's intervention into the male domain, as well as her attempt to protect an underclass domestic: 'The ASP smiled and said, "Now don't you fret yourself about him, Mrs. Chelvaratnam." He looked ruefully at the boy. "Unfortunately, dishonesty is instinctive of his class"' (FB 131). Underpinning his superficial interest in the woman and her child is the ASP's reaffirmation of his masculinity. Arresting the boy is only a token gesture, designed to placate the 'weaker' characters, to silence them. They are not worthy of knowing the full implications of what is going on. Moreover, the question of respectability is invoked here. Norms of respectability are defined by the patri-archal institutions—state, family and religion, and codes of female behaviour are class-marked. The respectable woman is a figure cut to the measure of middle-class society and incorporated into the image of the Nation.[60] During times of nationalist crisis, as we see in the novel, these norms are rigorously applied, even though, paradoxically, it is at these very times when 'normality' breaks down that conventional norms become meaningless.

Differentiations in class impinge upon nationalism in another way in the novel. Class boundaries separate the Colombo Tamils from the Jaffna Tamils. This distinction has an effect on the ideological formulations and affiliations of the characters. Jaffna Tamils are looked on with suspicion by the Colombo Tamils as involved with the Tamil Tigers. In the chapter 'Small Choices', Selvadurai foregrounds the concept of a homeland for these groups (*FB* 155-208). The demands of the separatists are described as 'Tiger nonsense' by Arjie's father (*FB* 157). Despite the fact that Arjie's family do not see themselves as Tamil, and like Sita in *Rasanayagam's Last Riot* try to divorce themselves from politics, they are forced to come to terms with the reality of being seen as on the 'other side'. This 'other side' has very little meaning for them, except to 'learn to play the game. [...] Go around quietly, make your money, and don't step on anyone's toes' (*FB* 173). For such characters, the choices are limited. Class background and westernisation preclude them from aligning themselves with their ethnic group, and ultimately the choice is to relinquish their home and homeland.

Perhaps the most poignant scene in the novel is Arjie's return to his former home. A close reading of an excerpt fuses the politics of home, gender, sexuality and nation.

How naked the house appeared without its door and windows, how hollow and barren with only scraps of paper and other debris in its rooms. I felt hot, angry tears begin to well up in me as I saw this final violation. Then, for the first time, I began to cry for our house. I sat on the

verandah steps and wept for the loss of my home, for the loss of everything that I held to be precious. (*FB* 311)

The fragmentation of the family home can be construed as a
symbolic enactment of the politics of the Sri Lankan nation—the
wanton destruction wreaked by ethnic animosity. On a literal
level, the above passage charts the events of a traumatic moment
in the protagonist's life. The description of the charred ruins
captures the extent of the profound emotional bonds towards the
home. Destruction of the material composition of the house
denotes political and psychological fragmentation. Political
fragmentation results in psychological fragmentation. It is also a
violation of the self, and Selvadurai deliberately deploys
metaphors linked to sexuality to suggest the nexus with home and
nation. It is crucial that his final encounter with home occurs
immediately after his final meeting with his lover, Shehan. The
narrative energy devoted to this episode evokes a dual despair:
'for the loss of everything [he] held to be precious'.

In her analysis of 'home', Rosemary George has mapped out its
multiple connotations: 'the private sphere of patriarchal hierarchy,
gendered self-identity, shelter, comfort, nurture and protection'.
Dynamics of gender, yoked with other ideologies such as class,
religion and ethnicity 'complicate the relationship between the
home and the self'. [61] Right throughout the novel, Selvadurai lays
bare these complications in Arjie's definition of self. Home, like the
nation, is sometimes frightening. Its patriarchal overtones are
emphasised in his father's anxiety to instil a rigorously masculine
identity in his sons. This identity is predicated upon the display of
'machismo' which includes the ability to endure any physical or
emotional hardship, as well as project and promote hetero-
sexuality. In the novel it emerges as the suppression of emotion,
especially crying. Even in his home, Arjie cannot cry in the presence of other family members, as this contravenes the dictates of
his father. His homosexuality, likewise, is proscribed in the home,
even though, when his hotel is used for the purposes of homo-
sexual activity, Arjie's father is dismissive, even indulgent (*FB*
170). Ironically, therefore, is only when the security of his home is

annihilated that Arjie can give vent to his emotions. Sitting on the step of the charred remains of his home, he weeps uncontrollably. This moment problematises and interrogates what George calls the 'seductive pleasures of home'.[62] The parameters of home, its exclusions and inclusions, enable us to read the narratives of nations; their obsessive preoccupation with sexuality, loyalty, identity and image have a valuable starting point in the novel.

Conclusion

Since 1983, creative writing in Sri Lanka has awoken to the cries of communal violence and the sound of gun-fire. Democratic values and the recognition of plurality and heterogeneity collide with one of the tacit commitments of the Nation: its defence of peace and stability. As I have illustrated here, prolonged and organised internal conflict throws into crisis the certitudes of the nation-state, and militant separatism has contributed to the politicisation of an English-educated middle-class literati that had languished in apathy and ambivalence amidst socio-political chaos. Ernest MacIntyre's *Rasanayagam's Last Riot* and *Village in the Jungle* remind the audience of the harrowing nightmare of political violence. Jean Arasanayagam's poetry grapples with the relentless suffering inflicted upon the innocent civilian and the inextricable interlinking of personal and political violence. Her poetry is probably among the most evocative and emotionally concise of written art forms dealing with issues of conflict in Sri Lanka. In *Funny Boy*, Selvadurai signals the tensions of adhering to the behavioural codes of a male-dominated society, even as these codes are thrown into crisis within the realm of conflict. These writers also make the reader or audience aware of the material costs incurred by conflict, of impoverishment and death.

Often this writing acutely reveals the contradictions between cultural reality and cultural expectations by exposing the range of mechanisms within nationalist discourse which silence, negate or deny the political opinions of women. MacIntyre contests the nationalist ideological construct of the rural woman as custodian of moral values in *Village in the Jungle* through his sensitive por-trayal of the women characters. It is through such portrayals that we realise that the two-dimensional, gendered representations of the nation, which influence both public debate and private opinion, fail to account for the empowering possibilities that arise when individuals struggle for a sense of meaning and identity in their personal and political worlds.

In opposition to the 'authentic' nationalist ideal are the representations of the different forms of 'hybridity', whether it is of mixed ancestry or intermarriage. These images are also a political and disempowering device designed to deliver society's condemnation of women who do not conform to traditional norms and expectations. Jean Arasanayagam forcefully vocalises her predicament as a minority, and her utterances serve to confound the validity of the negative symbolism assigned to the Burgher. She is also aware of the inherent dangers and connotations that western lineage carries in the contemporary socio-political landscape.

Through the perspective of a child, Selvadurai evocatively captures the gendered anxieties of a nation, the divisions of race, and their impingement upon personal relationships. Compromises made for the sake of race, family and home are often the cause of psychological trauma. Manifest in the novel, these traumas interrogate the process of selection of membership of a nation, and the underlying rubrics such as sexuality, gender and class which determine the violence and the security of the nation.

These authors have not divorced themselves from the urgent questions within their nations. Their role and responsibility in contesting and challenging repressive power structures, from both outside and within, is clearly a way of staking a claim in their country's future. Literature participates in the formulation of ideology and serves as a form of 'ideological insemination', and nations 'depend for their existence on an apparatus of cultural fictions in which imaginative literature plays a decisive role'.[63] While the Nation employs the condition of denial to prevail against the challenges and trauma of revolutionary change, literature need not be complicit in reinforcing such myths, but can provide a critical illumination and potentially empowering site for change.

Notes

1. This kind of propaganda material is also deployed by the LTTE. Sitralega Mauneguru outlines the prominent 'poster campaigns' in the North. She notes that 'old legends and classics were reconstructed which idealise mothers who send their sons to the battlefield with pride'. In addition, 'the LTTE's publication "Women and Revolution: The Role of Women in Tamil Eelam National Liberation" carries a prominent photograph of a Palestinian woman cadre holding a gun and a baby' ('Gendering Tamil Nationalism: The Construction of "Woman" in Projects of Protest and Control', *Unmaking the Nation,* ed. Qadri Ismail and Pradeep Jeganathan [Colombo: Social Scientists Assoc., 1995] 161, 164). The security conditions in Sri Lanka have prevented me from visiting the LTTE-controlled areas to obtain empirical evidence of the propaganda material. I am grateful to Sitralega Mauneguru, Mala de Alwis and Kumari Jayawardena for their time and generosity in discussing their work with me and enabling me to develop my own ideas on these issues.
2. Helen Gilbert and Joanna Tompkins, *Post-Colonial Drama: Theory, Practice, Politics* (London: Routledge, 1996) 3.
3. The insubstantial number of original plays performed between Independence in 1948 and the early 1980s were confined to the comical or historical genres. The historical genre attempted to rehabilitate the indigenous literature which had hitherto been suppressed by cultural colonisation. While this strand of writing was in keeping with the mood of decolonisation, the plays did not address contemporary issues. In the 1970s, despite some attempts to situate the theatrical productions within a more socially-relevant context, the comic and historical modes continued to hold sway. On the whole, critics, audiences and theatre practitioners recognised that the theatre was not catering for the sensibilities of the nation. In an analysis of the English-language theatre in Sri Lanka up to the early 1980s, Tissa Jayatilaka describes this lack of relevance. I am grateful to Jayatilaka for his ideas on this area.
4. Senaka Abeyratne, a young playwright, has been writing and producing plays in English in the last 2-3 years. His plays touch on political issues.
5. Aijaz Ahmad's contention with Fredric Jameson's reading of 'third world texts', that the telling of the individual story and the individual experience cannot but ultimately involve the telling of the experience of the collectivity itself, is useful here (*In Theory: Classes, Nations, Literatures* [London: Verso, 1992] 109).
6. Ernest MacIntyre, *Rasanayagam's Last Riot* (Sydney: Wordlink, 1993) xi. (Cited hereafter as *RLR.*)
7. Daphne Marlatt, 'Difference (em)bracing', *Unbecoming Daughters of the Empire,* ed. Shirley Chew and Anna Rutherford (Sydney: Dangaroo 1993) 183. Marlatt discusses the need to recognise 'the real differences of life-experience, privilege and accessibility to the centre' (184).
8. Philippa Rothfield, 'Feminism, Subjectivity and Sexual Experience', *A Reader in Feminist Knowledge,* ed. Sneja Gunew (London: Routledge, 1991) 109-11.

9. Nayantara Sahgal, 'Some Thoughts on the Puzzle of Identity', *Journal of Commonwealth Literature* 28.1 (1993) 30.

10. The burning of the Jaffna Library, allegedly by Sinhala militants, exacerbated the mounting tensions between the Sinhalese and Tamils. It led to a more vehement agenda of militancy on the part of the LTTE, since the Library was considered a symbol of Tamil culture.

11. See Ernest Gellner, *Nations and Nationalism* (Oxford: Blackwell, 1983) and Partha Chatterjee, *Nationalist Thought and the Colonial World* (London: Zed, 1986). Senaka Abeyratne says that after the performances of his plays, audiences felt that he was dealing with 'outdated themes which is *history*, because things in Sri Lanka are different now and more *civilised*'. For instance his plays worked to expose the repressive structures at work in the political arena. One play in particular, *Por La Libertad* uncovered the flagrant effects of political repression. He stated that the majority of his audience failed to make the connection. (Personal interview, Colombo, Aug. 1994.)

12. Stephen Slemon, 'Monuments of Empire: Allegory/Counter-Discourse/Post-Colonial Writing', *Kunapipi* 9.3 (1987): 7.

13. This kind of polarity pervades ideologies of protest in the Sinhala theatre. I have discussed this issue in my article 'Representation as "Othering the Other"': The Non-Sri Lankan in the Sinhala Theatre'.

14. The Prevention of Terrorism Act (PTA) brought in after 1983 is enforced against any person suspected of subversive acts.

15. Ernest MacIntyre, *Village in the Jungle* (Sydney: Wordlink, 1994) 10. (Cited hereafter as *VIJ*.)

16. Deniz Kandiyoti, 'Identity and Its Discontents: Women and the Nation', *Colonial Discourse and Post-Colonial Theory*, ed. Patrick Williams and Laura Chrisman (London: Harvester, 1993) 380.

17. Lynda Nead, Myths of Sexuality: Representations of Women in Victorian Britain (Oxford: Blackwell, 1988) 91.

18. Kadiatu Kanneh, 'The Difficult Politics of Wigs and Veils: Feminism and the Colonial Body', *The Post-Colonial Studies Reader* (London: Routledge, 1995) 346-47.

19. R. Radhakrishnan, 'Nationalism, Gender, and the Narrative of Identity', *Nationalisms and Sexualities*, ed. Andrew Parker, et al. (London: Routledge, 1992) 84.

20. Rothfield 128.

21. Rothfield 128.

22. Kandiyoti 382.

23. Personal interview, Kandy, Sept. 1994.

24. I am indebted to Reggie Siriwardene for his valuable insights into Arasanyagam's work, enabling me to situate her work within the oeuvre of Sri Lankan poetry in English.

25. Jean Arasanayagam , 'Narcissus', *An Anthology of Contemporary Sri Lankan Poetry in English*, ed. Rajiva Wijesinha (Colombo: British Council, 1988) 43.

26. Arasanayagam feels very strongly about the sense of alienation she experienced during the historic moments in post-Independence Sri Lanka.

These feelings, which were voiced during her interview with me, find their expression in her poetry. (Personal interview, Kandy, Sept. 1994.)

27. Regi Siriwardene, 'Jean Arasanayagam: In Search of Identity', *Anthology of Contemporary Sri Lankan Poetry* 95.

28. Arasanayagam , 'Nallur', *Anthology of Contemporary Sri Lankan Poetry* 1.

29. Since 1983 several Buddhist temples in the sacred cities of Anuradhapura and Polonnaruwa have been attacked.

30. Arasanayagam, '1958 ... '71 ... '77 ... '81 ... '83', *Anthology of Contemporary Sri Lankan Poetry* 11.

31. Homi Bhabha, *The Location of Culture* (London: Routledge, 1994) 51.

32. Siriwardene 96.

33. Jean Arasanayagam, *Colonial Inheritance and Other Poems* (Kandy: Ariya, 1985) 46.

34. See 'Portrait of a Ceylonese Victorian and His Forebears' (*Colonial Inheritance* 20-21), 'William Henry Solomans—Grandfather, 1853-1936' (*Colonial Inheritance* 22-23), 'Exiled Childhood' (*Shooting the Floricans* [Kandy: Samjna, 1993] 9-14), 'My Mother' (*Shooting the Floricans* 19-22) for similar portrayals of her European heritage. In her insightful analysis of Jean Arasanyagam's war poetry, Neloufer de Mel has also pointed to Arasanayagam's celebration of her colonial heritage, an aspect which I too feel is problematic ('Static Signifiers: Metaphors of Women in Sri Lankan War Poetry', *Embodied Violence: Communalising Women's Sexuality in South Asia*, ed. Kumari Jayawardena and Malathi De Alwis [New Delhi: Kali for Women, 1996], esp. 170-76).

35. Arasanayagam, *Colonial Inheritance* 7.

36. Arasanayagam, *Colonial Inheritance* 7 (emphasis added).

37. W. D. Ashcroft, 'Intersecting Marginalities: Post-colonialism and Feminism', *Kunapipi* 11.2 (1989): 32.

38. Arasanayagam, *Colonial Inheritance* 1 (emphasis added).

39. Siriwardene 98.

40. Arasanayagam, *Colonial Inheritance* 53 (emphasis added).

41. Samita Sen, 'Motherhood and Mothercraft: Gender and Nationalism in Bengal' in *Gender and History* 5.2 (1993): 234.

42. The Tamil mother's governing ideology is explained by C. S. Lakshmi. She feels that 'attempts to invest the maternal body—as if it is one universal body with one meaning—with "truths" about the meaning of women's existence have been fairly constant in the Tamil cultural ethics. [...] A mother with breasts and womb to create only sons who are warriors and fighters is a construct which the Tamil mothers think is their own internal, natural, biological power' ('Mother, Mother Community and Mother Politics in Tamil Nadu', *Economic and Political Weekly*, 20 Oct. 1990: 72-73).

43. Arasanayagam, *Colonial Inheritance* 54.

44. The distinction between 'feminine' and 'female' corresponds to the established usage among many feminists to make 'feminine' represent social constructs (patterns of behaviour imposed by cultural and social norms), and reserve 'female' for the purely biological aspects of sexual difference.

45. Norman Simms, introduction, Jean Arasanayagam, *Reddened Water Flows Clear* (London: Forest, 1991) x.

46. Arasanayagam, *Reddened Water* 49.
47. Arasanayagam, *Reddened Water* 50-51.
48. Judith Butler, *Gender Trouble* (London: Routledge, 1990) 131.
49. Marlatt, 'Difference (em)bracing' 184.
50. Arasanayagam, *Reddened Water* 95.
51. Arasanayagam, *Reddened Water* 97. *Nona* is the Sinhala term for 'lady'.
52. Arasanayagam, 'Ancestors', *Colonial Inheritance* 9.
53. Arasanayagam, 'A Question of Identity', *Reddened Water* 82.
54. Simms ix.
55. Simms xi. This point has also been made by Neloufer de Mel ('Static Signifiers', esp. 170-76).
56. Arasanayagam, *Shooting the Floricans* 19.
57. Shyam Selvadurai, *Funny Boy* (London: Granta, 1994) 3. (Cited hereafter as *FB*.)
58. Veena Das, ed., *Mirrors of Violence: Communities, Riots and Survivors in South Asia* (New Delhi: Oxford UP, 1992) 12, 14.
59. Das 12, 14.
60. Susie Tharu and K. Lalita, eds, *Women's Writing in India*, Vol. 2 (London: Pandora, 1993) 82-3.
61. Rosemary George, *The Politics of Home: Postcolonial Relocations and Twentieth-Century Fiction* (Cambridge: Cambridge UP, 1996) 1, 170.
62. George, *Politics of Home* 197.
63. Timothy Brennan, 'The National Longing for Form', *Nation and Narration*, ed. Homi Bhabha (London: Routledge, 1990) 52, 49.

Territorial Pains or Gains:
Writing the Canadian Far North and the Australian Outback

Lars Jensen

This essay seeks to explore the relationship between national space and post-colonial experience in Canada and Australia. I wish to focus on the position of the contemporary Australian and Canadian writer in relation to the idea of space as a shaping force in constructions of national identity: an exploration that situates these writers inside the debate between a post-colonial versus a nationalist discourse in former settler colonies. However, rather than getting myself entangled in the complexities of this debate, I shall instead look at the specific problems involved in situating Canadian and Australian writing inside post-colonial literature, and how such positioning difficulties are related to understandings of national identities in Canada and Australia.

At the centre of discourses about national identities are the perceptions of colonial beginnings and their significance for understanding contemporary post-colonial experience. It is my contention that the preoccupations of contemporary post-colonial writers constantly return to an early colonial moment to explain the fabric of their own contemporaneity, and to problematise received myths about colonial beginnings.

A particularly illustrative example of how past and present concerns coexist in contemporary Australian and Canadian writing is Thomas Keneally's novel *The Playmaker*, published in 1987, on the eve of the Australian Bicentennial.[1] As the novel is set in the early period of the first Australian colony, the reader implicitly expects a conventional representation of Australian

Translating Nations, ed. Prem Poddar, *The Dolphin* 30, pp. 88-114.
© 1999 by Aarhus University Press, Denmark.
ISBN 87 7288 381 2; ISSN 0106 4487.

colonial beginnings. However, the novel does not open with the arrival of the First Fleet and Governor Phillip's proclamation, but begins instead with events that take place over a year later. Only in the second part of the novel do we return to the weeks immediately following the arrival of the First Fleet. This inverted chronology draws attention to the constructedness of imperial (and national) histories, and shows that any point in time after the First Fleet's arrival could represent a beginning, and also suggests that even originary moments have a pre-history. In this way Keneally challenges the staged imperial history that Paul Carter draws attention to in *The Road to Botany Bay*, although *The Playmaker* can also be seen to challenge constructions of national history,[2] where Carter's position is more ambivalent. The idea of history unfolding on a stage is particularly congenial to my reading here, for Keneally's novel opens with the recruitment of convicts for the production of a play, *The Recruiting Officer*. The actors in the play are presented, as in a theatre programme, with the details of their careers, or in this case their criminal records. They are then both on the stage in the play, as well as on the stage of Australian history—as anti-heroic petty-thieves engaged in a nation-building activity. Keneally thus implicitly hints at one of the dilemmas of the Bicentennial; how to celebrate a 'nation's birth', when that nation came into existence primarily because it was the perfect dumping ground for Britain's unwanted people. Australia's most attractive aspect was, from the outset, its isolation, not its potential as a colony; in fact the primary value of its location was that it virtually guaranteed the convicts would never return to Britain. *The Playmaker* then writes itself into the debate surrounding the Bicentennial through an interrogation of the nature of that colonial beginning which the Bicentennial is staged to celebrate. Thus the novel represents an intervention into the debate between nationalist and post-colonial readings of Australia's colonial infancy.

Where then lies the split between nationalist and post-colonialist representations of colonial beginnings? Both embark on a return to colonial beginnings to reach an understanding of present-day Australia. Yet where a nationalist representation returns to the colonial beginning to explain the present by showing the contiguity between past and present processes, a post-colonial representation will challenge the assumptions on which such linear and chronological explanations of national histories are built. The politics involved in representing history as a linear progression are foregrounded by Keneally's dedication of *The Playmaker* 'to Arabanoo and his brethren still dispossessed', which situates his narrative of early colonial times within the political discourse and soul-searching that was characteristic of the period around the Australian Bicentennial, and which continues to haunt questions about Australian identity. This is evidenced by the current stalemate in white–Aboriginal relations, particularly in relation to the issue of indigenous land rights. Hence this post-colonial representation challenges nationalist constructions through the foregrounding of their inherent contradictions.

Australian nationalist representations lay claim to a formative colonial experience, such as the arrival of the First Fleet or carving out an existence in the bush, and continuously construct a gaze back into the past which is selective and exclusivist. The creation of the national moment is placed in an epic past that can only be paid allegiance to, not altered. Thus if a nationalist return to the beginning stresses the dispossession of the Aborigines, it is unable to explain how these people can return two hundred years later and lay claim to parts of a continent, whose history they have long since been written out of. The post-colonial approach in *The Playmaker* and other contemporary Australian and Canadian writing consists in the acknowledgement that it is impossible to consider new beginnings, new ways of articulating Australian and Canadian identities without constantly re-negotiating colonial histories. This is a perception that requires an understanding of history as a continuous process of engagement and re-writing, rather than as the representation of fixed moments/events in the past.

The nationalist and post-colonial strands in Australian and Canadian writing are the manifestations of the double position of the non-indigenous writer as both coloniser and colonised. A similar doubleness characterises the indigenous writers' position, although the tensions here are between traditional and western-ised cultures.[3] Through the definition of my own post-colonial approach in this article, and my inclusion of both 'white' and indigenous writers, I have, of course, already taken a position on the ringside of the group of post-colonial settler critics, such as Helen and Chris Tiffin, Alan Lawson, Gareth Griffiths, Diana Brydon and Stephen Slemon, whose pioneering efforts have contributed substantially to the establishment of post-colonial studies. I do not point this out to postulate that their efforts grant them a special charter on definitions of the post-colonial field *vis-à-vis* other post-colonial schools, nor to ignore other earlier contributions by, for example, Fanon, Cesaire and Cabral, but I do find their critical writings enabling for my own desire to delimit a post-colonial approach to Australian and Canadian writing. Furthermore, all these critics are themselves either Australian or Canadian, and write with an acute awareness of the critical discourses concerning the literary output in their respective countries.

It is important to note that this group of critics acknowledges that the inclusion of settler cultures within post-colonial discourse is far from unproblematic,[4] particularly at a time when Australia and Canada have become regional powers, exercising their own imperialistic policies towards less powerful nations in their regions, and perpetuating paternalistic attitudes towards their own indigenous populations. Keeping this in mind, it is also important to remember that writers are not their nation, and those writers associated with post-colonial writing problematise and challenge the power paradigms characteristic of the post-in-dependence nation. Evidently not all Canadian and Australian writings are post-colonial, but the same argument could be used about writings from 'Third World' post-colonial nations.[5]

The crucial argument for the inclusion of Canadian and Australian writings in the post-colonial field is that some of this literature is written from the margins, and subverts perceived notions about the fabric of the nation in ways that cannot be satisfactorily explained through metafictional, postmodernist readings. This literature challenges the binaries which inform the idea of the Nation—self/other, us/them—and which find expression in constructions such as the 'typical Canadian' or 'Aussie'. Not surprisingly, the critique of such constructions is most clearly expressed in literature produced from the most marginalised groups, particularly migrants of a non-European background. Indigenous writers occupy a particularly contradictory site in the national frame, because they often find themselves at the centre of debates concerning what constitutes a genuine Australian or Canadian experience. Yet regardless of whether migration or settlement is the current catchcry, the indigenes find themselves disqualified as 'typical material', because central to constructions of national identities in both countries is the idea of converting alien space to familiar place. In Australia the emphasis has shifted from multiculturalism and migrancy back to settlement, a move epitomised in the resurrection of 'the Aussie battler' to a position of national prominence.

The non-indigenous creative writers I shall consider in the following pages include Margaret Atwood, Aritha van Herk, David Malouf and Les Murray. All these writers are preoccupied with rewriting Australian and Canadian beginnings, and with redefining the impact of unsettled space on the Australian and Canadian imagination. Whilst these writers have established themselves as cultural critics via their creative writing, my exploration of their work here centres on how they state their critical position. They may be considered to be marginal because of their provincial, ethnic or gendered positioning—though they may be said to be cosmopolitan as well. Their cosmopolitanism reaches beyond the immediate confines of a struggle over how to define the criteria for Canadianness or Australianness, to consider issues in a wider post-colonial context. The strength of their writing may be said to originate from their 'double' position, which I identified earlier, because their writing demonstrates a radical questioning of the formation of national identities in former settler colonies, as well as of the cultural parameters inherited from European parent cultures. In the context of indigenous writing, the post-colonial position problematises the homogenising discourses of the 'authenticity' or 'purity' of experience in relation to 'Third World' countries and indigenous peoples. These are issues whose relevance has been demonstrated in relation to fragmented post-independent nations such as Nigeria and Sri Lanka, but which are equally relevant to questions of what constitutes Aboriginal or aboriginal Canadian writing.

I have already suggested that the differences between the relative positions of indigenous and non-indigenous writers, and particularly their degree of marginality, are significant, but I also wish to try to define the space which they share. This space I shall problematise through the trope of resistance. Though resistance has been widely discussed in post-colonial criticism,[6] the debate has tended to focus primarily on anti-colonial resistance. Here I wish to concentrate on how contemporary writers deploy resistance as part of a narrative strategy to foreground the contemporary Australian and Canadian colonial legacy. In the following paragraphs I shall focus on how the trope of resistance is employed in connection with former settler colonies, and then move on to consider Australian and Canadian writers' responses to their own positions in the light of the post-colonial issues I have raised.

Slemon identifies two kinds of resistance; the first is aimed at ridding 'a people of its oppressors'. Here '*literary* resistance ... can be seen as a form of contractual understanding between text and reader, one which is embedded in an experiential dimension and buttressed by a political and cultural aesthetic at work in the culture'.[7] However, while Slemon accepts the importance and validity of raising the previously unacknowledged voice of protest, he also warns against the implicit dangers of this position. He argues that resistance under these circumstances risks the mere substitution of one inscription for another, in which case the underlying assumption is that all indigenous literature is concerned with resistance as an intentional strategy. Furthermore, while resistance may in itself establish an alternative platform, Slemon argues this will in turn displace Foucault's theory 'that power *itself* inscribes its resistances and so, in the process, seeks to contain them'.[8]

The second form of resistance identified by Slemon highlights the ambivalent space occupied by post-colonial literature, 'between systems, between discursive worlds, implicit and complicit in both of them',[9] and this kind of resistance is crucial for Slemon's argument for including writing from former settler colonies in post-colonial discourse. For Slemon the settler text represents a *reading position*, which gains its strength precisely from the foregrounding of its own ambivalent position. Slemon here quotes Alan Lawson, who argues that 'the inherent aware-ness of both "there" and "here," and the cultural ambiguity of these terms ... are not so much the boundaries of its cultural matrix, nor tensions to be resolved, but a space *within* which [the Second-World, post-colonial] literary text may move *while* speaking'.[10]

Slemon uses Lawson's argument to legitimise the inclusion of Australian and Canadian writers in post-colonial discourse, but also to point out that there are fundamental differences between the respective positions of non-indigenous and indigenous writers. Where indigenous writers' resistance has grown out of the protest movement against the history of colonial invasion and the subsequent paternalistic policies of national and territorial governments, the position of the non-indigenous writer is more ambivalent because it is voiced from within the dominant power, yet also works in opposition to it. The positions are in both cases circumscribed by the given power structures, yet the choices for manoeuvring are quite disparate. Hence, to put it crudely, the white writer has a choice of identifying with a marginalised position, whereas for the indigenous writer marginality is a given position.[11]

To define the writer's position is to reach an understanding of the writer's idea of place in relation to his/her sense of a operat-ing in a communal space. I find it enabling to think of communal space in terms parallel to Benedict Anderson's definition of nations as 'imagined communities'.[12] Anderson uses his term to problematise nationalism, particularly in relation to the question of belonging and non-belonging. The writer's position reflects this, as s/he is both part of and detached from her/his own community,[13] and while writers' allegiances tend to be to smaller communities, e.g., regional (Western Australian or Albertan), metropolitan (Sydney or Toronto), or ethnic/indigenous communities (Chinese, Aboriginal or Inuit), their writings often have wider national implications.[14]

To understand what is meant by place, I wish to begin by considering the definition made in *The Post-Colonial Studies Reader*:

'Place' in post-colonial societies is a complex interaction of language, history and environment. It is characterised firstly by a sense of displacement in those who have moved to the colonies, or the more widespread sense of displacement from the imported language, of a gap between the 'experienced' environment and descriptions the language provides, and secondly, by a sense of the immense investment of culture in the construction of place. [...] Place is thus the concomitant of difference, the continual reminder of the separation, and yet of the hybrid interpenetration of the coloniser and colonised.[15]

This definition speaks of place in the broadest post-colonial sense, and is more readily applicable to former settler colonies than to at least some former 'coloured' colonies. However, my concern with this definition springs from the enabling way it draws attention to the double vision of the Australian and Canadian writer, where place operates as an affirmation of belonging, while exposing the elements of unbelonging. This explains the tendency in Canadian and Australian writing to narrate buried colonial stories that continue to haunt the contemporary place until they have been excavated.

Naturally, not all writers engage to the same degree in locating their own position. The writers I shall now move on to discuss are, in their critical writings, particularly concerned with the relationship between whites and indigenes, and between individual place and 'national' definitions of space. The Canadian writers I shall discuss are Margaret Atwood, Aritha van Herk, Robert Kroetsch, Mordecai Richler and Thomas King, and the

Australian writers are David Malouf, Les Murray, Oodgeroo and Eva Johnson.

Margaret Atwood is both an established writer and critic, but in her Clarendon Lectures on the Canadian North, *Strange Things: The Malevolent North in Canadian Literature*, it is her role as writer she draws upon. Here she begins by looking at how the North continues to be an intrusive force in Canadian literature, despite its physical remoteness to the vast majority of contemporary city-dwelling Canadians:

'The North' is thought of as a place, but it's a place with shifting boundaries. It's also a state of mind. It can mean 'wilderness' or 'frontier'.... In the Canadian North of popular image, the Mounties with their barking dog teams relentlessly pursue madmen.... The ends pursued by literature are more obscure, its pathways more oblique, but the chief features of the terrain—the signposts—have remained strangely constant although the values ascribed to them have varied considerably. [16]

It is these signposts, rather than a spatial definition, that are pivotal to Atwood's idea of North, because she considers such markers central to a Canadian experience, not as defining moments, but more as constantly recycled motifs. Hence she uses the myths surrounding the fatal Franklin expedition as an example of a British story of self-sacrifice that gradually becomes incorporated into a Canadian mythology, in other words, as one of the processes through which Canadians become 'of their place'. As Atwood concludes, 'because Franklin was never really "found", he continues to live on as a haunting presence; certainly in Canadian literature'.[17]

But what about Atwood's demarcation of her own place? What do these motifs mean to her as a writer? Here, she does not speak of her own creative relationship with the Franklin myth, although in her short story, 'The Age of Lead', (published in the same year as her lectures), the female protagonist watches a television documentary about the forensic expedition, which, nearly 150 years after the event, dug up the deep-frozen bodies of three Franklin expedition members. The forensic expedition revealed their deaths to be caused by lead poisoning; a conclusion that involves its own ironies, as the heroic expedition sent out to forge its way through the Northwest Passage was actually undermined by something as trite and domestic as its own food supplies. The epic Franklin story is linked to the 'ordinary', usually unrecorded experience in metropolitan Canada via the female television watcher, whose friend dies from some mysterious illness. As the friend comments 'it must have been something I ate'.[18] As the poisonous tinned food on the Franklin expedition is linked with industrialisation in nineteenth-century Britain, so the death of the protagonist's friend is linked to twentieth-century concerns about the environment and ecology. In a broader context, when Atwood juxtaposes the humanity of the frozen body with the universality of individual experience, she seeks to de-mythologise the Franklin expedition without challenging its status as a central Canadian story.

What then constitutes Atwood's distinction between story and myth? In order to answer this it is necessary to return to her lecture series, where she connects the writer's territory and Canadian space in her discussion of Mordecai Richler's novel, *Solomon Gursky Was Here*. Atwood argues that the project of Richler's Jewish character is to get '*in*, and getting in means getting into the mythology',[19] and thereby identifies one of the dominant strategies in post-colonial writing, that is, to undermine, subvert and question perceived historical truths.

Yet post-colonial writing does not merely seek to destabilise, but also to establish alternative visions to perceived national myths. In other words, resistance also implies the existence of an(other) vision to replace an existing nationalist one. Let me problematise this from a different angle: as long as debunking myths is both the aim and only goal, then the defining criteria of Canadian identity, will continue to revolve around those 'white' myths. My point is that the debate is not necessarily about interpretation only, but also about questioning the relevance of these particular myths and envisaging ways to establish alternative readings of Canadian space. I would argue that in a post-colonial exposition of Canadian mythologies it is necessary to distinguish between an insider's and an outsider's view. The insider's view holds that it is possible for other writers to inscribe themselves into a Canadian tradition by questioning national myths, whereas for the outsider it is necessary to establish new myths that are not derived from the established tradition.

What Atwood describes as Richler's 'fart in a church' is a limited form of rebellion, and I would argue that her own questioning of exploration stories is also circumscribed by her gendered approach, which aims to debunk self-congratulatory male projections, but does not challenge the relevance of the activity itself. To draw a blunt parallel, Inuit and First Nations writings do not need to rewrite exploration accounts to mythologise the North. By pointing this out I do not wish to suggest the answer for the white writer is to 'go native', but rather to show the predicament of the 'white' post-colonial Canadian writer's position as both here and there, or perhaps even neither nor. Later on, I shall return to consider the indigenous side of this equation, but first I wish to briefly consider other contemporary Canadian writers, who are preoccupied with the idea of landscape and its impact on the Canadian imagination.

Aritha van Herk writes from a position different from Atwood's; her perspective is that of a second generation, Dutch migrant growing up in the west, where Canadian space is seen as relatively new and the idea of writing is intimately connected to 'mapping the unknown'. The process of articulating place is for van Herk a reversible process, hence 'as landscape and space map/make the writer, so does the writer impose her map of language on her place … Language is the ultimate arbiter; language, by naming a place, gives it life, existence.'[20] For van Herk it is the undefined and unnamed status of space that presents the observer with infinite possibilities. Hers is a migrant's vision which derives pleasure from newness. It is the vast flatness of the prairies, and the newness of the west as opposed to the 'old', established settlements in the east (and Europe), that informs van Herk's cartographic vision of Canadian space, even if she does then conceive this newness as a defining characteristic of Canadian national identity:

It is no wonder that the concept of mapping is so inherent to the way we see ourselves—as nation, as people, as literature. Because we are such a new country, we have almost perfect records of our own charting and because of our youth, we continue to participate in that mapping; it remains both an on-going process and a metaphor for our particularity.... There are not many places in the world where one can know that one is standing where no human being has ever set foot. I have stood in such a place, a place never before seen by eyes, a place unnamed and unmapped.[21]

Van Herk's reading of Canadian space does not represent the vision of the traumatised exiled mind, but the view of the migrant, who sees space in its refreshing novelty, unconcerned with and unconnected to the heavy burdens of white male sacrifice in the form of exploration and colonial settlement. The disconnection in van Herk's writing arises from her double position as migrant and woman, and is legitimised by her location outside the paradigm of nineteenth-century white male exploration, and his twentieth-century descendants. Yet it could also be argued that the migrant's emphasis on novelty is another inscription that obliterates native presence, whether there is evidence of its particular physical presence or not. Hence the marginalised position which grants migrant writers their reading position is far from unproblematic in relation to an indigenous perspective.

Van Herk's position is also regionalistic, and her view is shaped by an awareness of the brevity of white history on the prairie in the west. In this definition of place her position is similar to that of her fellow Albertan writer, Robert Kroetsch. In particular her idea of Canada as unnamed, unmapped and hence unclaimed and undefined corresponds closely to Kroetsch's question 'how do you write in a new country?'[22] which he asks not about Canadian literature in general, but specifically about the literature from the prairie.

In a particularly revealing statement Kroetsch compares a Canadian and an Australian landscape painting,[23] and draws a parallel between their divisions of space:

The geography of middle space is a peculiar problem in these two countries, which both like to talk so much about great distances. The middle space becomes, if you will, unquotable.... Both these paintings with their empty middles are post-colonial, and speak to us of genealogical anxieties. The originary occasion has gone blank.[24]

Kroetsch here articulates a space that shares similarities with what Bhabha defines as the Third Space, where 'claims to the inherent originality or "purity" of cultures are untenable'; a space which Bhabha somewhat mysteriously argues is 'unrepresentable in itself'.[25] Bhabha's argument finds a parallel in Kroetsch's conclusion that 'the artist ... insists that the middle ground is unreadable' (although Kroetsch provides a tentative answer in his suggestion to look at the passage or process).[26]

The 'middle space' of course also illustrates the duality of the settler's position I discussed earlier, as both here and there, and articulates a dilemma similar to that of the European explorer who confronts a landscape that lacks correspondence. Between the foreground and background in the painting, or between place and space in literature, the post-colonial inserts itself through disruption, distortion and undermining. The middle space is then a meddling space that insists on its presence. It does not undermine the position of the subject, but belies the illusion of cohesion. However, this does not necessarily lead to a sense of loss or alienation, for as van Herk asserts, 'the edge is a fine place to write from'.[27]

There are many overlappings between the articulation of the indigenous writer's place in Canada and Australia, which is perhaps unsurprising, considering these writers investigations of the space between a white and an indigenous position. This naturally foregrounds indigenous concerns about creating a voice, re-inventing indigeneity, the legacy of colonialism and post-decolonisation patterns of oppression. Here, I shall not deal with indigenous writers who seek to establish an indigenous platform outside a white-Aboriginal contact universe, but instead focus on those writers who define an indigenous identity inside the complex field of white-native interrelations, and also more widely within a network of writers as an international community.

The double position of the Canadian white writer has interesting parallels to that of the indigenous writer, even if their positions are also inherently different. Where the white writer is concerned with the links between national/regional space and personal place, the Native writer focuses on the relationship between the individual and the Native community. Hence the Native writer, Thomas King, opens the anthology on Native writing, *All My Relations*, with the following observation:

'All my relations' is the English equivalent of a phrase familiar to most Native peoples in North America. It may begin or end a prayer or a speech or a story, and, while each tribe has its own way of expressing this sentiment in its own language, the meaning is the same. [28]

This accurately pinpoints the concerns which I have located in three major anthologies of Native writing, *All My Relations*, *Northern Voices* and *Native Writers and Canadian Writing*.[29] King evidently attaches much importance to the bond between the individual indigenous writer and his/her community, but also implies the existence of a wider community of all Native groups. In contrast to, for example, Kroetsch and van Herk, King's idea of the community extends immediately from the local group to a continental scale, and there is no reference to the signification of 'nation' to the activity of writing. This omission is far from coincidental—for King it constitutes a major difference between an indigenous and non-indigenous position:

Being Native is a matter of race rather than something more transitory such as nationality. One can become a Canadian and a Canadian writer, for example, without having been born in Canada, but one is either born an Indian or one is not.[30]

King's distinction appears to be uncomplicated and natural, yet it reveals its own ambiguities, both in relation to white-indigenous definitions of Canadianness, and also in connection with an indigenous defined universe. If we look first on the

'white' side, what is then to be made of those that came to the east
centuries ago? Is there no difference between a tenth generation
and a first generation migrant? And even if we are looking at the
Canadian west, which was settled in comparatively recent times,
where can one place writers like van Herk, Wiebe and Kroetsch,
who are themselves immigrants of non-Anglo-Saxon descent,
with an acute awareness of being marginal in relation to other
more predominant definitions of Canadianness? The answer to
these questions is that King's distinction attempts to define what
separates Native Canadians from other Canadians, and is not
concerned with the identity problems of non-aboriginal
Canadians.

However, if we turn to consider the indigenous side of the
equation, a similar set of difficulties emerge due to the destruction
in many places of much of the original Native culture. King seeks
to strike a balance between, on the one hand, the need to escape
fixed labels of identity, and on the other, to unite Native writers
in order to strengthen the Native platform. The dilemma resulting
from these two contrary positions is clear in King's description of
the situation:

In our discussions of Native literature, we try to imagine that there is a
racial denominator which full-bloods raised in cities, half-bloods raised
on farms, quarter-bloods raised on reservations, Indians adopted and
raised by white families, Indians who speak their tribal language,
Indians who speak only English, traditionally educated Indians,
university-trained Indians, Indians with little education, and the like all
share. We know, of course, that there is not. We know that this is a
romantic, mystical, and, in many instances, a self-serving notion that the
sheer number of cultural groups in North America, the variety of Native
languages, and the varied conditions of the various tribes should
immediately belie.[31]

An indigenous community cannot be based on narrow
definitions of cultural purity. Displacement, cultural as well as
physical, is in most cases the predicament of the indigenous
writer. The binary erected by an authenticity based discourse not
only reproduces earlier 'white' ways of categorising indigenes, it

may also disadvantage current indigenous demands for the recognition of their rights. An alternative may exist in building bridges between the indigenous community and those parts of the white community who are willing to listen. Whilst King emphasises the need for indigenous representations to counter Native stereotyping by non-indigenous people, he opposes Native self-representations of authenticity, and instead seems to advocate the right to mix Native and non-Native experience to create a hybridity based on self-determination.

The concerns of Native Canadian writers are in many ways similar to those of Aboriginal writers. Like their Canadian counterparts, Aborigines write literature that explores the belief in the survival of traditional values, attempts to retrieve or reconstruct roots of a traditional Aboriginality, or seeks to articulate an Aboriginal voice within a white-Aboriginal contact space. These different positions are to some extent the consequences of quite different white-Aboriginal contact histories. The history of colonisation in the Tiwi Islands north of Darwin, and more generally on the Torres Strait Islands, has been relatively short and often haphazard in comparison with the longer and more systematic colonisation on the coastal fringe of the continent further south. There are obviously also significant differences between various regional Aboriginal cultural practices. However, in the following pages, I shall focus on Aboriginal writing that concerns itself with the consequences of colonisation, and with establishing an Aboriginal writer's position.

Two characteristics which lend themselves readily to my discussion of the writer's position are generally found throughout Aboriginal writing, namely, a tendency to include explicit autobiographical material and a strong political commitment to Aboriginal causes. In the light of the history of colonisation and its systematic silencing of the other, it is not difficult to understand why such elements are prominent. Protest is intrinsic to the Aboriginal writer's position and to the writing process. This is illustrated, for example, by Eva Johnson's response to the question of why she writes: 'Writing has the power to unveil almost any conscious or unconscious thought. I write to that consciousness, the conscious demon that arrived in this country two hundred years ago.'[32] Yet while Johnson's comment shows the Aborigine's desire to draw attention to colonial and post-colonial binaries, it does not point to political writing as a goal in itself, but rather to how the political inevitably informs the writer's position.

Like Canadian Native writers, Aboriginal writers are also concerned with what constitutes an indigenous point of view, a search that is intrinsically linked to colonial history, but also to European ancestry, as many Aboriginal writers are of both Aboriginal and European descent. Thus positionality is fore-grounded through an explicit engagement in politics, as in the case of Oodgeroo (formerly Kath Walker): 'No one recognised my white blood in me all these years—why the hell should I have to declare it now? I don't want to declare it. To hell with the white blood in me! I'm black. ... It's been forced upon me, I'm glad it's been forced upon me now.'[33]

Oodgeroo's outraged comment reveals that Aborigines occupying a marginal position in relation to tradition-oriented definitions of Aboriginality, have had to establish their own position. As mainstream culture seeks to address Aboriginality in terms of a fixed 'primitivism', it simultaneously tries to deny non-traditional Aborigines the right to call themselves Aborigines. Furthermore, Oodgeroo's comment shows that her own overtly politicised position is historically determined by the forces that have shaped white-Aboriginal relations. In comparison with Canadian Native writing, Aboriginal writing is generally more radical, and more directly exposes the ways in which colonialism and later nationalism have attempted to silence Aboriginal protests. In Aboriginal writing resistance takes many forms, e.g., mimicry, protest, parody, irony and the juxtaposition of a white and an Aboriginal universe. All of these approaches centre on the function of language in post-colonial texts. The Aboriginal writer Herb Wharton, in an interview in the Melbourne paper, *The Age*, draws attention to the function of linguistic parody as a strategy of resistance: 'Just because someone could speak English didn't mean they had some superior intelligence, because it wasn't too long that the English landed here than the cockatoos and the galahs could speak English.'[34]

Wharton's comment shows how the coloniser aims to naturalise his own position. If this seems an obvious point, it may be pertinent to draw attention to the uneasy parallel between the use of standard language teaching and literature studies in the education system. This situation is also related to the emergence of Aboriginal anthologies which bring together the collective efforts of Aboriginal writers. One such anthology is *Paperbark*, in which the editors assert: 'This anthology is underpinned by the conviction that Aboriginal writing, like Uluru—two-thirds of which is hidden underground—is still largely unknown to most Australians. It is our hope that this collection will contribute to the process of 'learning the country' for the reader, both in this nation and overseas.'[35] The choice of Uluru as a metaphor is not coincidental. Uluru has become a central icon for Aboriginality, and as such has a universal appeal to Aborigines across regional, and traditional versus westernised divides. However, the quotation above also draws attention to the importance of Uluru beyond an indigenous context, as a symbol of unity for all Australians, albeit a unity that has remained elusive. Hence, with this collection, the editors hope to give the uninitiated reader an insight into Uluru. Naturally such concerns reflect both the realities of the publishing scene and the desire to win support for the indigenous cause. Hence the position taken by the editors of *Paperbark* reveals the gulf between the different double position held by Aboriginal and white writers, i.e., that Aboriginal writers are dependent on a white audience and are always negotiating a balance between a traditional and a westernised point of view.

In my discussion of non-indigenous Canadian writers, I drew attention to the double position they hold in relation to the idea of the Canadian west as new, unmapped and unnamed, compared both to a European place of origin, and to the history of settlement in the east. Contemporary Australian writers may also talk of Australia in terms of refreshing novelty and the 'exiled mind', but the sense of a place that is already known and mapped by a different culture is pronounced. The migrant's own mapping process must be seen against the backcloth of this pre-existing map, fully inscribed and understood within an Aboriginal geographical mythology. In the following paragraphs I shall try to illustrate how the awareness of the unknown space and Aboriginal presence influences white Australian writers' perceptions of their own position.

There is a pronounced wariness among white writers when the issue of Aboriginality is raised. The legacy of fixed representative modes in the non-Aboriginal literature that creates Aboriginal characters has made the use of Aboriginality or an Aboriginal viewpoint controversial, even when that incorporation of Aboriginality is part of an effort to counter prevailing settlement myths. I shall consider this theme in the work of two Australian writers, David Malouf and Les Murray, both of whom engage with the issue of Aboriginality, and whose viewpoints provide productive polarities for my exploration of the links between representations of Aboriginality and Australian space.

Les Murray's essay 'The Human Hair Thread' gives a revealing analysis of his own use of Aboriginality in his poetry. However, it is also necessary to say that Murray's position reflects the sensitivities of the decade in which it was written. In the 1970s, when the systematic silencing of Aboriginal demands had finally become an important national issue, it was acknowledged that Aboriginality lent its presence to a great deal of Australian writing in numerous, although not always explored, ways. Today, however, the situation is very different. There is now an established corpus of Aboriginal literature, although not quite yet of Aboriginal criticism, and the field has also become more sharply politically defined among different Aboriginal groupings, for example, in the debate between tradition and renewal, which revolves around the question of how westernised Aboriginal writing and art should become. The divide between Aboriginal and 'white' writers is also marked. Though efforts such as *Paperbark* show that white editorial intrusion is acceptable, and perhaps also a precondition for reaching a wider white audience, there is remarkably little overt cross-fertilisation between white and Aboriginal writers. However, in the wake of this stalemate it is also important to note that a whole group of white writers actively engage in imagining an Aboriginal viewpoint that often treads a careful balance between a spiritual and a radical histori-cal oriented universe. In this concluding section I shall consider how the writers themselves define what Murray calls 'Aboriginal presence' in their work.

Although 'The Human Hair Thread' was written in another decade, it speaks of divisions that have lost none of their signifi-cance. Drawing attention to the benefit he has derived from including Aboriginality in his poetry, Murray declares that he is less interested in 'what I have been able to do with one of the great Australian cultural heritages' than he is in 'what that heritage has given me'.[36] He then considers how that influence has manifested itself in his writing:

There has been an Aboriginal presence in my work almost from the start. This is natural enough, in one coming from the country. Until quite recently, the original Australians were almost exclusively a country people, and the white culture they had to resist or assimilate with was the Australian rural one. Growing up outside the cities, one couldn't fail to be conscious of them, living on the fringe of things, mostly in poverty, hanging around the pubs in Taree. ... In my part of the North Coast of New South Wales, they were not really poorer or more broken down than the poorest farm families or seasonal workers. ... One knew there were special laws about the Aboriginals—to some extent, the modern Aboriginal people is a *creation* of discriminatory laws working against the declared policy of assimilation.[37]

Murray's position here is fraught with ambivalence. He begins by claiming a kind of kinship between country people and local Aboriginal groups that appears to grow out of coexistence and experience, and moves beyond racial difference. Yet how is 'resist or assimilate with' to be understood? That country people have a sort of stubborn endurance, which ensures their survival and successful adaptation, and that Aborigines are as such what Murray terms them 'country people'? Murray is trapped by his reading of both country people and Aborigines as 'of the land' and is therefore unable to differentiate between different—in

certain ways even antagonistic—ways of belonging. The bridge
between Aborigines and Murray's country people consists in their
similar material status as 'rural poor'. In other words Murray
postulates, without problematising it, a particular kind of rural,
spiritual fellowship, which the city with its alienation does not
allow. Furthermore, it is tempting to ask whether Aborigines who
fled to the city to escape the systematic discrimination in the
country, could not equally well be said to share working-class
conditions with the city poor.

If his rural image of white-Aboriginal relations is inconsistent
with political realities, his statement that the modern Aborigine is
to some extent created by discriminatory laws is even more
problematic, because it takes the agency away from the Aborigines, and also indirectly supports the common white view of
Aborigines as the lost people from forgotten tribes. Although
resistance is mentioned in connection with the rural situation, it is
of the past, when resistance meant fighting the invasion. Again
one might venture a few plausible reasons why Aboriginal
resistance was revived from the city, not from the bush. Murray's
political agenda emerges more fully, when he talks about the
whites' relationship with their own history:

The Aboriginals were partly a people, partly a caste, partly a class,
though really that last term is inaccurate: they were actually part of a
larger class of the rural poor, and it is still often more useful to see them
in that light than in currently fashionable radical-racialist terms. We, my
family, were almost in the same class ourselves. ... Really, I am not at all
sure about white conquest-guilt; it may be no more than a construct of
the political Left, that great inventor of prescriptive sentiments and
categories. It certainly isn't a reliable sentiment for outsiders to invoke
among country people.[38]

Perhaps Murray's saving grace is that he does not completely
allow for total identification between the white rural poor and
Aborigines. Yet, he is unable to articulate what constitutes that
difference precisely, it seems to me, because it would entail
unravelling the whole colonial history, and make his own position as one of the victims untenable. Murray misconstrues two

arguments, one that deals with economic reality and another that deals with the historical differences between white and Aboriginal positions. Thus, Murray postulates a dichotomy between city and country experience that supersedes the systematic racial oppression that has been the Aboriginal experience throughout Australian history.

Murray's political stance lands him in severe problems in relation to the incorporation of Aboriginal presence in his poetry. Aboriginal trails and tracks can be seen both in his poetry and in the countryside (in the poetry by, for example, invoking an Aboriginally inspired mythological reading, in the countryside through the preservation of Aboriginal names). Yet Aboriginality is presumably not there to be made use of without adequate recognition of the tradition of the local Aborigines. If an acknowledgement of Aboriginal histories does not include the transitional phase between a traditional Aboriginal universe and the modern Aboriginal existence, through the experience of colonial history, Murray ends up trapping the Aborigines in the past—and represents modern Aborigines as essentially non-Aboriginal. I use the word 'essentially' deliberately to draw attention to the fact that essentialising can not only trap indigenes inside traditionalism or primitivism, but can equally well trap modern indigenes outside their own culture, denying them access to express indigeneity in whatever degree of westernisation, they may desire.

David Malouf represents an opposite pole in the representation of Australian space. Les Murray draws attention to their differing views, when he quotes Malouf towards the end of 'The Human-Hair Thread':

It is only through Caliban that we get this sense of the richness of the island, its tumbling fecundity. His capacity to name things, and by naming evoke them, is a different sort of magic from Prospero's but no less powerful and real. It might remind us of the extraordinary way our own Aborigines have possessed the land in their minds, through folkstories, taboos, song cycles, and made it part of the very fabric of their living as we never can.[39]

By drawing attention to Caliban, Malouf immediately conjures up images of a common cause among the oppressed, and shows more importantly the ability of the oppressed to present an alternative agenda. Malouf also creates a link between the situation of the Aborigines and the white writer who wishes to question perceived national Australian myths about the formative experience of mateship in the bush, as the only valid form of voicing an Australian experience.

I will turn shortly to consider how Malouf has more recently spoken of the writer's place in Australia. But first I wish to return to Murray's response to Malouf's romantically inspired idea of a unique Aboriginal perception of nature, which non-Aborigines can hope to glimpse, but never achieve:

My contention is that of course 'we' can, and some of us do possess the land imaginatively in very much the Aboriginal way. We have recently been awed by the discovery that the Aboriginals have been here for thirty or forty thousand years, but I think too much is often made of this. Forty thousand years are not very different from a few hundred, if your culture has not, through genealogy, developed a sense of the progression of time and thus made history possible. Aboriginal 'history' is poetic, a matter of significant moments rather than of development.[40]

Murray's response is to seek to liberate the image of Aborigines from the idea of portraying them as mysterious and inscrutable. Yet he sets an agenda that comes disturbingly close to a colonialist view, where white culture becomes a natural successor to a redundant, static Aboriginal culture.

In his Bicentennial piece for *The Age* in January 1988, Malouf continues to stress his view of Australians as essentially migrants in their own country: 'There is, at the centre of our lives here, a deep irony: that the very industry that gives us a hold on the earth has no roots in the land itself, no history, no past; and the sort of past—the experience of having developed along with the land and its creatures—may be precisely what one needs.'[41] Malouf here gives voice to an extreme reading of the settlement experience, where the past does not exist, where the bridges to the past have been burnt, and where, consequently, the most has to be made of the present, because it is the present that gives vitality to the migrant experience. What Malouf suggests is not merely Patrick White's idea of an empty Australian soul, but also that there is a missing sense of purpose in the new migrant place, as if the displaced history has failed to impregnate the new place with significance:

There is, and always has been, something rootless and irresponsible about our attitude to the land. We treat it, we go at things 'as if there were no tomorrow', using, wasting, making the most of everything while it lasts, stripping assets, taking the short view.

What comes across in Malouf's vision is an awareness of the land as stolen, not rightfully claimed and therefore only there until the theft is detected, when it will be returned to its rightful owner. However, if this may lead to the assumption that Australia is still trapped inside a colonial mentality, Malouf also draws attention to the land's significance as a place for new beginnings and its potential as a regenerative force. This is clear from his juxtaposition between his Brisbane school-days (in the 1940s) and Australia in 1988:

Once you left the coast and the wheatlands beyond, there was nothing out there to hang on to. The centre, imaginatively speaking, was blank.
Now the centre of Australia, the Centre, is fixed, occupied by a vivid symbol, a natural phenomenon so powerful that it rivals and counter-balances our man-made ones, those unmistakable marks of our presence, the Bridge and the Opera House. ... I mean Ayers Rock. ... Still unknown 40 years ago, and therefore invisible, its emergence in a thousand forms (as a big hamburger or as the mould that breaks open to reveal the new Ford) is one of the few significant events of our history: the hero as rock. It has become the true naval of our consciousness, the great belly-button of the land.

Malouf's statement constitutes a suitable conclusion to the problems involved in fixing the position of the Australian and Canadian writer in relation to the idea of a national, geographic centre. As the focal point for the Canadian and Australian search for national identity, this centre—fluid rather than fixed, process-oriented rather than static, and open to constantly changing interpretations of history—is seen to reflect the doubleness of the Canadian and Australian writer's position.

Notes

1. Thomas Keneally, *The Playmaker* (London: Sceptre, 1988).
2. Keith Windschuttle in his otherwise unnuanced attack on those who dare question traditional historiography does point out the problem in Carter's sweeping generalisations concerning what constitutes imperial history (*The Killing of History: How a Discipline Is Being Murdered by Literary Critics and Social Theorists* [Sydney: Macleay, 1996] 108-10). Although I follow Carter's idea of the staging of history, I find it more productive to make a distinction between imperial and national history.
3. The post-colonial discourse on definitions of Canadian and Australian identity is also closely related to gender and multicultural discourses. Hence when for example a migrant writer from China writes about the difficulties involved in carving out a space for his/her own writing in one of the Canadian or Australian metropolises, s/he is questioning perceived monopolies on definitions of Canadian or Australian national identities, which are traditionally linked to the settlement experience. It lies, unfortunately, outside the scope of this article to pursue the topic of ethnic or gender based challenges to mainstream definitions of national space further than to point out that the question concerning definitions of Australian and Canadian identity revolves around the (often conflicting) ideas of migration, the pioneer legend, or the male sacrifice stemming from fighting displaced wars for Canada and the British Empire in Europe or South Africa as the leitmotifs in Australian and Canadian identity. Nationalist representations of Canadian and Australian identity place the formative experience in the past, and are as such exclusivist or at least assimilationist, whereas multicultural models are by nature constantly reformulated, that is process-oriented rather than fixed in relation to an archetypal past.
4. See for example Stephen Slemon, 'Unsettling the Empire: Resistance Theory for the Second World', *World Literature Written in English* 30.2 (1990), and Helen Tiffin, 'Post-Colonial Literatures and Counter-Discourse', *Kunapipi* 9.3 (1987). Bart Moore-Gilbert also challenges an easy inclusion of Canada and Australia in the post-colonial fold (*Post-Colonial Theory: Contexts, Practices, Politics* [London: Verso, 1997] 10-11 and 32), although he tends to map the positions rather than inserting himself directly in the debate.
5. As Slemon points out 'subjected peoples are sometimes capable of producing reactionary literary documents' (33). The point is, however, not to dilute post-colonial discourse by making it wider in its implications (a trend that is already threatening to undermine the shaky stability of the

field), but instead to see the benefits which will come from including Australian and Canadian writing.

6. In my discussion of 'resistance' I draw upon arguments from Moore-Gilbert's discussion on Bhabha's use of 'resistance' (*Post-Colonial Theory* 130-40), Gareth Griffiths, 'The Myth of Authenticity', *De-Scribing Empire: Post-Colonialism and Textuality*, ed. Chris Tiffin and Alan Lawson (London: Routledge, 1994), Slemon, and the section, 'Representation and Resistance' in *The Post-Colonial Studies Reader*, ed. Bill Ashcroft, Gareth Griffiths and Helen Tiffin (London: Routledge, 1995).

7. Slemon 36.

8. Slemon 36.

9. Slemon 37.

10. Quoted in Slemon 38.

11. It may be tempting to argue that the current infatuation with indigenous cultures grants indigenous writers a privileged position. However, it is important to recognise that this fetishism is circumscribed by its own infatuation with indigeneity in the form of native 'authenticity' or 'primitivism', which first of all locks indigenes in fixed pre-modern, representational modes, and secondly that 'primitivism' is conveniently disconnected from indigenous, political aspirations (for land rights and for self-determination, to mention just two of the areas). For a fuller explication of this industry see Nicholas Thomas, *Colonialism's Culture: Anthropology, Travel and Government* (Oxford: Polity, 1994), esp. 170-95, where Thomas describes the commodification of primitivism.

12. Benedict Anderson, *Imagined Communities: Reflections on the Origin and Spread of Nationalism*, rev. ed. (London: Verso, 1991) 5-7.

13. Writing may be seen as a process of commitment and detachment. On the one hand to write is to define a stand, that is a process through which writers inscribe themselves into a tradition that grows out of a particular perspective, and the idea of a geographically as well as a culturally defined space. On the other hand writing is also a process of detachment from the community, where the writer steps outside or beyond the confines of the community to imagine it.

14. The link between literature and nationalism is well-established by for example Timothy Brennan, 'The National Longing for Form', *Nation and Narration*, ed. Homi K. Bhabha (London: Routledge, 1990). Anderson also discusses the relationship between literature and nation (29-33).

15. Ashcroft, Griffiths and Tiffin 391.

16. Margaret Atwood, *Strange Things: The Malevolent North in Canadian Literature* (Oxford: Clarendon, 1995) 8-9.

17. Atwood, *Strange Things* 16.

18. Margaret Atwood, 'The Age of Lead', *Wilderness Tips* (Toronto: McClelland-Bantam, 1992) 168.

19. Atwood, *Strange Things* 32.

20. Aritha van Herk, *A Frozen Tongue* (Mundelstrup: Dangaroo, 1992) 25.

21. Van Herk 54-55.

22. Robert Kroetsch, *The Lovely Treachery of Words: Essays Selected and New* (Toronto: Oxford UP, 1989) 5.

23. The two paintings he compares, Tom Thomson's *The Jack Pine* (1916) and Russell Drysdale's *The Drover's Wife* (1945), are now considered to belong to national schools of painting.

24. Kroetsch 36-37.

25. Homi K. Bhabha, *The Location of Culture* (London: Routledge, 1994) 37.

26. Kroetsch 38.

27. Van Herk 74.

28. Thomas King, ed., *All My Relations: An Anthology of Contemporary Canadian Native Fiction* (Toronto: McClelland and Stewart, 1990) ix.

29. Penny Petrone, ed., *Northern Voices: Inuit Writing in English* (Toronto: U of Toronto P, 1988), W. H. New, ed., *Native Writers and Canadian Writing* (Vancouver: U of British Columbia P, 1990).

30. King x.

31. King x-xi.

32. Anna Rutherford, Lars Jensen and Shirley Chew, eds, *Into the Nineties: Post-Colonial Women's Writing*, (Hebden Bridge: Dangaroo, 1994) 11.

33. Oodgeroo [Kath Walker], interview, *Meanjin* 36.4 (1977): 434.

34. Herb Wharton, interview, *The Age* 11 May 1996.

35. Jack Davis, Mudrooroo Narogin, Stephen Muecke and Adam Shoemaker, eds, *Paperbark: A Collection of Black Australian Writings* (St Lucia: UQP, 1990) 6.

36. Les Murray, 'The Human-Hair Thread', *Meanjin* 36.4 (1977) 550.

37. Murray 550-551.

38. Murray 551.

39. Quoted in Murray 569.

40. Murray 569.

41. David Malouf, 'Putting Ourselves on the Map', *The Age* (Melbourne) 23 Jan. 1988.

The First Rainbow Nation?
The Griqua in Post-Apartheid South Africa

David Johnson

Two concerns run through this chapter. The first is a theoretical concern: to consider how history is read in different contexts, and in particular how the reading of history within the academy differs from how history might be read outside the academy. My second concern is to reflect upon the status of minority groups within a nation, and in particular upon how ethnic group identity confronts an ideology of nationhood. To pursue these two concerns, I focus on the claims of a particular ethnic minority, the Griqua in South Africa, and consider their recent claims to the South African government for recognition.

What are the claims of the Griqua? These are best summed up in a memorandum presented by the Griqua National Conference to the United Nations Working Group on Indigenous Populations on 27 July 1995.[1] To quote from the Memorandum:

Notwithstanding South Africa's dramatic, praiseworthy and unprecedented transformation into a democratic nation state committed to realising the full human rights potential of South Africa's self-styled Rainbow Nation, the Griqua people, as a self-identified, autochtonous [sic], non-dominant and first self-identified nation having
    * traditional lands
    * historical continuity
    * distinctive cultural characteristics
remain marginalised and constitutionally disempowered.

Taken together, these factors qualify the Griqua for First Nation status, and in political terms, this allows the Griqua National Conference to make the following demands:

Translating Nations, ed. Prem Poddar, *The Dolphin* 30, pp. 115-28.
© 1999 by Aarhus University Press, Denmark.
ISBN 87 7288 381 2; ISSN 0106 4487.

* the restitution of land rights resulting from the violation of treaties that pre-
    date 1913
* the formal recognition of the distinct identity of the Griqua people
* representation in the newly-formed provincial Houses of the Traditional
    Leaders at central government level.

The Memorandum to the United Nations was accompanied by a short history of the Griqua. The origins of the Griqua nation are located in the eighteenth century, when the Griqua 'evolved from the semi-nomadic aboriginal group of people with a common identity, culture and language essentially known as the Khoi-Khoi'. As a result of colonial expansion, 'displaced remnant clans withdrew from Colonial subjugation and oppression and came to be known and united as the Griqua'.[2] After 1820, two substantial Griqua communities emerged, one based in Griquatown under Andries Waterboer, and one under Adam Kok II in Philippolis. Their nomadic lifestyle abandoned, the Griqua successfully cultivated the land, and ruled themselves as an independent state for approximately sixty years. In the second half of the nineteenth century, '[c]olonial encroachment and the breaking of treaties resulted in the further diaspora of the Griqua people, [with the result that] after the death of Adam Kok III, the Griqua people were in disarray and dispersed'.[3] After a paragraph on the charismatic Griqua leader of the early twentieth century, A. A. S. Le Fleur, the present structure of the Griqua movement is set out, with details of the paramount chief, the Griqua Independent Church, and the various Griqua cultural groups.

This Griqua version of history challenges in fundamental ways the national historical narrative as set down in the Preamble of South Africa's new constitution. Where the Griqua history insists upon the particularly cruel oppression of the Griqua nation under colonialism and apartheid in South Africa, and the need for appropriate reparation, the Preamble emphasizes the collective suffering of *all South Africans*, and the need for a collective *national* re-constitution:

We, the people of South Africa,
Recognise the injustices of our past;
Honour those who suffered for justice and freedom in our land;
Respect those who have worked to build and develop our country; which
Belongs to all who live in it, unified in our diversity.[4]

The pronouns 'we' and 'our' include all races, thus blurring the line between oppressed and oppressors, and a new unified South Africa is imagined, which transcends the differences of the past.

This is not to say that the South African government has dismissed Griqua claims entirely. In a speech in May this year (1997) opening the new Council of Traditional Leaders, Nelson Mandela referred specifically the Griqua, whose 'long resistance forged leaders of the stature of Waterboer, Le Fleur and Adam Kok'.[5] More significantly, two historians, John Kitching and Johan Meiring, were appointed last year to investigate whether the Griqua represent a special case, and should therefore be treated differently.[6] In July 1997, they produced *A Conceptual Report on Griqua History, Griqua Interest Groups and Leadership*, which provides a 50-page summary of the main events in the history of the Griqua, as well as 28 appendices of key documents. Though the Report declares on the cover that it has no official status, it is being made available both to Griqua groups for comments and criticism, and to members of parliament, who will ultimately vote on the legitimacy of Griqua claims.

The Report provides background on two questions: (1) the origins of the Griqua (are they indeed indigenous people in terms of UN definitions?), and (2) whether they have suffered especially severe deprivations as a result of colonialism and apartheid. If both are answered in the affirmative, Griqua claims to political representation and the restitution of land will be much strengthened. Though strong on detail, the Meiring/ Kitching Report is weak on analysis, and no clear answers emerge. To establish how these questions have been answered over time, I want now to turn to three different histories.

Dr John Philip

Starting in the nineteenth century, perhaps the most influential version of Griqua history is the one provided by London Missionary Society leader in the Cape Colony, Dr John Philip.[7] Of Scottish evangelical training, Philip arrived at the Cape in 1819, and until his death in 1851 energetically tried to defend the interests of Christian missions among African communities against Boer settlers and the British colonial government. In evidence to the British House of Commons Select Committee on Aborigines (British Settlements) in 1837, Philip describes the origins of the Griqua in the eighteenth century as follows:

[T]hey are a race of mulattos whose ancestors were the offspring of the colonists by Hottentot females. These Bastards, as they were termed, finding themselves treated as an inferior race by their kinsmen of European blood, and prevented from acquiring land, or any fixed property, within the colony, about 50 years ago sought a refuge from contumely and oppression among the native tribes beyond its limits, where their numbers were gradually augmented by refugees of the same caste from the colony, and by intermarriages with females of the Bushmen and Coranna tribes around them. In the year 1800, when Mr Anderson went among the Griquas (as they are now denominated), they were a herd of wandering naked savages, subsisting by plunder and chase. Their bodies were daubed with red paint, their heads loaded with grease and shining powder, with no covering but the filthy caross over their shoulders. Without knowledge, without morals, or any traces of civilisation, they were wholly abandoned to witchcraft, drunkenness, licentiousness.[8]

Philip explains how it was the missionaries who first convinced the Griqua to establish stable settlements, and then oversaw the creation of Griqua political institutions. Philip cements his version of events by quoting in full a letter from Chief Andries Waterboer to the Reverend Peter Wright, which confirms the beneficence of the missionaries:

We owe everything to the blessing of God upon the labours of the missionaries in the service of the London Missionary Society. We were no people when the missionaries found us, and it was under these circumstances we became a people. We had no country of our own when the missionaries came among us, but were wandering about as fugitives without a settled abode; and it was the missionaries that found a country for us, and persuaded us to settle on it and cultivate the land.[9]

What answers does Philip provide to our two questions? As to whether the Griqua are indeed an indigenous group, Philip answers in the affirmative, though his myths of Griqua savagery would now be dismissed as symptoms of a nineteenth-century racist pathology. As to the second question, the Griqua as described by Philip could not be seen as only the victims of colonialism: even if they suffered at the hands of Boer farmers and the British colonial governments at the

Cape, their relationship with the missionaries as described by Waterboer clearly brought some benefits. More than just victims, they might also then be seen as having for a significant period benefited from colonialism.

A. A. S. Le Fleur

Moving on to try and find a Griqua history written in its own terms, the writings of the early twentieth century Griqua nationalist leader, Andries Abraham Stockenstrom le Fleur provide an appropriate source.[10] Born in the Orange Free State in 1867, Le Fleur moved as a young man to Kokstad where he married the eldest daughter of the last Kok *kapteyn*, and in the process acquired the Griqua symbols of political authority. In 1894, Le Fleur became a full-time political activist, and he spent the remainder of his long life campaigning tirelessly for the cause of the Griqua. In the 1920s, he published the *Griqua and Coloured People's Opinion* from Cape Town, and it is here that his version of Griqua history is elaborated.

He sets out the origins of the Griqua as follows:

In 1624 our Forefathers lived in South Africa as Heathens under their Chiefs. They have migrated from the North of Africa, and came across the Eastern shores to the South. Our race was a mixed race, and had our own language and in every mode of thinking and acting a similarity ever existed between us, and the Jews. They mixed with the Bantu and Bushman and got to where we were before the Europeans came here. Then came the time, in 1652, the Europeans ... became settled here, and from them the Intermixture began; then we became a mixed Race and lived amongst the Europeans, then we began to form a distinct race with a Chief. ... [A]t Mamre the Mixed Race got the name of Griquas; from their mixture with the European.[11]

Le Fleur goes on to describe how slaves were integrated into the Griqua community, and then lists the succession of Griqua chiefs, emphasising the Kok line, and making only the briefest mention of Waterboer.

As regards the oppression of the Griqua, Le Fleur provides ample evidence of Griqua poverty and suffering, but he never directly blames colonialism. He mentions only in passing the villainy of Sir Harry Smith, and treats colonial and settler authorities of the 1920s with great deference. The pages of the *Griqua and Coloured People's*

Opinion reproduce letters of homage and support from Le Fleur to J.C. Smuts, to J. B. M. Hertzog, and to the visiting Prince of Wales.[12] An editorial celebrating the Government's release of Rehobother prisoners captures the tone of Le Fleur's attitude:

We can assure General [Hertzog] that his actions will go down in history as the first in which greatness has been shown to our people. ... So General Hertzog's name will go down in the History as one of our greatest men with a great mind. Let us not forget general Smuts, who did great in the Johannesburg Strike, in the same direction. ... You have an example of what affection can do, the Prince of Wales, by his greetings, has won the affection of every race, yet He is the Highest Prince in the world.[13]

Responsibility for Griqua suffering is located with 'the Reds' and 'the Asiatic Problem', but Le Fleur also concedes that the Griqua have themselves been complicit in their decline due to 'the loss of National instinct and National honour or respect for each other'.[14] The solution, he argues, is to promote Griqua self-sufficiency: 'Let us cease to look abroad for assistance for our advancement. We must look into our own country for this; improve our conditions.'[15] A combination of benevolent paternalism and vigorous self-help are therefore seen as the route to Griqua redemption.

How then does Le Fleur answer these two questions? Again, the autochthonous pre-colonial origins of the Griqua are confirmed, but as with the Philip history, the relationship with colonialism presents complications. Keenly aware of the political advantage to be gained by flattering the powerful, Le Fleur's addresses to Hertzog and the Prince of Wales—not unlike Waterboer's letters to Philip and Wright—might be read as strategic attempts to win sympathy for the Griqua people. However, it is impossible to read any irony in his views on 'Reds' and on 'Asiatics'. As in the case of Philip's history then, Le Fleur fails to tell us unambiguously whether the Griqua were victims of colonialism or unsuccessful collaborators.

Robert Ross

Moving finally to more recent Griqua histories,[16] social historian Robert Ross complicates Philip and Le Fleur's insistence on indigenous Griqua origins by placing somewhat greater emphasis upon their mixed heritage:

The Griquas were descendants of early Boer frontiersman; of the remnants of Khoisan tribes—hunters, gatherers and pastoralists; of escaped slaves from wine and wheat farms of the south-west Cape; of free blacks from the colony who could find no acceptable place for themselves in it; and of African tribesman, detached from their tribes by war or by choice.[17]

In his short chapter on the early history of the Griqua, Ross stresses the role played first by mixed-race refugees from the Cape Colony like Adam Kok, and by missionaries like John Campbell, who claimed that in August 1813 he convinced the Griqua to abandon the name 'Bastards' and assume the name 'Griqua'.

Ross focuses on the later period of the Philippolis Captaincy (1834-1861), and after setting out in scrupulous detail the shameful treatment of the Griqua at the hands of the colonial authorities during Adam Kok II's reign, Ross concludes by stressing the ambivalences of the relation:

The Griquas were collaborators of the British, not because the British provided some advantage in recompense, but because there was no other way in which the Griquas could hope to fulfil the aspirations which they held as a community. After the British found ... that the Griquas could not perform the functions of collaborators in maintaining the peace beyond the Orange, and consequently began to scout the Highveld for other, more effective ones, even then the Griquas remained loyal to the British.[18]

Ross's answer to the second question would then be: Yes, the Griqua *were* collaborators with colonialism, but crucially, they were forced into this compromising role by the British, as they had no alternative means of guaranteeing their survival as a community.

Contexts of Griqua Histories

Having set out very briefly these different versions of Griqua history,[19] I want to turn to the question of where, and by whom they might be read, and to this end want to introduce two quite different readers: the postcolonial critic faced with a conference deadline; and the South

African member of parliament faced with the urgent political demands of the Griqua National Conference.

How is the postcolonial critic in the 1990s likely to view these competing Griqua histories? The vocabulary of the discipline insists that such histories be read through the theoretical lenses of post-68 literary theory. Thus an act of translation is called for, as the primary texts—the Griqua National Conference history, the Kitching/Meiring Report, Philip, Le Fleur and Ross—are first re-coded in appropriate theoretical terms, and then transmitted within the academic circuits of the conference and scholarly journal.

This might be done in any number of ways. First, any reflection on the origins of the Griqua might well be influenced by the methodological prescriptions of Michel Foucault. In his essay 'Politics and the study of discourse', Foucault rejects the search for origins:

I would like ... to challenge again the theme of an indefinitely receding origin, and the idea that in the realm of thought, the role of history is to awaken what has been forgotten, to eliminate the occultations, to efface—or to lift anew—the barriers. Against this, I would like to propose the analysis of discursive systems, historically defined, to which one can affix thresholds, and assign conditions of birth and disappearance.[20]

Histories taking their cue from this position would then re-orientate their researches away from the kinds of essentialist pre-occupations facing the earlier historians, and focus instead on the 'historically defined discursive systems' constituting Griqua national identity. That this paper has been influenced by such an emphasis should be clear.

Secondly, in reading the Griqua relation to colonial rule, the postcolonial critic would almost certainly turn first to Frantz Fanon. Waterboer's relation to the British colonial authorities might well be seen as a version of what Fanon in *The Wretched of the Earth* describes as the native intellectual in the first phase of colonial domination, who 'has thrown himself greedily upon Western culture', and gives 'proof that he has assimilated the culture of the occupying power'.[21] Alternately, s/he might seek an explanation for Waterboer's pro-British writings in Homi Bhabha's formulations of how colonial subjects practise a 'sly civility' and 'subversive mimicry' as forms of defensive warfare. As Bhabha explains, extending Fanon, 'beyond the psychic choice ... "turn white or disappear" ... [t]here is the more ambivalent, third choice: camouflage, mimicry, black skins white masks'.[22] This subtle and sophisticated critical vocabulary will surely see progress in making sense of Griqua history.[23]

The second imaginary reader of these histories—the South African member of parliament—will be under rather different pressures. In particular s/he will have to decide pressing political questions, including whether the Griqua should be represented in the Council of Traditional Leaders, and whether their land claims pre-dating the 1913 Land Act should be treated. The histories are inconclusive: depending on how literally 'indigenous' is defined, the white colonial strand of Griqua ancestry might compromise claims to authentic autochthonous status. Also, strong cases could be made either way as to whether the collaborative relationships the Griqua had with the British were chosen or enforced. My suspicion is that rather than being interpreted according to standards of historical or theoretical accuracy, history will be mobilised to suit current political and economic imperatives. In political terms, can Griqua claims which foreground an ethnic particularism be accommodated without threatening the fragile national 'unity-in-diversity' the ANC government presides over? The chances are slim, according to journalist Melanie Gosling:

Khoesan appeals to the government for First Nation recognition have been largely ignored. Academics say South African politicians are reluctant to grapple with ethnicity, having thrown off the oppression of apartheid which was underpinned by race. If the government were to recognise an aboriginal people, it would mean a major paradigm shift for the country.[24]

Furthermore, with only around 100,000 members,[25] the Griqua community is at this stage too small and dispersed to exert much political pressure on the new government. Economic considerations will also be to the fore: even with the necessary political will, can the provincial governments of the Free State and Kwazulu-Natal afford to pay compensation to white farmers around Philippolis and Kokstad so that Griqua communities can re-occupy land stolen from them in the nineteenth century?

Finally, as regards the theoretical questions of audience and address, it is a familiar routine to gesture to the university's responsibilities to the world beyond its limits. Thinkers as different as Jacques Derrida and Jürgen Habermas agree on this: Derrida writes of the need for universities 'to transform the modes of writing, approaches to pedagogy, the procedures of academic exchange, the relation to languages, to other disciplines, to the institution in general, to its inside and its outside',[26] and Habermas in only slightly different terms insists upon the need 'to make the connections of research processes to the lifeworld transparent in terms of those processes themselves, and ... especially their connection to culture as a whole, to general processes of socialization'.[27] Extending this appeal to postcolonial studies is also not especially original—Edward Said and Gayatri Spivak have frequently made the same point—but I would add a caution: references in postcolonial studies to contemporary political struggles function all too often as rhetorical flourishes; my belief is that greater attention should focus on these struggles, and further that the barriers between institutions generating postcolonial theory, and the subjects of postcolonial theory, should be a central theme in all such inquiries.[28]

As regards the place of minority groups within the nation, this swift survey of Griqua claims in South Africa in 1990s South Africa reveals that no matter how inclusive the official myths, symbols and historical narratives of nationhood claim to be, there remain ethnic minorities like the Griqua who complain of exclusion. Politically oppressed, and denied access to land under the apartheid regime, many Griqua anticipated that with the coming of the new rainbow order, their mixed heritage would qualify them for sympathetic treatment. Yet their hopes have been frustrated, and their marginalisation has continued. I have suggested that part of the explanation for this apparent anomaly lies in the uneven contest between the discourses of South African rainbow nationhood and Griqua ethnicity. From the point of view of the state, however, Griqua claims pose a further threat because they expose the contradiction between the political equalities promised by the new constitution and the continuing economic inequalities produced by a capitalist economy.

Notes

1. I am indebted to Mansell Upham, the legal representative of the Griqua National Conference (hereafter GNC), for spending time explaining current Griqua politics to me. I also learnt much during an interview with the youth representatives on the Executive Council of the GNC, Elmo Abrahams, Lisa

Dirkse, and Roderick Williams. The GNC claims to be the largest of a number of Griqua political groups. For a comprehensive summary of the competing Griqua political and cultural organisations, see John Kitching and Johan Meiring, eds, *A Conceptual Report on Griqua History, Griqua Interest Groups and Leadership* (Pretoria: Constitutional Assembly, 1997) 31-44.

2. GNC, 'Statement by the Griqua National Conference to the United Nations Working Group on Indigenous Populations' (1995), Kitching and Meiring, Appendix E, 1.

3. GNC, 'Statement' 2.

4. Republic of South Africa, Constitutional Assembly, *Constitution of the Republic of South Africa Bill* (1996) 3.

5. Nelson Mandela, address, inauguration of the National Council of Traditional Leaders, Pretoria, May 1997.

6. The 1997 government report by Kitching and Meiring is only the latest in a long line of such state-sponsored enquiries into the Griqua. In the nineteenth century, there were two British commissions of inquiry which looked *inter alia* at the Griqua, the *Report of the Select Committee on Aborigines (British Settlements)* in 1837, and the *Report from the Select Committee on the Kafir Tribes* in 1851. Following a Griqua uprising in 1878, the Ministerial Department of Native Affairs of the Cape of Good Hope published the *Report of a Commission Appointed by His Excellency the Governor and High Commissioner to inquire into the recent outbreak in Griqualand East* (Cape Town: Solomon, 1879). More recently, the National Party government published the *Report of the Constitutional Committee of the President's Council on the Needs and Demands of the Griqua* in 1983.

7. For a detailed biography of Philip, see Andrew Ross, *John Philip. 1775-1851: Missions, Race, and Politics in South Africa* (Aberdeen: Aberdeen UP, 1986). There are of course many nineteenth century missionary accounts of the Griqua. In chronological order, they include: John Campbell, *Travels in South Africa* (1835; Cape Town: Struik, 1974) 249-58; William Shaw, *A Defence of the Wesleyan Missionaries in Southern Africa* (London: Mason, 1839) 73-79; James Backhouse, *An Appeal on Behalf of the Griquas and Other Coloured People of South Africa* (York: John Lewis Linney, 1841); Great Britain, House of Commons [J. J. Freeman], *Report from the Select Committee on the Kafir Tribes* (1851) 31-42; William Thompson, *A Word on Behalf of the Down-trodden in South Africa* (Cape Town: Solomon, 1854); Nathaniel Merriman, *The Kafir, the Hottentot, and the Frontier Farmer* (London: Bell, 1854) 80-87; and Edward Twells, *An Account of the Bishops to the Griquas in 'No Mans Land'* (Birmingham: Hodgetts, 1866). With the exception of William Shaw, most of the missionaries were in broad sympathy with Philip's championing of the Griqua. Beyond the missionaries, however, the white settler community was deeply hostile towards the Griqua. These more negative perceptions are evident in many of the travel diaries of the period. See, for example, the descriptions of the Griqua in William Burchell, *Travels in Southern Africa* (1822; Oxford: Oxford UP, 1935), and R. G. Cumming, *Five Years of a Hunter's Life in the Far Interior of Southern Africa* (London: Murray, 1856). The most extreme anti-Griqua prejudice is expressed by George Stow, who describes the missionaries' relation with the Griqua as follows: 'A more humiliating picture of a waste of energy and total failure of missionary enterprise could not

be found than that shown in the present of these people [the Griqua]. The folly of teaching a barbarian race confused ideas of equality and Christianity, without impressing upon its members *the necessity* of cultivating habits of industry and the arts of civilisation, was never more strongly marked than in the present condition of the Griquas. ... The pure Griqua, with all the teaching he has received, is at the present moment one of the most insolent and degraded of all the races found in the southern portion of Africa' ('Griqualand West', *Cape Monthly Magazine* 5 [1872]: 76).

8. Great Britain, House of Commons, *Report of Select Committee on Aborigines (British Settlements)* (1837; Cape Town: Struik, 1966) 698.

9 . Great Britain, *Select Committee on Aborigines* 624.

10. For a description of A. A. S. le Fleur's life and work, see Robert Edgar and Christopher Saunders, 'A. A. S. le Fleur and the Griqua Trek of 1917: Segregation, Self-Help and Ethnic Identity', *International Journal of African Historical Studies* 15.2 (1982). Other Griqua histories written by the Griqua themselves include those of R. Beddy, *A Brief History of the Griqua People of South Africa* (Northern Cape Griqua Land Affairs Committee, n.d.) and T. Carse, 'Die Onstaan van Griekwa Kore', *Griqua Centenary Programme*, 9 May 1989. Linda Waldman, 'The Past: Who Owns It and What Should We Do About It?', *South African Historical Journal* 35 (1996) provides a short survey of Griqua histories. The *Griqua and Coloured People's Opinion* re-commenced publication in March 1997, with the first issue dedicated to the memory of Saartje Baartman.

11. *Griqua and Coloured People's Opinion*, 23 Jan. 1925: 2. Cited hereafter as *GCPO*.

12. *GCPO*, 23 Jan. 1925: 2; 13 Mar. 1925: 1-2; 8 May 1925: 1-3.

13. *GCPO*, 15 May 1925: 1.

14. *GCPO*, 13 Feb. 1925: 1.

15. *GCPO*, 8 May 1925: 1.

16. Ross was one of a number of social historians in the 1970s who brought a sympathetic 'history-from-below' perspective to the study of the Griqua. Martin Legassick's unpublished PhD thesis, 'The Griqua, the South-Tswana, and the Missionaries, 1780-1840: The Politics of a Frontier Zone', U of California, 1969, was the most considerable contribution, but other histories written in this spirit include William F. Lye, 'The Emergence of the Griqua Culture: An African response to Colonialism and Christianity', *Profile of Self-Determination*, ed. David Chanaiwa (Northbridge: California State UP, 1976), Peter Carstens, 'Opting out of Colonial Rule: The Brown Voortrekkers of South Africa and their Constitutions', *African Studies* 42.2 (1983), Margaret Kinsman, 'Populists and Patriarchs: The Transformation of the Captaincy at Griqua Town, 1804-1822', *Organisation and Economic Change*, ed. Alan Mabin (Johannesburg: Ravan, 1989), and Timothy Keegan, *Colonial South Africa and the Origins of the Racial Order* (Cape Town: David Philip, 1996) 170-84.

17. Robert Ross, *Adam Kok's Griquas: A Study in the Development of Stratification in South Africa* (Cambridge: Cambridge UP, 1976) 1.

18. Ross, *Adam Kok's Griquas* 65.

19. I should emphasise that the three 'schools' of Griqua history-writing schematically outlined above by no means represent the full range of extant work. There have also been histories of the Griqua by Trotskyists like Dora

Taylor [as 'Nosipho Majeke'], *The Role of the Missionaries in Conquest* (Johannesburg: Soc. of Young Africa, 1952) 77-86; by anthropologists like George T. Nurse, *The Origins of the Northern Cape Griqua* (Johannesburg: Inst. for the Study of Man in Africa, 1975); by early sympathetic liberal historians like J. S. Marais, *The Cape Coloured People, 1652-1937* (London: Longmans, Green and Co., 1939) 32-73; by historians writing for a popular, non-academic audience like Samuel Halford, *The Griquas of Griqualand: A Historical Narrative of the Griqua People: Their Rise, Progress, and Decline* (Cape Town: Juta, 1949), Roy Harber, *Gentlemen of Brave Mettle* (College of Careers, 1976), John Shepherd, *In the Shadow of the Drakensberg* (Durban: T. W. Griggs, 1976), and Alf Wannenberg, *Forgotten Frontiersmen* (Cape Town: Howard Timmins, 1980); and by Afrikaner historians like P. J. van der Merwe, *Die Noordwaartse Beweging van die Boere voor die Groot Trek* (The Hague: Stockum, 1937), D. H. van Zyl, *'n Griekwa 'Ietsigeit'* (Cape Town: Nasionale P, 1947), and Izak W. van Tonder, *Geel en Bruin: 'n Verhaal oor ons Oudste Inboorlingrasse* (Cape Town: Juta, 1952) 154-68.

20. Michel Foucault, 'Politics and the Study of Discourse', *Ideology and Consciousness* 3 (1978): 16. Jacques Derrida makes a similar point in *Margins of Philosophy*, where he warns: 'In order to mark *effectively* the displacements of the sites of conceptual inscription, one must articulate the systematic chains of the movement according to their proper generality and their proper period, according to their unevenness, their inequalities of development, the complex figures of their inclusions, implications, exclusions, etc. Which is something entirely other than going back to the *origin* or to the foundational ground of a concept, as if something of the sort could exist, even if such an inaugural and imaginary limit did not revive the reassuring myth of a transcendental signified, of an archaeology before any trace and difference' (Jacques Derrida, *Margins of Philosophy*, trans. Alan Bass [Hemel Hempstead: Harvester, 1982] 72).

21. Frantz Fanon, *The Wretched of the Earth*, trans. Constance Farrington (1961; Harmondsworth: Penguin,1967) 176, 178.

22. Homi Bhabha, 'Signs taken for Wonders: Questions of Ambivalence and Authority under a Tree outside Delhi, May 1817', *Europe and its Others*, ed. Francis Barker, et al., vol. 1 (Colchester: U of Essex, 1984) 103.

23. Though in a different vocabulary to the one proposed by Bhabha, the 'subversive mimicry' of the Griqua has been noted. Legassick writes of Andries Waterboer, for example, that he became a successful state builder once he 'became better versed in the dichotomous rhetoric of the missionaries, which separated people uncompromisingly into "good" and "bad"' (455), and he then quotes examples of Waterboer strategically echoing the myths of missionary superiority.

24. Melanie Gosling, 'New Official Language Bid', *Cape Times*, 14 July 1997: 1.

25. The official number of Griqua is much disputed. In the Population Census of 1986, in response to the question 'what race are you?', about 100,000 replied 'Griqua'. Spokespersons for the Griqua National Conference believe the number to now be significantly higher.

26. Jacques Derrida, 'The Principle of Reason: The University in the Eyes of its Pupils', trans. Catherine Porter and Edward P. Morris, *Diacritics* 13 (1983): 17.

27. Jürgen Habermas, *The New Conservatism: Cultural Criticism and the Historians' Debate*, trans. S. W. Nicholsen (Cambridge: Polity, 1989) 118.

28. The fraught nature of the exchange between academics and groups such as the Griqua National Conference is a recurring theme. This is brought home by one of the GNC's affiliates, the Working Group of Indigenous Minorities in Southern Africa, based in Windhoek, who argue: 'Academics ... have often ignored present socio-economic realities, cultural transition process and dilemmas facing the San. They have frequently treated us as objects of research, they have rarely involved our people in setting their research agendas and thereby ignored our needs and desires. ... [What this means is that] the socio-economic position and dignity of the San is declining in spite of all this research' (Working Group of Indigenous Minorities in Southern Africa, 'A San Position: Research, the San and San Organisations', abstract, Conference on Khoisan Identities and Cultural Heritage, Capetown, 12-16 July 1997).

South African and Danish Literary History from a Comparative, Personal and an Ethical Point of View

Hans Hauge

> Lo, Smuts and Botha! Has there ever been
> Such proof as these of nationhood serene
> In heights of greatness, for our land in store?
> Thank God who gave South Africa the Boer.
>
> Ethel Campbell

1. Inclusion and exclusion

When I was a boy in the early sixties we had a chemistry teacher who was a Baptist and a pacifist. He always attacked apartheid in South Africa. We collected evidence from newspapers and other sources where apartheid was defended. We presented him with the evidence; he got so angry and talked and talked about how evil racism was and how we were all created equal, thus we could make him forget chemistry and physics. That was the whole idea. It is also a little scary. We became quite good at defending Verwoerd. Today I know nothing about chemistry because of apartheid.

'The Commonwealth discourse was one of inclusion.'

Roxanne Lynn Doty, 'Sovereignty and the Nation'

Can the Union of South Africa from 1910 and onwards at all be called a nation-state[1] if nationalism implies one people (*ein Volk*, one–many) with one language, one religion and one culture? At least it was never an ideal nation-state and perhaps never aspired to be one. At the other end of the world, and in 1910, Denmark had become an ideal nation-state by chance. In Denmark nationalisation was homogenisation and hence, sociologically speaking,

Translating Nations, ed. Prem Poddar, *The Dolphin* 30, pp. 129-60.
© 1999 by Aarhus University Press, Denmark.
ISBN 87 7288 381 2; ISSN 0106 4487.

inclusion. Peasants (*Bønder*) into Danes. One state with one nation. Inclusion or assimilation was easy, peaceful and non-violent because there was no one to exclude or assimilate. Why not? We lost the others in wars we lost. First went Norway plus the Sami population in 1814 to Sweden. Then the Prussians took the German speaking third. And if one forgets—and we do—the small colonies in India, the West Indies and in the North, Denmark woke up after defeat in 1864 with one language, one religion and one culture without having done anything to bring it about. Danish decolonisation was different. We sold colonies; and kept the rest even after decolonisation was more or less completed. The Faeroe Islands have now started a process which will perhaps lead to independence and will become yet another nation-state like Nauru and Kosovo.

In South Africa nationalisation resulted in (or came to, after Jan Smuts) apartheid or many nationalities, and hence anthropologically speaking exclusion or 'bantustans'. This policy is also called 'dissimilationist' or 'differentialist'.[2] Peasants (*Boers*) without Coloureds (Afrikaner Christian nationalism). One state, many nations. In Denmark everyone was created equal by the state and hence came to be similar; in South Africa different. In South Africa, the more 'union', 'unification', 'university', 'universalism', the more difference. In Denmark, just the opposite. By 'similarity in Denmark', by 'homogenisation', I shall mean 'shared culture'. In South Africa the rulers did not want to share (or mix) culture. Having said that much, not very much, I have not committed myself to any belief in the existence of such a shared culture. I tend to agree with Roy Wagner that cultures only exist in the heads of cultural anthropologists.

Inclusion and exclusion of peoples; that is the core of the issue. Although often confused, there is a difference between literature and human beings. Literature may have something to do with human rights and freedom of speech, but it does not have such rights itself. Literatures can and should, in certain eras and for certain purposes (especially teaching purposes), be excluded. One of many reasons is economical. Today there is far too much literature on the market. Choices have to be made. The market calls this choice the bestseller list; the school calls it a curriculum;

culture (the state) calls it a canon. Much or most literature is necessarily excluded (from the school), is actively and happily forgotten (by the market) and left unread in no-man's land without a supportive literary history.

How much South African or Danish literature ought to be included in a canon, if it exists, of world literature? Probably none at all. A literary history is not an encyclopaedia; literary histories should never come to resemble, too much, stamp catalogues. In the process of constructing a Danish national literary history, all non-Danish and not-in-Danish literature got excluded and, more importantly, was successfully forgotten. By whom and where? The excluders, needless to say, were the teachers; that is to say the whole school system—we used to call it the ideological state apparatus—plus newspapers and 'cultural life'. This process has not stopped after the reluctant Danish entry into the European Union. On the contrary, Danish Golden Age painting and Romantic literature are receiving more and more special attention, and are being appreciated and even exported.

In South African literary history the process of exclusion somehow failed; what will be remembered and what was read even in pre-Mandela times was more often than not *the excluded literature*. Did literature only exist outside? A void in the middle of the Union's literature? I speak as an outsider, of course, about the fragments of the literature we received, on what escaped from South Africa, and what we could hear up here so far away. There were established national poets 'showered with prizes and public awards', as Jack Cope and Uys Krige write in their introduction to *The Penguin Book of South African Verse* (1968). Their problem, incidentally, was how to anthologise verse written in several different languages. They had to exclude a lot of the best Afrikaans literature and colonial literature too. If there is a South African literature that will survive from the past, will it be a women's literature—and novels—just like old Canadian and old Anglo-Indian? The (white) founding mothers: Lady Anne Barnard, Olive Schreiner, Pauline Smith, Sarah Gertrude Millen, Daphne Rooke. (Cope and Krige had Roy Campbell as their founding father). Will it be anti-racist or protest literature?

It is no secret that one cannot include without excluding (or vice versa). You can't make bonds without bars as the linguist Firth taught us. However, such exclusion is never wholly successful. The excluded inevitably leaves a mark or trace on the included. In the Danish case, however, the birthmarks are almost invisible, but can be spotted with an effort. To give just one example, most Danish students (98%) study Ludvig Holberg as Danish literature; but he was Norwegian; that is to say if nationalities were meaningful prior to the nineteenth century. All pre-1814 'Norwegian' literature was excluded from Danish literature and still is. Although we know Faeroese literature is not ours we treat it as if it were. It is true that once one has introduced such concepts as inclusion and exclusion the distinction between them is blurred. To borrow Niklas Luhman's words, '"Inklusion" bezeichnet dann die innere Seite der Form, deren äußere Seite "Exklusion" ist'.[3] I am fully aware that Danish literary history is also exclusivist. It depends on where one stands.

One must take into consideration that to exclude can be an aesthetic gesture, too. New Critics excluded for aesthetic reasons. Uncritical inclusion can mean a lack of taste, an inability to distinguish. Criticism means to exclude. Critical literary histories exclude for other reasons than national ones. In a Danish canon works are included not because they are good but because they are Danish.

One means of making the marks of the excluded visible is through an unprecedented comparison between two incomparable entities such as this one: between Danish and South African literature; two literatures never in contact, with no influence on each other, absolutely non-contiguous, but perhaps after all a bit similar. Here, I am not suggesting any affiliation between *négritude* and Germanity.

So far, I have not really made a case for my claim that in South Africa, the exclusion of texts was unsuccessful in the sense that it was precisely the excluded texts that were, let's say, the 'best that had been thought and said in South Africa', and were therefore read and studied outside. My only argument here is: what was addressed to us via translation up here from down there was such writers as Nadine Gordimer, J. M. Coetzee and André Brink. We were probably also the addressees, and we politely received them. If a South African literature of the centre existed we would not have known it and did not want to know, just as no-one would willingly read official socialist realism from the pre-1989 GDR or the Soviet Union, or Algeria, if it exists, after 1962. We knew that socialist realist literature existed, but one read the dissident writers—naturally.[4]

Why was it not possible to exclude 'them' in this particular South African case? And by 'them' I mean the *good* anti-apartheid or anti-racist writers. To be sure, a great number of South African writers lived outside—exiles and expatriates and refugees. From William Plomer, Daphne Rooke and Pauline Smith to many contemporary writers like Alex La Guma and Ezekiel Mphahlele. South Africa had her share of Hemingways and Gertrude Steins. Exile is, we should recall, the nursery of nationalism.[5] Sol Plaatje stayed inside, at home, almost like Williams Carlos Williams; they both created languages. *Cry, The Beloved Country* was written in Trondheim, just as the most national of all Danish books, *Nøddebo Præstegaard*, was written in the heat in Egypt. Denmark in the winter is found in the Orient.

What I am looking for in the middle is the official 'national' literature of the South African centre, a home-made world, and poets, dramatists, and novelists who write in defence of apartheid. Poets with copious creative racist imaginations. Just as there were socialist realist writers, state writers, in the socialist countries, there must have been 'racist' realists in South Africa. They do not exist for me by name. I can't look them up—or can I? Will they turn up one day like many forgotten women poets? Like Ntsikane? My question is: was there any good racist literature? Or can poetry not be racist? We know that people can, the law can; and both can be quite explicit. Below I shall be quoting someone who claims that literary texts can help to sustain the colonial vision. If that is true did the apartheid regime use imaginative literature the way religion and the law was used? In that case what literature? Which poets? They must have, since we learn from many postcolonial theorists that literature is effective in maintaining racism. I am not an expert on South African literature; far from it, but I have been looking around for examples.

Perhaps, one day I will find one. Where is the great South African racist narrative? Or was the nation itself an artwork and Verwoerd its author? Like expressionist Germany in the thirties?

My claim is that if there is no good pro-apartheid literature, the practical reason for this is *ethical*. This can be made more explicit, like a principle: one cannot write a good novel, poem or play praising apartheid or racism. Such things cannot be made beautiful or sublime. Truth and silence are not beauty in South Africa. I have seen Nadine Gordimer make a similar point somewhere, without my being able to find out where. The claim appears to be anti-modernist and anti-aesthetic. Anti-modernist in the sense that much genuine modernist art was pro-fascist, pro-totalitarian, pro-Stalinist, pro-communist, ultra- or-anti-nationalist, anti-Semitic, racist, sexist and what have you. What decent C. P. Snow called 'politically wicked'. Anti-aesthetic in the sense that an aesthetic concept of art separates the ethical from the aesthetic. Let me formulate my claim once more and a little broader. Why did the British (or the French) empire not produce great art? It was an historic event and an achievement. A certain Oaten, who wrote about Anglo-Indian literature, was the one who asked the question many years ago. He had no answer. I have—it could be I have. The ethical one, to be made more explicit. But before I come to ethics and aesthetics I first have to deal with unethical epistemology.

2. The Neo-Kantianism of postcolonial discourse

As a boy I collected South African stamps. I liked best the stamps from before 1910; from Transvaal, Cape of Good Hope and so on. Stamps were my only contact with South Africa. They communicated. and one of the few things one could buy from South Africa. In 1964 I attended Gymnasium (high school). The very first full-length English (or Scottish) or South African novel I read , in English, was John Buchan's Prester John. *In 1967 I entered university to read English. I forgot all about John Buchan and never imagined I would have to reread my first English novel—from 1910—because of postcolonial theory and Foucault and all that. The only South African writer I read whilst a student was Roy Campbell because I was interested in Eliot and Pound.*

'Projection was a mode of cognition.'
Elleke Boehmer, *Colonial and Postcolonial Literature*

'Their solution is in no way advanced by inventing a bogy called Orientalism—and still less by the insinuation that if the bogy is overcome, all will be made plain.'
Ernest Gellner, *Encounters with Nationalism*

Postcolonial discourse or theory often adopts a (neo-)Kantian (or Vichian) but anti-universalist epistemology which some may miraculously escape if reality an sich helps. (When 'savages' begin to represent themselves.) Its aesthetics, if it has one, or ethics, which it has, are almost never Kantian; on the contrary. Such an epistemology is probably due to pressure from the academic market. Elleke Boehmer's, I guess, popular Colonial and Postcolonial Literature is a good (cynical) example. 'As we know, literary texts helped sustain the colonial vision, giving reinforcement to an already insular colonial world.'[6] We don't know that. But it is a way of legitimating the study of such texts in English departments full to the brim of students sick and tired of English literature. There these texts help to sustain the teaching of postcolonial theory and revitalise the teaching of literature. If Boehmer is right, aesthetics is wrong; this is, admittedly, a possibility to be entertained. Aesthetics is wrong because of its formalism and its insistence on the disinterestedness and uselessness of the work of art; if useless how can it sustain colonial visions? Literary texts also face the charge of being unethical if they really did help to sustain that colonial vision and if the vision was immoral, which we don't know.

Here, then, finally, an example of the unacknowledged neo-Kantian epistemology:

Colonialist discourse, [...], embraced a set of ideological approaches to expansion and foreign rule. Sometimes called Orientalist or Africanist, depending on the *categories of representation* involved, colonialist discourses thus *constituted* the systems of *cognition*—interpretative screens, glass churches—which Europe used to *found* and guarantee its colonial authority. Contemporary postcolonial theories of discourse are associated most typically with the work of Michel Foucault and Louis

Althusser concerning the involvement of textual practices in relations of power. Such theories were influentially brought to bear on colonial writing by Edward Said in his analysis of Orientalist discourse, *Orientalism* (1978). [...] His book explicates at length what we have been seen happening above—the ways in which European linguistics conventions and *epistemologies* underpinned the *conception*, management, and control of colonial relationships.[7]

I have italicized words sounding Kantian. I am not saying this is neo-Kantian epistemology proper, but it states something about epistemology which is sort of Kantian; makes a claim that we are, or rather that they were, governed by such a one, and finally that epistemologies can be relativised by being characterised as European. Are there non-European alternative epistemologies? No. Perhaps it is too much to call Foucault's epistemes neo-Kantian, but I think it is true to say that Althusser's theory was.[8]

This specimen, Boehmer's, of popular postcolonialism transforms literature first into literary texts, second into colonialist discourse, and third into interpretative screens; further into crude epistemologies, into constitutive discourses, into categories of representation. A simulated counterfeit philosophical language is used. And one wonders what's behind the screen? Nothing? The Other? Reality? Or can there be no post postcolonial? We can only know what we have made ourselves. This is Edward Said's Viconian credo—and E. D. Hirsch's.[9]

Boehmer holds that a Victorian writer was unable to 'resist the prevailing representations of Empire' since this would have 'meant resisting the very self-perceptions on which late-nineteenth century grounded itself'. If this includes Macaulay it would have to include that other Victorian, Marx as well, though he isn't mentioned. Victorian writers (Marx and Haggard, for example), or colonialist discourse, created or constructed a world of their own. This world constituted by European linguistic conventions (whatever that may be) and epistemologies, was not and never could be an imitation (in the good old-fashioned sense of the word), an empirical reflection, an *Abbild* of the world out there: Arabia, Africa, Australia. In short, since the colonialist discourse tells us nothing about its object—all objects have to be constituted first—it only provides us with information about the writers or the producers of the discourses themselves; about us, them, the Victorians, the colonialists, the imperialists, the British. By studying colonialist discourse you may learn something about colonialist discourse. Hence, if you study this discourse you end up, once again, studying not only English but even the English, and then we are back where we began. English Studies Regained.

Colonialist discourse can be made into an object of study since it studies an object constituted by itself. The same must be true of postcolonial theory. How can it resist today's European episte-mologies or the self-perceptions on which the late-twentieth century grounds itself? How can it avoid not constructing the Victorian imperialists in its own postcolonialist image? How could one at all escape the epistemological prison house? How can a neo-Kantian Althusser be of any help? How can we know anything if what Boehmer says is true? The answer is: we cannot. In schools, therefore, in literature departments, we don't study colonial and postcolonial literature but *Colonial and Postcolonial Literature*.

No wonder that Edward Said was taken to task after first having revolutionised theory with a paradoxical iconoclastic constructivism. First Harold Bloom (and Hartman) Judaised theory,[10] and after, Said 'Palestinised' it. This American Jew–Arab duo practised the sublime prohibition against images. Oriental-ism is making an image. Said said: don't make an image which he called a 'discourse of power'. But then came the imaginative critics. Why did they resist the message? Because they were unwilling to accept constructivism 'most people [outside univer-sities?] resist the underlying notion: that human identity is not only natural and stable, but constructed, and occasionally invented outright'.[11] Notice the comforting words that identity is *also* 'natural' and 'stable'. Is constructed identity merely a kind of superstructure to be stripped off at demand? Subtly, the differ-ence between primordialists and constructivists is softened and blurred. Can Islam survive constructivism? Probably not.

Let's go back to where modern constructivism was reborn, in Germany in the early twenties when constructivism was called neo-Kantianism. Anti-neo-Kantian philosophers (phenomenolo-gists) discussed how the Other, the Real, at that time called *Du* or

Gegenwart could avoid being internalised or how to destruct or de-obstruct the mind's constructions. The question was if there is anything outside our own constructions. If we remove the interpretative screen called 'Orientalism' what will we see? Nothing or something? The French neo-Kantian Brunschvicg is reported to have said, jokingly, 'Egyptology invented Egypt'.

Literary texts helped sustain the colonial vision. As we all know. But where?[12] Who read them? Where were these texts studied in the late nineteenth century? Were the schoolboys who read Haggard involved textually in imperialism? Boehmer mentions Benjamin Jowett's advice that men destined for colonial service in India be taught Greek and Latin classics. He would never have said Rider Haggard, Ballantyne, Buchan or Marryat; but Homer, Pindar and Virgil. How did Virgil sustain the colonial vision? That would have been a worthwhile question. The reading, study and teaching of national literatures in schools (and universities) is a very recent, very short-lived, never successful, almost mid-twentieth century and *post-imperialist* enterprise, in most cases designed for women. And it would never have included John Buchan or any of the writers mentioned by Boehmer. Imagine Leavis analysing Haggard. English poetry, before Leavis, was mainly something to be learnt by heart and not something to be appreciated or analysed by men.

Young people, in practice boys, in all European countries read the classics, especially Virgil, and they did so for centuries. If literature is what is taught in schools, then Virgil is European literature, and he was still for T. S. Eliot almost the only classic. Children in Europe never read a literature of their own in schools although they may have done so on their own. Who has not, in Europe, for centuries been colonised by Roman culture? No one. For a very simple reason; nationalism and self-determination did not exist when it happened. Today, resisting classical culture is pure *Asterix*. In the nineteenth and early twentieth century resistance was called nationalism and nationalism is canon busting. Prior to that, the barbarians (us up here) adopted the language, culture and religion of the people 'we' conquered.

The idea of teaching one's own literature did not begin to take hold until the advent of nationalism; in the 1880s in Denmark, a little earlier in Italy, much later in England. The advent of nationalism coincided with the formation or unifications of several new nations, Canada and South Africa, but also of Germany and Italy. The two first without literatures and languages of their own; the Germans had a lot of literature plus a complex language; the Italians had no language but one Dante. The United States, by the end of the century first really united by the Civil War, had had a head-start. They already had Longfellow, Cooper, and especially anti-European Emerson. Then came Canadian federation in 1867. They had no literature whatsoever, and they knew it and somehow learnt to cope with it—by teaching English instead as *Ersatz*-Latin. They had a number of women writing 'texts' somewhere out in the prairies, but who read them? These women writers were converted into literature in the late twentieth century.

The three Scandinavian countries also tried to create a union; but they failed even though they had literature and three almost identical languages. Unions only succeed if one of the states is militarily strong. Sweden was not strong enough, like the Yankees in the North, Ontario, the British in the Cape, Piemonte[13] and Prussia. After Canada, Italy and Germany—younger nations than Canada—came Australia and the Union of South Africa in 1910. In 1917 another kind of union was created: the Soviet Union based on national Marxism. Soviet imperialism lasted longer than British—even in Africa. The colonialist Russians haven't left Latvia yet. Canada, Australia and South Africa did not possess literatures as yet like Germany and Italy. One Thomas Pringle or Tiyo Soga doesn't make a literature. By the end of the nineteenth century several European nations had managed to produce classics of their own, national classics who could claim universality: Goethe in Germany, Dante in Italy (perhaps, like pizza, it was the New England Americans who made him a classic),[14] Racine and Corneille in France, and Shakespeare and Milton in England. The Scandinavian countries had none but they struggled to make some.

In 1947 Ernst Robert Curtius could say: 'European literature of the nineteenth century has not yet been sifted, what is dead has not yet been separated from what is alive. It can furnish subjects for dissertations.'[15] And: 'The founding hero (*heros ktistes*) of European literature is Homer. Its last universal author is Goethe.'[16] It is a sobering thought. We haven't had much in the nature of literature in the last two hundred years.

3. 1910

Some years ago I was writing a book parts of which dealt with Kant's aesthetics. I went, as one does, to the library and searched for studies of Kant's third Critique. *I found a rather good one. It had the advantage of being in English. It was written by a country vicar in South Africa. Kant in a South African vicarage! Why not? His name was R. A. C. Macmillan. His book was published in 1912. He called the reflective aesthetic judgement divine and compared it to open roadways. His book's title is* The Crowning Phase of Critical Philosophy. *Who will write the book:* Kant in Natal?

'To the end of the eighteenth century the Afrikaners produced no literature, no painting, no music.'
Leonard M. Thompson, 'The South African Dilemma'

In 1910 there was no South African nation-state. There was a state, a little later a Dominion (said some), a union (but no unity), a republic, and several unrecognised 'nations', one Nationalism[17] (Afrikaner, later to be challenged by African Nationalism), many languages (or two official literary ones, like Canada, with Dutch as English and English as French), a Greek democracy (no universal suffrage), parliamentarism, many religions (or perhaps I am overdoing this?), one legal tradition (Roman-Dutch). The Union was surrounded by colonies: Portuguese, British and German. And, like West Berlin before 1989, inside it were two British protectorates (Basutoland and Swaziland). This was the difficult beginning of the modernisation of the South; an independent or at least self-governing settler colony encircled by dependent pre-modern colonies.

Modernity is a triangle consisting of industrialisation, democratisation and nationalisation. If nationalisation, i.e. homogenisation, fails then democracy does not follow. A free market may develop, and it did, but it cannot produce other freedoms, e.g. of speech, although freedom of speech and other freedoms cannot exist without a free market economy. South Africa had a strong state; weak nationalisms (two or many? Boers and Black), English-style liberalism (threatened by Sovietico-African communism), and it had a small but beautiful civil society: the church(es)—and literature might be described as performing functions like a civil(ised) society,

What did Denmark look like in 1910? State and nation were almost identical. There was a Christian-National alliance. Therefore very little civil society. South Africa got bigger, acquiring Südwestafrika from defeated Germany in 1920. We, too, got some land back from Germany that same year. The world is interdependent.

In the nineteenth century Denmark got smaller and smaller. Denmark had 'lost', as we say, Norway to Sweden in 1814—and there's an intriguing 'correspondence' here: this was the same year the British (our enemies, then, too) conquered or bought the Cape Colony. This our 'loss', we seldom realise, is related to the founding of the 'Second Empire' (Ernest Barker's words). The English also acquired Ceylon that year, and in today's Denmark, as a result, Sri Lankan Tamils are part of everyday life.

Civil war and war with Prussia resulted in the 'loss' of the German speaking parts of the realm in 1864 (our Orange Free State and Transvaal). Colonial settlements in India (Tranquebar and Serampore) and in Africa (the Gold Coast) had been sold to the British. But three Danish West Indian islands, the Faeroe Islands, Iceland and Greenland were still part of this Northern benevolent mini-Empire. Denmark seen in isolation, which is how it is always seen, appeared to be, and in a sense was, a model or ideal nation state. One language,[18] a homogenised people, one faith, one rich literature, a national music, a landscape nationalised by painters, internal colonialism,[19] one university (three had been lost—one to Norway, one to Germany and one in India). It was unnecessary to invent a national language like it was in Norway, Italy and South Africa. In Norway the old so-called New Norwegian was resurrected; in Italy only 2.5% (around 1870) of the population spoke and understood Italian, i.e. the Tuscan dialect.

Michael Green mentions how Isabel Hofmeyr has shown that the Afrikaner nationalism, like Irish and Norwegian, has 'retro-actively created a tradition of a homogeneous language for itself' and Green himself says that Sol Plaatje also had to construct a language. Plaatje was, after all, an accomplished linguist.[20] There is nothing extraordinary about this. The same happened in the same way all other places.

What about today? A Centre for the Study of Southern African Literature and Languages announced in 1995 that it was going to produce a 'South African national literary history'.[21] Is this desirable, Michael Green asks? The producers, Green informs us, never commit the worst academic sin you can commit— namely being an essentialist. The question is; once you have lost your essentialist or realist faith in literature and become a post-apartheid constructivist, is a literary history any longer possible? It is to commit the constructivist fallacy if you believe that once you have given up your essentialist illusions you can design (con-struct) something new? To be a constructivist is not, paradoxi-cally, constructive but the opposite. And once everyone is a constructivist it has to be abandoned. Like Diana Fuss has done.[22]

Green mentions what I believe is one of the most challenging ideas in recent literary theory: that the teaching of English literature began in India. Colonialism thus speeded up secu-larisation in England[23] in the sense that a national literature, as a canon, is meant to replace the teaching of the Bible. Only, one should add, the resistance towards teaching national literature was much stronger in England than in the rest of Europe, which was secularised much more easily, it seems, the fewer colonies it possessed.[24] If you have no colonies you have little sense of service, trust and mission. As late as 1947 Oxford Vice-Chancellor Sir Richard Livingstone thought with horror on how in Germany before the war attempts had been made to replace the classics with German literature in order to foster a narrow pan-Germanism.

It seems that the South African literature professors, discussed by Green, have difficulties in agreeing on how to invent a new national literary history after they have all become constructivists. Why did the end of apartheid (and of communism—the two are interdependent)[25] also mean the end of essentialism and the advent of constructivism? Some want the new literary history to be comparative (and multilingual?); some comprehensive and encyclopaedic, some thematic, some narrative, and Green rhetorical. The pressure to make a new one seems to come indirectly from a great number of new students with new and different backgrounds entering tertiary education. Michael Green has not noticed that it is not what literature one should teach these students, there and here, which is the problem. The inclusion and exclusion debate has nothing to do with including oral traditions and forgotten women writers and excluding Roy Campbell or racist Afrikaner poetry but whether to teach literature at all. Should literature as such be excluded from the school; that's the issue. This is what the so-called canon-debate was about.

American universities faced similar problems with new students in the 1950s. They solved the problem by inventing the New Criticism. Meaning: forget literary history and nationality. That was the only way of salvaging the teaching of literature to students from many different backgrounds and interested in film, sports and pop music. Remove the author; gender and race disappear. Remove the reader; his biography disappears. Remove mimesis; reference disappears.[26] This pedagogical strategy is probably not feasible today. But it did work once. Maybe it only postponed the death of literature as something to be taught in universities.

If South Africa is not going to become a nation-state in the global future there is little reason why it should continue to support large English or literature Departments. Literature has very little use value as a cohesive force in a non-national state's educational system. We see this in post-industrial Denmark where state and nation are getting a divorce. This radically diminishes the value of the teaching of national literature as such. It is still being taught but no one really knows why. It becomes even more absurd when one teaches it to immigrants. Why teach Danish romantic national literature to a bunch of Somali, Tamil and Turkish kids? In Sweden there are no Swedish Departments.

Religion or Christianity might instead, I premise, become a nation-building force in South Africa. This suggestion comes from Charles Villa-Vicencio's A Theology of Reconstruction where he describes the transformation of a theology of liberation into a theology of nation-building. He says: 'In South Africa's apartheid history there are few resources available and waiting to be appropriated in a culture of national unity. Hidden within the long history of black resistance there are at the same time memories of non-racism, democracy and struggles for human values and rights.'[27] Villa-Vicencio never mentions literature as a present or past resource and I don't think he is a philistine. Do we witness a new querelle between constructivists and reconstructivists? In South Africa or elsewhere?

4. A literature of one's own

I went to California to study Ezra Pound in the seventies. Not the best of times to do so. Paul de Man was beginning to become a cult figure. Habermas lectured at the university. Earlier I had written my speciale *(something like a 'thesis') on T. S. Eliot. I wrote a few articles on Pound and Eliot to be buried in certain obscure journals. That was when I first heard about Pauline Smith. Eliot visited Arnold Bennett. They talked about fiction and Virginia Woolf. They both agreed Pauline Smith was a better writer than Woolf.*

'With Shakespeare and poetry , a new world was born [...] I lived in two worlds, the world of Vrededorp and the world of these books.'
Peter Abrahams

'By what right does anyone classify amongst the great poets the author of the views this elite Fascist [Ezra Pound] embodies in his work? [...] T. S. Eliot's views are those adopted and being applied by Dr. Verwoerd and Dr. Eiselen.'
Sam Kahn

'Marx himself, of course, loved Shakespeare.'
David Johnson

All these quotations are taken from David Johnson's *Shakespeare and South Africa*. It is really a book about two Shakespeares, or the ways in which one can use him for political purposes. Shakespeare is part of a history of 'imperial violence' and in that history the actor (Shakespeare) has played his last role: 'a central and deeply compromised role'.[28]

The Peter Abrahams quotation illustrates beautifully the aesthetic idea of art: art is another nature as Kant formulated it. We enter this other world, created by the imagination, when we find life too 'alltäglich'. Apparently Peter Abrahams believed he could escape the exigencies of racist life by entering into the Shakespearean world of romance, but if Johnson is right, Abrahams was deluded.

Sam Kahn's more modern sinister statement is a blueprint for censorship. His vision is reality in today's Algeria.[29] And let's not forget that Pound was put into a cage in Pisa. It is obvious, if Kahn is right (which he isn't), that the English departments in South Africa which taught students the poetries of Eliot and Pound supported Verwoerd and W. W. M. Eiselen's social anthropological defence of exclusion, anti-integration or separation (*apartheid*). Was English literature (was Dutch literature never taught—Erasmus, for instance, or Hildebrand?) the wicked literature in the centre I have been looking for, with South African literature from Pringle to Chris van Dyck and such, the excluded and the good? If that is so, South Africa again looks like Canada. Why did they not teach their own literature in the schools like we have done for the last hundred years? Why English? Why Shakespeare? David Johnson records how successive generations of teachers of English have, without interruption, imported theories from either Britain or the United States (or the Soviet Union):[30] all the way from Cornish Sir Arthur Quiller-Couch via Leavis and Williams to Birmingham cultural studies. And now it seems literary studies are to be converted into cultural studies— like in the rest of the English-speaking world. At this point South Africa is normal, ordinary, not apart.[31] David Johnson no longer has to worry. Shakespeare's occupation has gone.

The ANC Policy Framework of General Education and Training has other ideas: '[t]he curriculum of General Education will be committed to national development and social responsibility [...] and to the development of a national identity'.[32]

Shakespeare is not part of that curriculum. One can easily imagine future conflicts between the Anglophilia of the cultural studies English professors (like David Johnson) and the state's interest in creating unity and national identity (like the *nieuw* literary history people and the theologians of reconstruction). Interestingly this, once more, makes South Africa normal: old nation-states experience identity crises just like S.A. Just think of Britain and England.

Literary and cultural studies are incompatible paradigms. Cultural studies did not destroy literary studies but was made possible by the decline of the importance of literature as cultural capital. Such at least is John Guillory's persuasive argument.

Why English studies and Shakespeare in the first place, in that particular place? There have been English departments in most European countries also. Many in Denmark have studied both racist Eliot and imperialist Shakespeare without us being, I hope, totally corrupted by it.

The attacks upon English studies, as documented by David Johnson, are comparable to similar ones made by Danish nationalists in the middle of the nineteenth century against Roman civilization, culture, imperialism, literature and language—Latin. Søren Kierkegaard fought unironically in order to be allowed to write his MA-thesis (on irony) in Danish and not in Latin. These attacks upon classical education led to its replacement by a national one and in universities slowly to the establishing of national philologies that were imitations of classical philology. The idea of living languages was invented, but they were studied as dead. English, German, and French were studied in the same way one had studied Latin and Greek. To this should be added that a national language was a language with a (written) literature and a dictionary. Without it, it was just a dialect.

It did not happen in the same way in the settler colonies or fragment societies *because they had no classical education to fight against*. They had the language of the country they had left. The teaching of English was from the beginning *modern and liberal* not classical and aristocratic. Thus English, since it was the language of the Empire and modernisation, came to function like Latin; Shakespeare and Milton like Virgil and Homer; but it did not replace classical studies. No culture existed in the colonies to humanise and slow down civilisation. Two different things, culture and civilization in Europe, were the same outside of Europe. German Romantics could use Shakespeare, as *Kultur*, to fight civilization with. In South Africa Shakespeare was civilization-as-*cultuur*. In that way English literature could get universalised in the colonies but not at home where it remained the 'poor man's classics' and where it even prided itself on its insularity, Englishness and particularity (Blake). In England, English literature would always be compared with classical and it would never 'win', but in the colonies it had no competition except for in British India or Egypt and Palestine with a classical literature already there. This already existing literature was religious and therefore the secularism of English literature could be emphasised and claimed as a sign of its modernity (English literature has never been really modern, but it looked modern compared with sacred Sanskrit or Arabic literature).

To teach a foreign language—when teaching Afrikaners and Africans—involved teaching literature.[33] One simply couldn't teach another language without, for if it had no literature it wasn't a language. We still think it a bit curious to teach or learn Bavarian, for example. Indirectly though, classical culture was communicated to South Africans *as fiction* in the writings of Mary Renault. She belongs to South African literature too.[34] Or classical Greece was present as architecture in the buildings of Sir Herbert Baker and in Cecil Rhodes's library.

Today, however, second language learning has developed in new anti-literary philistine directions. It has emancipated itself from the humanities and the arts and has become a secular instrumental and technical enterprise; in that way it has proved to be much more efficient than old-fashioned language pedagogy which might insist on teaching Shakespeare. In short: one can and does teach English as a second language without cultural and literary delaying detours. So perhaps even David Johnson's occupation has gone at the University of Natal's English department.

Have I also solved my problem about identifying the racist and imperialist writers? I kept looking into South African literature where they did not exist and which was not taught in schools in a systematic and historical way like we have been used to doing it with our 'own' literatures in the Nordic countries. It was English literature as such and English liberal culture that was racist (or taught by teachers silent about racism?). There are several problems involved in this; problems perhaps created by myself when I say what I do about English in this way. I promised at the beginning to develop my claim about ethics and literature. In fact, I said something like this: literature cannot be racist or unethical. Literature is goodness. Ethics and aesthetics cannot be divorced. This contradicts all that has been said so far and indeed the modernist separation between the two. I shall add another claim. Liberalism or liberal universalism (with its idea of rights) is not racist. It was and is an Enlightenment philosophy about equality, human rights, freedom and so on. It was also 'the art of separation' (M. Walzer).

One of my heroes, K. E. Løgstrup, Danish philosopher of religion, in a book from 1961 (*Kunst og etik*), contended that art is always ethical.[35] If it isn't, it isn't art. I cannot go into details here. Suffice it to say that in literature evil will always be condemned. I have already said that good literature cannot be a celebration of apartheid. Racism cannot be made beautiful. When we read such a statement, what do most mistrusting literary critics do? Try to find an example where it isn't true. But it isn't so easy as one might think. And why would anyone wish to resist the idea? What are the consequences if one doesn't accept the idea?

Can anyone imagine or find an example of, say, a novel where the torturer—let's imagine him to be a stereotypical white, brutal, South African policeman—is the hero; and the victim, an innocent black woman, the scoundrel? A novel which ends by showing that the torturer was right and just? A novel which persuades us to love the torturer and hate the tortured? Can anyone imagine a good novel which was on the side of the guards and the regime behind the Gulag camps in the Soviet Union? I premise that even in socialist realist novels, supposed to give socialism a human face, one could find cracks allowing us to see the horror and the evil beneath the surface. An aesthetic FIS musical about slaughtering children? A play with a Nazi doctor in a KZ-camp as hero?

I am sure many have by now come up with counter-examples. Homer, Virgil, Cooper, or *American Psycho*, for example, or the Old Testament. Most literature is, it is true, about war and killing.[36] What about poor Kipling or the whole of Victorian literature (as in Boehmer), or the whole of Western literature (all marked by imperialism, says Australian nationalist Simon During).[37] Need I say that nobody dies in a text, not even God? So, either literature as such and as a whole is evil, or it is good.

One more thing. It is ethically necessary to separate teller from tale. It may contradict both logic, common sense, biographies and epistemology to do so, but still it is better for us to do so or else the result will inevitably be censorship and persecution. Authors may not be good people, in fact they may be just like us. The author of *The Satanic Verses* and Salman Rushdie are two different persons, just as, to use a famous philosophical example, *were* the author of *Waverley* and Walter Scott. Eliot did not, as a poet, express anything in his verse.[38] And so on. It is in this sense the author is virtually dead before he is actually killed. Without some sense of form, of art as virtual, or some version of formalism art can no longer be ethical and hence no longer be art. There are Sam Kahns in all societies. This is how Wendy Steiner has it: 'But if all that was missing were a content-oriented aesthetics, the Marxist, feminist, African-American, and postcolonialist criticism of recent years would surely fill the bill. These have, in fact, reconnected criticism to its preformalist days.'[39] Richard Rorty said about Heidegger something like 'the greatest twentieth century philosopher just happened to be a nazi.' This can be transferred to South African literature, to English, to imperialist Shakespeare and anti-Semite Eliot. Many great writers happened to be racist.

5. Ordinary South Africa

I visited our Department's library which holds one of Europe's best collections of Commonwealth literature due to the efforts of Anna Rutherford who invented Commonwealth literature in Denmark. There were not so many books about South African literature as I had expected. Then suddenly I found one book

which caught my eye me because it was so familiar-looking. It was Acta
Germanica: Jahrbuch des Südafrikanischen Germanistverbandes.
Imagine, they had had Germanisten *there all the time just as we have. And
why not? There were* Germanisten *in it writing dull articles about Brecht,
Heine and Busch, just like we do. Especially the life story of one professor Bernd
Schneider I found fascinating. He died in 1984. He came from Berlin to
Swakopmund in 1919. He did his doctoral work on Gerhart Hauptmann's
relationship to antiquity. Then he wrote about Klopstock's aesthetics in 1954. In
Pretoria he was head of the German Department. This is also South Africa.
How did this work on Klopstock's aesthetics influence life in the fifties? Was
this text better than Peter Abrahams's* Tell Freedom *which came out the same
year? 'Klopstock and Abrahams'. What a title.*

'Race [...] pretends to be an objective term of classification, when in fact
it is a dangerous trope.'
Henry L. Gates, Jr., 'Introduction: Writing Race and the Difference It
Makes'

In February 1998 six South African—or Johannesburg—poets and
playwrights visited Denmark and the Aarhus English Department. There were only a little more than six students who turned
up to listen to them. All sorts of reasons could be given for this
lack of audience; I suggest the reason was that today South
African literature is *ordinary* and the poets don't suffer anymore.
It's a literature like most other literatures. For some years to come
the writers will still write about the immediate past—like for
instance in Mark Behr's recent novel. But if a new literary history
is produced it will be *normal*. Some years ago South African
literature was studied, or read, because it was anti-apartheid and
anti-racist. It was an example, like dissident literature from the
East (think of Václav Havel), of committed literature.[40]

  Literary Denmark and literary South Africa are coming to
look more alike now; there's very little exotic about SA literature.
Blacks are no longer foreign, strange or other; they are our
neighbours. Africa is in the middle of European big cities. The
mediating role of ex-colonials and neo-nomads in the West has
resulted in a 'fusion of horizons' (Gadamer) between them and
us, or, as the fusion is called in postcolonial language: the anti-
binarisms of 'hybrid' narratives. No longer a temporal fusion of

horizons of past and present but a spatial one of coloniser and colonised, north and south.

What happens to Mill, if there is no (intelligent) Coleridge? Strange as it may sound, Lionel Trilling asked a question like this in his book about 'the politics of culture': *The Liberal Imagination.* He noted how in the United States at that time (1949) there was no conservatism or reaction. Liberalism, he said, was the 'sole intellectual tradition'.[41] This was true of South Africa too. It is even more true now after the demise of Marxism. Anti-universalist ex-colonial academics and neo-nomad poets in the West use liberal universal narratives to reinterpret their oppressed past. To say that this was also true in South Africa may sound untrue. But what other narratives were available? Now or then? A parallel narrative, supra-universalist, was Christianity (think of early ANC). Africans used and use the Christian narrative to reinterpret their past, but they lived already in a Christian society.

Louis Hartz formulates his main theory of fragment societies in this way: 'when a part of a European nation is detached from the whole of it, and hurled outward onto new soil, it loses it stimulus toward change that the whole provides'.[42] Since my concern here is literary history, let me immediately transfer this. The same loss of stimulus toward change is found in literary history as in the history as such of these nations. Hartz uses the formula 'immobilities of fragmentation'. I do not think this is a mere idiosyncrasy on my part, but is it not so with much of what we used to call Commonwealth literatures that it lacks something? Something is missing? No dynamism. We read them for cultural and not for literary reasons. This was what Northrop Frye said about Canadian literature (a literature he did not even mention once in his *Anatomy of Criticism*). The same is true of South African. We get a literature which is modern, yet at the same time wholly traditional, if we use that word in the traditional way. Traditional literature, the ancients, never was there and that is why English literature came to be a substitute for classical literature. Danish literature had an easier job in replacing Latin and Greek than Australian in replacing English. But is the Danish situation in the late nineteenth century at all comparable to the South African (or Australian or Canadian) then or now? If

English (not in England) in South Africa was from the beginning
a substitute classical literature can it successfully be substituted
by a 'national' literature which itself is a substitution? Or is it too
late? National literature's last word? But what comes after a
national literature? Here and there?

   Paul Gilroy has attempted an answer: 'autobiographical
writing, special and uniquely creative ways of manipulating
spoken language, and, above all the music. All three have
overflowed from the containers that the modern nation state
provides for them.' He may be right. These three exist. But who
would dream of making these three art-forms school texts,
university exam questions?[43] Above all the music (the honest man
sings, doesn't he?). Gilroy goes on, 'For the descendants of slaves,
work signifies only servitude': luckily then, for we live in capitalism without work anyway. 'Artistic expression [for the 'descendants of slaves'], expanded beyond recognition from the grudg-
ing gifts offered by the masters as a token substitute for freedom
from bondage, therefore becomes the means towards both
individual self-fashioning and communal liberation.'[44] This is
demanded of everyone today and has nothing to do with descendants of slaves. Everyone must fashion himself; it is not a choice,
it's destiny. *Gesamtkunstwerk Ich.* If Gilroy intends to reserve this
(image) for the same descendants he seems to repeat the worst
Eurocentric images of Africa[45]—Africans as premodern anti-
enlightenment musicians—singers, dancers and entertainers.
Gilroy's *British* cultural studies-cum-MTV-construction-of-Africa-
accentuated-by-drum-beats is not (South) Africa. South African
literature of the future will be ordinary. I guess.

6. Edward Said as an Egyptian Stanley Fish

When I take the bus from where I live I pass graffiti on a wall. It says 'Afrika
sulter' (Africa starves). Is it a rock song? Or a political slogan? While I waited
for the bus today a man, Danish, begged money from me. He said he starved. In
the windows one could see Time Magazine's *front page. It said 'Africa*
Rising'. It was a Norwegian , by the way, who wrote Hunger. *And more by the*
way. SWA. Namibia. It is now part of Weltliteratur. *Made immortal in*
Thomas Pynchon's V.

'Die Völker haben gewöhnlich nur ein unklares Bewußtsein davon, wie sie sich in einander spiegeln.'
Walter Benjamin, 'Deutsch in Norwegen'

I am not an Africanist; I once almost became a Canadian Studies person; I am most certainly not an Orientalist.[46] Or are we all, in the West, 'Orientalists'? 'Orientalism', in one particular sense of the word, has, since 1978, Israel's 30th birthday, become the name of something, a symbol, a presence, an obstacle, a trope in literary theory, literary criticism, literary history—even if you confine yourself to medieval Danish literature or Shakespeare's romances you can't hide from it. There is a 'question of Palestine' even there. We can say: I am not an Africanist; but is it so, now, that we are all Orientalists? Yes, we are. Can we escape it? Yes, we can if we become non-ironic postmodernists. This means going 'Arabic'. Explanation follows.

In the early eighties the trope 'Orientalism' emerged in literary theory together with such strange words as *kabbala*, *zimzun*, *midrash*, as if the Hellenised, secular, Aristotelian, American, Arnoldian vocabulary of literary criticism was about to lose its hegemony. Edward Said's interpretation of the interpretation 'Orientalism' was a de-christianisation[47] of American lit. crit. just as Harold Bloom's intervention was. We came to realise just how (Jew)Greek Frye's Canadian-Commonwealth literary theory was despite of its Christian-Methodist biases. Frye combined Greek theory and Christian imagery much in the same way as Milton did in Paradise Lost. Israel, as symbol, was very present in the Anatomy, but not Palestine, and not South Africa (nor Canada). Heidegger and Nietzsche were Greeks. Even Derrida, the Jew-Greek. But Edward Said is 'Egyptian'. Can the Egyptian speak? Most certainly so. He spoke Orientalism.

Palestine is an interpretation, says Said, 'one with much less continuity and prestige than Israel'.[48] Only a literary critic could say so. The 'Orient' is an interpretation too. Having said so much another deracinated Jewish-American contemporary comes to mind: Stanley Fish. What is an interpretation an interpretation of, is his question. We don't know. Is his answer. Palestine may be an interpretation, but of what? That's the question. A name given to

Arabic-speaking Levantines, as a British officer observed back in the twenties.[49]

Are the Palestinians 'like' the Africans and Coloureds in apartheid South Africa? 'Like' is a dangerous word. So, differences must be mentioned also. It was not the Africans but the Afrikaners who sympathised with the Nazis; but so did the representative Palestinian 'leader', the Mufti of Jerusalem, and the Iraqi Rashid 'Ali. The Ba'th Party's origin is related to him. That party's ideology is a mixture of Marxian economics, Nietzsche's Superman and Chamberlain's race theory. Rashid 'Ali came from that Baghdad which George Bernard Shaw believed would become the future capital of the British Empire. The Palestinians are (not) like the Boers? Gaza is (not) Transkei. But the philosopher and logician Verwoerd can be compared with the Mufti; they shared an admiration for Hitler and anti-Semitic views. Was this not the point of comparison between T. S. Eliot and Verwoerd? There are as many Jews in South Africa as Palestinian Arabs in Israel. The Jews came before the English. But Jews are not objects of study for Orientalists, and, if in Africa, not even for Africanists?

How tempting was not once the Cold War comparison(s) between the isolated Israel and white excluded South Africa? The Palestinian Arabs were 'there', as Said believes, and similarly the Khoikhois ('Hottentots') were 'there' when Van Riebeeck came. Palestine is both trope and topos. Orientalism is somewhat like an interpretative community but not quite. There is nothing outside Orientalism; Said interprets Orientalism in a Vichian way. As I said: We can only know what we have made; we, in this case being the Orientalists, have 'made' the Orient. This 'construction' of the Orient does not correspond to the brute reality also called the East. This brute reality is the East *an sich*. The Orientalists themselves were not Vichians nor constructivists and they probably believed they were studying something, the truth for instance, out there—or down there. They weren't. That is the message of Orientalism. 'But the phenomenon of Orientalism as I study it here deals principally, not with a correspondence between Orientalism and Orient, but with the internal consistency of Orientalism and its ideas about the Orient (the East as career) despite or beyond any correspondence, or lack thereof, with a "real Orient."'[50] Said treats Orientalism's truth as a truth of coherence or as consensual not as a correspondence truth.

Orientalism dominates the Orient (it is a relationship of power); but not the real Orient.[51] It is just like the way in which the transcendental subject dominates (vom Geist konstituiert) the object.[52] Can the object, the brute reality, speak or resist? The literary-liberal novel-noise from South Africa during the apartheid years could not be ignored. Yes, the object can speak. Orientalism opens with a discussion of a speech Balfour gave in 1910 (that year again) about 'England in Egypt'. Said comments: 'It does not occur to Balfour, however, to let the Egyptian speak for himself.'[53] Said, as I already said, became the 'Egyptian' who spoke.

Orientalism is, I suggested above, Arab postmodern. How? Does anyone remember 'What was postmodernism?' Anti-universalist and against generalisations. A postmodernist is a Nietzschean nominalist but an Orientalist is a realist—in the philosophical medieval sense of the two terms. Postmodern nominalism claims there are only individuals and singularities. It never uses the determining Urteil, only the aesthetic one, that is to say, the reflective one which our South African vicar called the divine. This judgement, we know, never subsumes singularities under general categories. Here is the reason why Orientalism became such a success in academe. It was not out of concern for the Arabs. No. The structure of the text was postmodern and aesthetic. Orientalism was unaesthetic because it generalised and subsumed. It was 'realistic'. But postmodern aesthetes knew their ethics: You must not generalise and never be scientific. There are only singularities. If you say just one thing, or any thing, about the Arabs—or a work of art—you have already made difference identical; many into one. Language generalises and subsumes. Therefore it falsifies, as Nietzsche taught that generation of poststructuralist students who were well-prepared for reading Edward Said. Thus the poststructuralists became postcolonialists. This was the end of Orientalism. Edward Said could not say anything about the 'real' Orient. 'There was, of course, an attempt in both of the later books to supply what was missing in Ori-

entalism, namely a sense of what an alternative picture of parts of
the Orient—Palestine and Islam respectively—might be, from a
personal point of view.'[54] Indeed, only from a personal point of
view. The Question of Palestine is an alternative picture from
such a view. The personal point of view is the alternative. The
Orient can make the Occident into an object of study, as the
Egyptian philosopher Hanafi once said in Aarhus. An Arab
Occidentalism will say nothing about the West. The twain shall
never meet, it seems.

Let me end this by quoting something from a very sensible
and clever Leo Marquard. He showed how we can generalise. His
book The Peoples and Policies of South Africa, appeared in 1952:
'It is as impossible to generalize about 'the African' as it is to
generalize about the 'mysterious East' or about 'the Englishman'
or about the inhabitants of the United States.'[55] Why had it
become impossible? After the Second World War it had for many
reasons become impossible in social science and history to
operate with such a concept as a fixed national character, something which had been quite normal and acceptable before. Let me
mention in passing that in another book about South Africa, also
from 1952 (when 'the tercentenary celebrations of the entry of
Western civilization into Southern Africa' were being prepared),[56]
Francis Brett Young's In South Africa did talk about the English
race in the old way: 'And here were these English, a race as
stubborn as themselves [i.e. the Dutch], speaking a foreign tongue
and expressing ideas that were equally foreign to them[…].'[57]

Leo Marquard, however, couldn't say such things. But he had
a pragmatic solution to his problem. If one cannot generalise one
cannot do science and only write from the personal point of view.
Marquard continued: 'Africans are individuals, each with his or
her [notice this proto-feminist gesture] own personality, likes and
dislikes, moods and hopes and fears.' If we are all individuals
then you can only write novels. The novel differs from history
and science because it deals with individuals; it never generalises.
And we have read many novels from South Africa. But Marquard
goes on: 'With this warning in mind, it is, nevertheless, convenient to describe a few general characteristics of the African.

Africans have dark skins[...].' And then he began to describe the peoples and policies of South Africa.

7. The last words: Miriam Tlali speaks

But first Francis Brett Young about Johannesburg:

Johannesburgers are justly proud of their city. [...] Its standard of life is high; its amenities and luxuries equal to those of any modern city in Europa or America, with a notable lack of the more sordid elements usually associated with industrial development on a large scale. Culture, too, which often wilts in societies which are mainly interested in the making of money, is not neglected. It has an admirable, though small, Art Gallery, fine libraries, a municipal orchestra and a lively and enterprising university. [...] If Johannesburg has a defect as a place of residence (and I fancy that its inhabitants will be generally loth to admit one) it is the absence of any attractive countryside in its immediate neighbourhood.[58]

And then Tlali:

It was mainly black faces. She dismissed with a smile the thought which came flashing into her mind that most whites seemed of late to avoid moving along the main thoroughfares leading towards Park Station at that time of day. She mused at the thought of the many arguments which often resulted in black-versus-white free-for-alls at such times. She remembered, chuckling, how she herself would become involved in the skirmishes. all through the shuffling and colliding of opposing waves of human traffic—whites maintaining that the blacks should remember to stick to their 'place' by keeping 'out of the way' and the blacks stubbornly refusing to accept the 'order' and dismissing it as a sign of nonsensical arrogance![59]

Notes

1. See Michael Green, *Novel Histories: Past, Present, and Future in South African Fiction* (Johannesburg: Witwatersrand UP, 1997) 44 ff.
2. These words Rogers Brubaker uses to describe interwar Poland's policy towards Germans and Jews in his seminal *Nationalism Revisited* (Cambridge: Cambridge UP, 1996) 86.
3. Niklas Luhman, 'Inklusion und Exklusion', *Nationales Bewußtsein und kollektive Identität*, ed. H. Berding (Frankfurt am Main, 1994) 20.

4. It is ironic that Anthony Sampson in his introduction to *South African Writing Today* compares the situation for SA writers in 1967 to that of Russian writers *before* the revolution (Nadine Gordimer and Lionel Abrahams, eds, *South African Writing Today* [Harmondsworrth: Penguin, 1967]). I compare them with dissident ones after the revolution.

5. Think of James Joyce; see Declan Kiberd, *Inventing Ireland* (Cambridge, MA: Harvard UP, 1996).

6. Elleke Boehmer, *Colonial and Postcolonial Literature* (Oxford, Oxford UP: 1995) 44.

7. Boehmer, *Colonial and Postcolonial* 50-51.

8. I base this entirely on the arguments of Vincent Descombes, *Modern French Philosophy*, trans. L. Scott-Fox and J. M. Harding (Cambridge: Cambridge UP, 1980).

9. Edward W. Said, *Orientalism* (Harmondsworth: Penguin, 1995) 5.

10. I owe the expression to Inge Birgitte Siegumfelt.

11. Afterword, Said, *Orientalism* 332.

12. This is pure university ideology. If it is true, we have a reason to study them and write dissertations about them.

13. It was not Mazzini but Vittorio Emanuele II and Cavour who united Italy. On Canadian unification and its literature see my 'Continentalism versus Nationalism: The US, the Canadian, and the Nordic Experience', *Informal Empire? Cultural Relations Between Canada, the United States and Europe*, ed. Peter Easingwood, Konrad Gross and Hartmut Lutz (Kiel: l & f, 1998).

14. Around 1800 he was more or less forgotten.

15. So can postcolonial literature, and it even does.

16. Ernst Robert Curtius, *European Literature and the Latin Middle Ages* (1948; New York: Harper, 1963) 16.

17. 'The British fragment has certainly not become a nation' (Leonard M. Thompson, 'The South African Dilemma', *The Founding of New Societies*, ed. Louis Hartz [New York, 1964] 197).

18. The other languages were never heard or read.

19. The peninsula Jutland was 'colonised' or 'discovered' by Copenhagen intellectuals and poets after the loss of substantial parts to Prussia.

20. He worked together with the renowned English phonetician Daniel Jones on the Sechuana language.

21. Information from Green, *Novel Histories* 291. Green believes that national literary histories were conservative. That is not true. They were progressive, since the triangle nationalism, industrialism and democracy are modernity as such. Conservatives would be patriots not nationalists.

22. Diana Fuss, *Essentially Speaking: Feminism, Nature and Difference* (New York: Routledge, 1989).

23. See also Gauri Viswanathan, 'Raymond Williams and British Colonialism', *Yale Journal of Criticism* 4.2 (1991).

24. Well, we have to forget about France.

25. In Norway, at a conference, I asked Nadine Gordimer if she saw any parallels between the collapse of communism and of apartheid. Apparently she had never heard such a question before. After having thought about it

she responded she could see no similarity, since for her communism was a good idea that had been destroyed by evil people. The same could be said about apartheid. Communism divides people into classes and apartheid into races.

26. This was more or less what Roland Barthes did in 1968 in Paris in order to save Balzac.
27. Charles Villa-Vicencio, *A Theology of Reconstruction: Nation-building and Human Rights* (Cambridge: Cambridge UP, 1992) 45. Villa-Vicencio is professor of religion and society in the University of Cape Town.
28. David Johnson, *Shakespeare and South Africa* (Oxford, 1996) 214.
29. Try to list all the writers who would have to be excluded from Kahn's canon. Just to mention a few obvious candidates: Bertold Brecht, Jean-Paul Sartre, D. H. Lawrence, Céline, Gottfried Benn, Heidegger, Paul de Man, and so on.
30. Theories travelled to South Africa more easily than other goods. Was there no theory boycott?
31. 'Indeed, Gardiner suggests the replacement of English studies with cultural studies' (Johnson, *Shakespeare* 203).
32. Quoted in Johnson, *Shakespeare* 204.
33. Mittee in Daphne Rooke's novel (*Mittee* [Boston: Houghton Mifflin, 1952]) reads English literature in the middle of nowhere or Transvaal; and the wife in Athol Fugard's *A Lesson From Aloes* reads English literature.
34. It would be interesting to do allegorical readings of Renault's works. She was clearly aware of the context in which she wrote. In *The King Must Die* (1958) she compares parts of the Theseus myth, which she believed was not really a myth but reality, to African folk tales. She talks about 'the levelling fashion' of our days and says we live in an 'Admass' society (see 'Author's Note' to *The Kind Must Die* [1958; London, 1974] 282-83). Mention should also be made of the literary magazine *The Classic*.
35. See my *K. E. Løgstrup: En moderne profet* (Copenhagen: Spektrum, 1993) for further details. 'Ethical' does not mean 'didactic'.
36. There is little difference in that respect between the opening lines of the *Aeneid* and *Bhagavad-Gîtá* ('Arma virumque cano' and 'Dhritirashtra: Ranged thus for battle on the sacred plain...').
37. Simon During, 'Literature—Nationalism's other?', *Nation and Narration*, ed. Homi K. Bhabha (London: Routledge, 1990). By 'literature', During means Australian literature, though he doesn't say so. After all Australia had quite a number of colonies after the First World War. They still have them—for instance Norfolk Island, where a famous novelist protests against the Australians. Who does not know the author of *The Thornbirds*?
38. One of our professors (a woman) believed Eliot was gay and therefore he ought not to be studied. She was a precursor of queering theorists who now don't read Eliot because he wasn't gay.
39. Wendy Steiner, *The Scandal of Pleasure* (Chicago: U of Chicago P, 1995) 210.
40. And even so readers were often disappointed. Anthony Sampson writes in his introduction to new South African writing: 'Some readers will be tempted to search in this collection for "committed" writers, and to award

marks according to the extent of political involvement. [Such readers] will be disappointed in this book.' *South African Writing Today* 12.

41. Lionel Trilling, *The Liberal Imagination* (1951; London: Mercury, 1961) ix.
42. Louis Hartz, 'A Theory of the Development of the New Societies', *The Founding of New Societies: Studies in the History of the United States, Latin America, South Africa, Canada, and Australia* (New York: Harcourt, 1964) 3.
43. Silly question. They already are, or Gilroy's text is. Why else was it written? Gilroy is in a literary theory anthology. Once a text is in there it is dead.
44. Paul Gilroy, 'The Black Atlantic', *Literary Theory: An Anthology*, ed. Julie Rivkin and Michael Ryan (Oxford: Blackwell, 1998) 977.
45. See Ulrich Beck, *Was Ist Globalisierung? Irrtümer des Globalismus- Antworten auf Globalisierung* (Frankfurt am Main: Suhrkamp, 1998) 55 ff. 'Afrika ist kein Kontinent, sondern ein Koncept.'
46. Although I own a book with the innocent title *Mastering Arabic.*
47. And I don't mean secularisation since that is a consequence of Christianity itself.
48. Edward W. Said, *The Question of Palestine* (1979; New York: Vintage, 1992) 10.
49. See A. J. Sherman, *Mandate Days: British Lives in Palestine* (London: Thames and Hudson, 1997) 26.
50. Said, *Orientalism* 5.
51. Said mentions K. M. Pannikar's classic *Asia and Western Dominance.* I mention Said mentioning this classic in order to mention a book which is not a classic, Raymund Pannikar's *The Hidden Christ of Hinduism* (London: Darton Longman, 1964).
52. After Kant it became easier for the Prussians to order around their servants (their objects).
53. Said, *Orientalism* 33.
54. Said, *Question of Palestine* 338.
55. Leo Marquard, *The Peoples and Policies of South Africa* (London: Oxford UP, 1952) 34.
56. Marquand, *Peoples and Policies*, preface.
57. Francis Brett Young, *In South Africa* (Melbourne: Heinneman, 1952) 10.
58. Young, *In South Africa* 102.
59. Miriam Tlali, *Footprints in the Quag: Stories and Dialogues from Soweto* (Cape Town: David Philip, 1989) 28.

Danish Imperial Fantasies: Peter Høeg's *Miss Smilla's Feeling for Snow*

Prem Poddar and Cheralyn Mealor

> In a little country like ours, you are a sensitive issue, Miss Jaspersen.[1]

> To me now, the very word 'Scandinavian' is a horror word, full of ice and death and sullen coitus.[2]

The publication of Peter Høeg's novel *Miss Smilla's Feeling for Snow* brought to the fore issues that, judging from their curious neglect in the critical reception of the novel in Denmark, certainly do appear to be 'sensitive': Danish imperialism, the Danish colonisation of Greenland, and postcolonial migrancy and identity. The majority of reviews and critical essays do not consider *Smilla* as a postcolonial novel, preferring to locate it within the detective/thriller genre, or debate its status as a modern or postmodern text: those which do refer to the important themes of colonialism and cultural hybridity in the novel tend to do so in terms of Western rather than Danish imperialism, and view hybridity simply as a generalised culture clash or as a psychological function of the novel's main character.[3] Both approaches, of course, indicate an evasion of the novel's critique of Danish colonial history and contemporary Danish society. It is perhaps unsurprising then that these critics also fail to consider the questions of Danish national identity that arise in a postcolonial reading of *Smilla*.

In fact, the positioning by one reviewer of *Smilla* in the postcolonial tradition of writing[4] has provoked the following rebuttals: '[it's] not so much a book about a real murder in Copenhagen to be solved, and about postcolonial conditions and contemporary

Translating Nations, ed. Prem Poddar, *The Dolphin* 30, pp. 161-202.
© 1999 by Aarhus University Press, Denmark.
ISBN 87 7288 381 2; ISSN 0106 4487.

relations between Denmark and Greenland. It's rather a meta-fictive narrative about the relation between reality and fiction'.[5] And again, '[p]ostcolonial Greenland is strangely absent in the novel, only in Smilla's reminiscences is it visible. And at the same moment that the novel sets course towards Greenland, it leaves the realistic narrative behind … At no point do we meet contemporary Greenlandic society.'[6] Such statements reveal certain misconceptions about the postcolonial. Understanding the term only as a temporal marker of societal progress (from the status of colonised to de-colonised) results in the maintenance of a centre/periphery distinction that diverts attention away from the interstitial reality (or present) of postcolonial migrancy.[7]

For some time now, migration from the colonies to the Western world has confronted the old imperial powers with their largely denied imperial histories:

The Western metropole must confront its postcolonial history, told by its influx of postwar immigrants and refugees, as an indigenous or native narrative *internal to its national identity*; and the reason for this is made clear in the stammering, drunken words of Mr 'Whisky' Sisodia from *The Satanic Verses*: 'The trouble with the Engenglish is that their hiss hiss history happened overseas, so they dodo don't know what it means.'[8]

It is precisely Høeg's positioning of the main character of *Smilla*, a postcolonial migrant, in the metropolitan centre that raises the issue of the trans-cultural third space inhabited by postcolonial migrants and diasporas, and enables a critique of Danish imperialism and the narrative constructions of Danish national identity.

This paper aims to examine these interrelated themes and issues as they appear in Peter Høeg's novel. In the first section, we will consider the more forceful aspects of *Smilla's* critique of Danish colonialism, paying particular attention to the description of imperial violence in the form of knowledge and surveillance—the so-called mapping of the other that has been the traditional task of anthropology and numerous other sciences. Drawing on postcolonial theorising on hybridity, the second section of the paper will focus on the question of identity raised in Høeg's text and will aim to reveal a certain ambivalence in its treatment of identity and show how this in turn serves to undermine its critique of Danish colonialism. The following section is concerned with the representation of Danish national identity in *Smilla*, which then finally leads us on to a discussion of the current debates in Denmark surrounding the 'sensitive issues' of immigration and multiculturalism.

Imperial Violence: 'put[ting] the past in order'

> *Ved* Hans Hedtofts *forlis i januar 1959 gik nemlig de sydgrønlandske arkiver tabt.* (For with the sinking of the *Hans Hedtoft* in January 1959, the southern Greenlandic archives were lost.)[9]

In 1950, at a time when decolonisation began to take place around the globe, marking the emergence of a new post-imperial era in world history, Hans Hedtoft, prime minister of Denmark, was busy defending the Danish presence in Greenland in terms of grand missionary zeal:

we know how to lead Greenlanders, in a humane way, from the more primitive stage up to the level at which we find ourselves. This is what legitimates our possession of Greenland to the rest of the world.[10]

This sensibility is underwritten by the very mechanisms of the modern state. It is precisely through such universal indices which allow the measurement of progress and/or backwardness that the contemporary world of nation-states is structured—some countries being (im)measurably more developed or advanced than others. This regime of perception that structures such comparisons makes up the liberal ideal of competitive pluralism and appears at various junctures—between perceived races, ethnic communities and nations. Dating back to the latter half of the eighteenth century, this ideal was contained within the notion of 'civilisation', a word that the French began deploying in the 1760s and which later lost out to 'progress' in the nineteenth century and to 'development' in the twentieth.[11] It remains with us today in the institution of development discourse as a replacement of colonial discourse.

A common justification for colonialism has thus been the coloniser's duty to provide enlightenment and speed the development of what are perceived as backward cultures. The virtues of benign colonisation have thus been emphasised along with the coloniser's responsibility towards and protection of its colonies. In *Den Hvide Races Sejrsgang* (1909; 'The White Race's Path to Victory'), for instance, W. Dreyer defended the Danish monopoly on trade by claiming that Eskimos were substantially better off under Danish rule, and that the colonisation of Greenland would 'protect the population by preventing too intimate a contact with foreigners, by keeping alcohol away from it and nurturing its enlightenment and spiritual development.'[12] This view has persisted in the portrayal of Denmark as the benevolent and nurturing parent, and Greenland as the grateful child: 'Greenlanders..., as one of them once said, will always feel like children who owe mother Denmark the child's genuine love and gratitude.'[13] The idea that colonialism managed to save Inuit culture from extinction is also present in *Smilla*. Although Inuit culture is celebrated for its closeness to nature, its pre-modern state of innocence, and colonialism is attacked for bringing about its near-extinction, it is also admitted to have 'irrefutably improved the material needs of an existence that was one of the most difficult in the world' (275).

Whilst there is a critique of the notion of the progress and/or backwardness of cultures in *Smilla*, because of the emphasis in the novel on the so-called 'dark side' of modernity, the critique of Danish colonialism is presented essentially as a critique of the evils of capitalism and materialist culture i.e., of greed and exploitation. The quest for the meteor is literally a 'gold-digging' colonial project, dangling the promise of great wealth and fame. This search is now in its third attempt with a new generation of colonial exploiters (Claussen, Seidenfaden and Tørk Hvid)[14] and a ship's crew who are, with the sole exception of Sonne, an important figure to be discussed in detail later, all corrupt in one way or another. The project is, of course, as demanded by the convention of hubris, doomed from the very start. The belief that technology will lead to man's complete mastery of nature is demonstrated to be false. The ice can never be controlled, and Western pride and self-complacency in its own cultural achievement will always result in the fate shared by the *Titanic* and, the somewhat significantly named *Hans Hedtoft* (257).

Following this logic to the plot, scientific knowledge is presented throughout the novel as holding more promise for the evil forces of greed and exploitation than for the advancement of the human condition anticipated by Enlightenment rationality: 'the attitude of Western science towards the world. Calculation, hatred, hope, fear, the attempt to measure everything. And above all else, stronger than any empathy for living things: the desire for money' (404). The production of knowledge is never autonomous, and in *Smilla* it is indeed scientific knowledge, with all its universalising claims, rather than military force, which constitutes the strongest weapon for the purposes of colonial exploitation and domination. In fact, in Høeg's text, the exercise of colonial power is shown to be so dependent on its ability to produce knowledge that Greenland has been transformed by the colonial gaze into a kind of giant laboratory, in which unprincipled self-seeking characters like Loyen and Moritz are let loose to conduct their scientific experiments on the indigenous population. However, it is not only medical science which is implicated in the project of exploitation, but the whole range of sciences at hand to the colonial authorities; geography, geology, meteorology, ethnography and so on.

Of these, the most elementary, one could say, for the colonial project, is cartography. In *Smilla* the real intention of the coloniser is 'to coerce … the Other, the vastness, that which surrounds human beings. It is the sea, the earth, the ice' (316). In order to control the 'Other', it must first be made visible and then become known. This 'Other', of course, must also include the native subject, and the basic methods of observation and inspection by which the land and native subject are rendered transparent and knowable correspond (e.g., the classificatory systems and procedures of colonial census, anthropological surveys, etc.). The never-ending process of mapping, surveying, measuring, classifying, plotting co-ordinates and drawing contours around the other constitutes in itself an act of possession and mastery. It is not only the amassing of useful data as a potential instrument for colonial exploitation and governmentality, but a *representation*, a configuring of Western/imperial-produced knowledges about both the land and native subject. Whilst there are

always spaces for resistance within colonial discourse, it nevertheless attempts to bind the native subject into the contours it draws
around them, into its closed, pre-established categories.

Thus, in a compulsive projection of its own fantasy of domination and exploitation, the colonial power constructs reality as it
wants to see it; the production of scientific knowledge is not so much
a reading of facts as a writing of fictions:

> ... the topographical maps of the Geodesic Institute. The red and green
> parabolas on the military maps of the ice pack. The discus-shaped,
> greyish-white photographs of X-band radar. The multi-spectrum scans of
> LANDSAT 3. The candy-coloured sediment maps of the geologists. The
> red and blue thermal photographs. ... *The text about ice.* (71, emphasis
> added)

But still, as mentioned above, this meticulous and evidently inexhaustible inspection is by no means limited to the ice alone.

In *Smilla*, the trope of pathology signifies that the native subject
has also been put under the knife of colonial inspection; thus an
analogy is drawn between the surveillance of land and people,
between ice and skin, between mineral samples and muscle
biopsies. The powerful image of Isaiah's autopsy resonates
through the text, linking these themes of ice, death and surveillance: 'his cold little body which someone has stuck a needle into,
that they have opened up and photographed and cut slices out of
and closed up again' (69). In fact, forensic medicine in *Smilla*
becomes a metaphor for the violent death of Inuit culture caused
(as the autopsy will reveal) by the Danish colonisation of Greenland.

In the novel, this enormous production of knowledge undertaken by the colonial authorities; the collecting, analysing, sam-
pling, surveying, diagnosing, observing, recording, etc., is all
stored in the archives tucked away in Copenhagen basements.
Historically, the archive has had a foundational role for the rule of
empire. In the case of the British Empire, the function of the
Victorian archive, as it was imagined, was to provide a centre
(though not necessarily at the same physical location) for the
collection and storage of information which could then be systema-
tised into a unified, coherent whole. The 'fantasy of empire' was

thus the aspiration of hegemony and unification of empire (as a kind of extended nation) which would be realised through the myth of positive and comprehensive knowledge.[15] The extent to which the fist of the metropole could hold its grip around the colonies would thus depend on an epistemology, on knowledge produced and assembled in the imperial archive, rather than the mere exercise of brute military force.

Whilst the imperial archive in Denmark by no means grew to the vast proportions of its British counterpart (reflecting, of course, the comparative size of empires), it is certainly extensive, comprising materials from numerous expeditions to Greenland, Central Asia and North Africa, and, of course, from the Danish colonies of Tranquebar, the Danish West Indies, and other possessions on the Gold Coast. The archival materials include written sources (maps, scientific studies, records of trade and administration, etc.) and artefacts (ethnographic, archaeological, etc.) and are primarily housed in The Danish National Archives (*Rigsarkivet*), The National Museum and The Royal Library in Copenhagen.

Greenland was by far the most significant source of archival materials. Whilst the importance of gathering artefacts and scientific data was already established by the time of the early expeditions to Greenland in the seventeenth and eighteenth centuries,[16] it was during the period of the scientific expeditions (from c. 1880 to the 1930s) that there was a dramatic increase in the volume of materials and data collected (archaeological, geological, botanical, ethnographic, cartographic, etc.). It was also during this period that a number of museums and institutions were expanded to house these growing collections, most notably the National Museum's Ethnographic Section, the various institutes for Polar research and Copenhagen University's Department of Eskimology.[17] Such expeditions were eventually made redundant by advances in modern technology, e.g., aerial photography, resulting in different and more rigorous technologies of measurement.[18]

Of course, the so-called scientific expeditions were not solely undertaken in a quest for pure knowledge, but were essential to the requirements of colonialist expansion. The mapping of the land and native subject commenced with the search for sea passages, the competition with other European powers over trade and the establishment of the early missions on Greenland; it continued with scientific expeditions in a race to mark out the land as a Danish possession (consider, for instance, the significantly named *Danmark-Ekspeditionen*, 1906-08). A regime of perception was set up that was structured by the notions of evolution and the progress of civilisations, gradually shifting from Hans Egede's 'wild savages' (see *Den Gamle Grønlands Perlustration*, 1741) to Knud Rasmussen's romanticised 'naturfolk' (Rasmussen himself was partly of Green-landic descent) and the ideal of benign colonisation.

The representation of Greenlanders was, of course, under-pinned by anthropological studies that employed various tech-nologies of measurement to map Eskimo bodies. Kaj Birket-Smith's influential book, *Eskimoerne* (1927), for instance, describes Eskimo physiognomy in some detail, and in a section on the cranium, before going on to discuss to what extent it can be compared to Neanderthal man, he asserts,

The most notable characteristic of the Eskimo cranium is perhaps its roof or crest-like form ... [which] can give the impression of something 'bestial', something which is remotely reminiscent of the gorilla and its powerful muscular attachments.[19]

The fascination with Eskimo craniums, hair types and eye colour, had a further significance for Danish anthropologists as it was believed possible to trace the descendants of the original Norse settlers on Greenland ('Nordboerne'). In *Eskimoerne*, Birket-Smith explains that in Icelandic sagas from the Middle Ages the term 'Greenlander' was used to denote 'Nordboerne' and no or little reference was made to Eskimos; Hans Egede's plan to establish the first mission on Greenland was based on his hope of coming to the aid of their descendants who, for 300 years, had lived without Christianity.[20] In fact, virtually all the expeditions to Greenland (early and late) had, to some extent, as one of their goals, the discovery of the so-called 'blond Eskimos' with Nordic features. In this way, the exploration and colonisation of Greenland was inextricably linked to the tracing of Danish origins. Indeed, Norse mythology and the Vikings are still very much a part of contempo-rary attempts to define Danish national identity.[21]

The interest in Eskimo origins and history, on the other hand, which combined the disciplines of archaeology and anthropology, again provides an illustration of the naturalisation of time in anthropological discourse, or of what Fabian terms 'the ethnographic present'.[22] In *Eskimoer og Stenalderfolk* (1929) ('Eskimos and Stone Age People'), Knud Rasmussen associates the Greenlandic landscape with that of Europe during the Ice Age, and considers there to be

Eskimos ... who not only themselves stood in the middle of an Ice Age as well as a Tundra Age, but even in the case of some tribes, found themselves in the middle of a Stone and Bone Age culture, which is comparable to the one Europe experienced about 25-30,000 years ago. (19)

For archaeologists, Greenland became a kind of living museum based on the notion that the study of a less progressed culture would illuminate the pre-history of European civilisation. This was reflected in the chronological classificatory system and the spatial ordering of ethnographic objects in the National Museum; Eskimo artefacts were collected and exhibited alongside collections of archaeological material on Danish pre-history.[23]

In *Smilla* the quantification, mapping, and classification of the land and native subject is shown to be a function of the archive which exemplifies the imperial fantasy of the systematisation of all human knowledge:

Merciless order ought to prevail in archives. They are quite simply the crystallization of a wish to put the past in order. So that busy, energetic young people can come waltzing in, select a specific case, a specific core sample, and waltz out again with precisely that segment of the past.

These archives, however, leave something to be desired. There are no labels on the shelves. There are no numbers, dates, or letters on the spines of the filed material. (73-74)

The disorderliness of these records testifies less to the impossibility of 'merciless order' in archival systems, than to the fact that 'the quivering vigour of imperialism' (60) has finally expended itself; that finding the prospects of exploitation greatly diminished, Denmark has gradually begun to withdraw (though not remove) its colonial gaze: Smilla asks, 'Is this a portrait of Denmark's relationship to its former colony? Disillusionment, resignation, and retreat? While retaining the last administrative grip: control over foreign policy, mineral rights, and military interests?' (72). Thus, the seemingly inexhaustible cycle of examination, classification and data collection belonging to the bureaucratic machinery that characterises modern state power has begun to crumble. That this decay of empire is coextensive with the disappointments of modernity, is confirmed through images of the disintegrating structures of the metropole: the degeneration and decay witnessed on the surface of Copenhagen (the semi-demolished building of the Cryolite Corporation, the White Cells) extends into the half-forgotten archives in the city's cavities.

Forgetting, as Ernest Renan has famously argued, is a necessary manoeuvre in the narrative construction of the nation. The archive itself is testimony to this selectivity of historical memory. Narratives of national unity proclaim national identity as originary, coherent, and pure and thus deny the influence of external agency and refuse to acknowledge difference within the national boundaries. Sonne, we are told, as a 'quintessential Dane' has the 'iron resolve to repress what's happening around him' (353). This repression of the other, of conflicting narratives, differences and oppositions by the drive towards national coherence, explains how certain issues become 'sensitive' (90). In terms of the archive, the nationalist 'iron resolve' to forget doubles the will 'to put the past in order' (73); the disavowal (or effacing) of otherness doubles the disavowal of chaos (whether archival order was achieved or, as more likely, was not).

The particular archive that Smilla infiltrates is housed in what remains of the Cryolite Corporation's building. Although the general collapse of the Cryolite Corporation symbolises colonial disillusionment, the continuance and reach of the imperial archive is evident; its institutions are as numerous as are the references to them in the text—the Cryolite Corporation Danmark, the Geodesic Institute, the Centre for Developmental Research, Geoinform, the Institute of Forensic Medicine, the Institute for Arctic Medicine, Copenhagen University, the Advisory Scientific Commission, the Institute for Eskimology, the Arctic Museum, etc., etc. Smilla not only infiltrates the basement of the Cryolite Corporation but also wreaks havoc in the archives there, and her visit to the Arctic Museum is shortly followed by its complete destruction (she symbolically escapes after being locked in). It should, however, also be noted that there is an ambivalence in the text, as 'the Western mania for control and archives and cataloguing' is also described as a 'back-handed blessing' as it is 'intended as a protection' (274).

The Arctic Museum enjoys a special status within this imperial archive. As the institution that most concerns itself with producing knowledge of indigenous cultures, it is primarily responsible for the systems of primitive classification to which Inuit culture is subjected. Commenting on the procedures by which anthropology constructs its object, Høeg writes,

In *The Last Kings of Thule,* Jean Malaurie writes that a significant argument for studying the interesting Polar Eskimos is that you can thus learn something about human progression from the Neanderthal stage to the people of the Stone Age.

It's written with a certain amount of affection. But it's a study in unconscious prejudices.

Any race of people that allows itself to be measured on a grade scale designed by European science will appear to be a culture of higher primates.

Grading is meaningless. Every attempt to compare cultures with the intention of determining which is the most developed will never be anything other than one more bullshit projection of Western culture's hatred of its own shadows. (169)

Such 'grade scales' are formulated by colonialist discourse on the premise that the paternalistic intervention of the West will elevate the non-West to a higher stage of modernisation, so that, ultimately, it will be transformed into a mirror-image of its Western benefactor (here we return to Hans Hedtoft and co.). This notion of time-lag provides the foundation for the modern ideology of progress, which sees the destiny of the nation in terms of its progression along the path of modernity, or through what Benjamin terms 'homogeneous empty time'. It is in Homi Bhabha's distinction between the pedagogical (homogeneous empty time) and the performative time of the nation, that the time of the archive becomes clear: the time of the archive is not coterminous with the performativity of the people but represents, in a sense, a concrete inscription of the homogeneous time of the nation.

That the colonialist agenda of transforming the non-West into its own image results in a form of perversion, of 'Western culture's hatred of its own shadows', is a point made by Bhabha in his discussion of Fanon's 'Manichaean delirium':

The representative figure of such a perversion ... is the image of post-Enlightenment man tethered to, *not* confronted by, his dark reflection, the shadow of colonized man, that splits his presence, distorts his outline, breaches his boundaries, repeats his action at a distance, disturbs and divides the very time of his being.[24]

In an attempt to recover its authority, colonialist discourse thus tries to fix its subject in what Edward Said calls the 'timeless eternal', i.e., to render it transparent and unchanging. According to Fanon, the colonial stereotype results in

a continued agony rather than a total disappearance of the pre-existing culture. The culture once living and open to the future, becomes closed, fixed in the colonial status, caught in the yolk [sic] of oppression. Both present and mummified, it testifies against its members ... The cultural mummification leads to a mummification of individual thinking ... As though it were possible for a man to evolve otherwise than within the framework of a culture that recognises him and that he decides to assume.[25]

The construction of the other as stereotype is described by Bhabha in terms of Freudian fetishism and the Lacanian Imaginary. The colonial subject is represented by the 'four term strategy' of the shifting positionalities of 'metonymic/aggressive' and 'metaphoric/narcissistic': in the same way that the child identifies aggressively with the mirror image of itself (for its difference from the self), yet simultaneously delights in its own image (for its similarity to the self), the colonial subject both fears and desires the familiar unfamiliarity of the stereotype it produces.[26] As Said writes, '[t]he Orient at large ... vacillates between the West's contempt for what is familiar and its shivers of delight in—or fear of—novelty'.[27] It is perhaps in this context that the relationship in the novel between Smilla's Danish father and her Inuit mother is best understood: he was 'imprisoned in a land which he hated by a love which he did not understand' (33).

But there are two further examples in *Smilla* that illustrate this link between colonial stereotyping and fetishism particularly well: the 'life-sized model' of the boxer Ayub Kalule made out of dark chocolate that stands outside a Copenhagen bakery (139), and the hollowed out Eskimo figure displayed in the Arctic Museum. Both of these objects, by their very form, mark the absence of the other that they supposedly represent:

What he's leaning on is a long harpoon. In his left hand he's holding a dart thrower. He is not in full dress, in high *kamiks* and a suit of bird skin and feathers. He isn't much taller than me. I pat him on the cheek. He is cast from hollow fibreglass and then cleverly painted. His face is attentive.

'Lifelike isn't it?' (130-31)

It is perhaps unsurprising that the curator of this museum, the mimic man of the novel 'looks exactly like the manikin' (131) which he considers so 'lifelike'.

In *Smilla* the theme of Eskimo culture reduced to a museum piece is underlined by the fact that Loyen[28] (an archetypal producer of knowledge for the imperial archive whose research includes Arctic medicine, X-rays, and history) has a special interest in mummification (127). Furthermore, it is also stereotyping and primitivism that informs the naive European belief that modernity has not arrived in Greenland. But it is precisely this naivety which opens the way for certain forms of indigenous resistance. Through a rearticulation of the coloniser's stereotype, Smilla's mother is able to trap them by their own blind prejudices; 'she paddled a kayak that was made in the same way they were made in the seventeenth century, before the art of kayak building disappeared from North Greenland. But she used a sealed plastic container for her hunting float' (68). The success of her subversive strategy depended precisely on the fact that 'No one *dared* to believe that [Smilla's] mother had violated the ban' (67, emphasis added)—the colonisers dared not believe in anything which had the potential of undermining the authority of their Self/Other constructions. It could, perhaps, also be said that her success as a figure of anti-colonial resistance is finalised in death, as she cheats the colonial power out of the autopsy it hopes to perform (to find out things that the ethnographer who studied her could not) thereby escaping the colonial gaze.

The curator of the Arctic Museum, Andreas Fine Licht, is greatly resented by Smilla for his transformation into a 'genuine, intellectual Northern Dane' (134). Fully recruited into the service of empire and archive, he represents not only the act of, but also the result of the coloniser's attempts to inscribe the hegemonic structures of the empire onto its colonies. Just as the archive's production of knowledge enables the colonial power to occupy the land, to possess it and civilise it (i.e. by controlling and cultivating it), knowledge is produced about the native subject so that this same civilising process can be enforced: Greenland is thus re-inscribed as 'Denmark's northernmost county' and the Inuit are 'educated' into docile 'Northern Danes' (105). This subjectification of the individual is effected through the various institutions operating the normalising technologies of what Foucault calls 'modern disciplinary power'; i.e., schools, churches, prisons—all of which Smilla herself has been subjected to or threatened with. Furthermore, the process of subjectification becomes associated in the novel with the trope of pathology: here the individual body is taken apart and reconstructed even in death. The brutal and meticulous probing, examination and suturing together again of the native subject, as on the slab of the autopsy table, proves ultimately to result in the mummification of Inuit culture rather than in its resurrection as a civilised Western copy.[29]

That Smilla, as a figure of resistance, is considered a real threat to the authorities is confirmed by their interrogation of her and their ongoing surveillance of her personal and political activities. However, what makes Smilla a particularly 'sensitive issue' (92) for them, concerns the imperial archive's relation to state security. First of all, Smilla possesses classified information; she has been trained to serve the imperial archive and has learned the 'nomen-clature, [the] system of symbols' (71) for reading maps, and having participated in knowledge-producing expeditions for the archive she has, of course, had access to secret knowledge. This access has furthermore not always been authorised i.e., her entry into the archive at the Cryolite Corporation. Second, Smilla's 'feeling for snow', a kind of folk-knowledge providing her with an intuitive understanding of ice, gives her an advantage over the scientific truth-producing procedures of the West. In contrast to the rigorous archival procedures of cataloguing and classifying (an exercise in putting a shape on things), this 'feeling for snow' is a kind of protean, shapeless metaphor. Whilst the imperial archive would most likely dismiss this type of indigenous knowledge, it would in any case refuse to be contained within the fixed co-ordinates of the archive's systematisation of knowledge and absorbed into its methodologies.

It is on this basis of trying to (re-)assert the authority of colonialist discourse that her interrogator, Ravn, warns her she is under surveillance. But Smilla also interrogates and defiantly throws back her own gaze, so to speak, on the colonialist project. The authority of the state as a producer of knowledge is under-mined in two important ways: colonial-produced knowledges are shown to provide the means for Smilla's empowerment, and, sceptical of the integrity of the official police investigation, she conducts her own investigation into Isaiah's death. Moreover, in this process, Smilla traverses Copenhagen, remapping and redefining the capital in terms of its imperial archive, and interro-gates a number of characters who are all, in one way or another, representatives of the imperial ideology (although not all of them are aware of it); Loyen, Lübing, Clahn, Licht, etc. It is this act of remapping from the postcolonial perspective, and of interrogating the authority of the colonialist discourse, that constitutes the driving force of the novel.

Imperialism, as some have argued, meant a de-territoriali-sation (i.e., emptying of previous significations) of the world's spaces, such that a 're-territorialisation' with new significations could take place.[30] Høeg's text, reminiscent of Kureishi and Rushdie's London, de- and re-territorialises Copenhagen as a location and setting for fiction. Cultural use can be made of what Lefebvre detects as 'a permanent tension between the *appropriation* and use of space for individual and social purposes and the *domination* of space' by institutionalised forms of power.[31] And as de Certeau explains, the use of racial and cultural dominants in the wake of Spanish violence 'nevertheless often *made* of the rituals, representations, and laws imposed on them [Indians] something quite different from what their conquerors had in mind... deflecting its power, which they lacked the means to challenge, they escaped it without leaving it'.[32] Smilla's itinerary through Copenhagen in relation to the totalised city of the map, is what 'the speech act is to language'.[33] Her footsteps actualise the city as a function of time and narrative, weakening its borders and deprioritising its properties of planned and organised place. But while Brickhall of *The Satanic Verses* becomes a space of difference and transformation within the metropolis, Høeg's localities in Copenhagen do not.

Hybrid Identities: 'living ... in transit'

Smilla is a hybrid—a product of the unhappy encounter between coloniser (her father/Denmark) and colonised (her mother/Greenland). Her hybridity manifests itself in several ways; in her appearance (her 'trace of something Asian' [11]), her uprooted existence and living 'in transit' (9) between two cultures, and, of course, in her passion for ice which is fuelled by a combination of her instinctive (Eskimo) 'feeling for snow' and expert (Western) knowledge in glacial morphology. It is worth noting, however, that Smilla's Greenlandic nature (her appearance does not give this away: 'There aren't many Danes who can tell by looking at me' [11]) is recognisable to only two other characters in the novel; Isaiah recognises her because of their sameness, their shared ethnic identity, or what, perhaps, Benedict Anderson would call their 'deep horizontal friendship',[34] whereas Loyen recognises her because of his professional expertise gained from years of experience as a technician of colonial surveillance.

The unhomeliness of Smilla's condition is further emphasised by her identification with the displaced and marginalised; 'Invalids, foreigners, the fat boy of the class, the ones nobody ever wants to dance with' (42). Living in-between cultural traditions, Smilla subverts and transgresses norms almost wherever she finds them. The subversive potential of hybridity is also indicated in the passages on Smilla's mother—the transgression of gender roles (also an important feature of Smilla's character) that causes her to become an object of ethnographic study is based on 'the natural acceptance in Greenland that each of the sexes contains the potential to become its opposite' (28). This bears much in common with the notion of the ambivalence of authoritative discourses. Her mother's behaviour is truly hybrid because also in Greenland, 'the collective could tolerate a change in sex, but not a constant transition to and fro' (28).[35] However, as this section aims to show, to argue that the binary relation of coloniser/colonised is deconstructed through the figure of Smilla as a hybrid or cultural composite of conflicting elements, is too straightforward.

Considering *Smilla* as an attempt to provide a counter-history to the Enlightenment master-narratives of progress and civilisation is problematic due to an ambivalence concerning the question of identity that runs through the entire novel. On the one hand, Høeg's text appears to undermine the notion of the sovereign, self-sustaining subject: its representation of fragmented identities and the hybrid character of postcolonial migrants certainly challenges this unified concept of identity. But on the other hand, it is quite clear that an essentialist view of identity is also asserted, and that what is consequently understood as the problem of identity is blamed on the displacing and alienating processes of modernity operating through colonialism.

Throughout the text identity is treated as if it were pure or true, fixed and self-contained, hence something which can be lost or abandoned, and should on all accounts be 'held on to' (134). The essence of identity is thus closed, secured within its boundaries and only becomes fractured or repressed by the various forms of subjugation which, in this instance, are exercised by the colonialist regime. Indigenous resistance to imperial power will, therefore, take the form of an attempt to regain or rediscover the authentic, pre-colonial identity. This recovery of a true identity is precisely what Smilla spends so much of her energies trying to achieve and is also, as she is well aware, the source of her frustrations as a hybrid.

There are, however, also moments of brief respite in which Smilla seems to express an apparently unproblematic sense of belonging to both cultures: 'I think about the 120,000 that the butcher lost. The annual net salary for *one of us* ordinary Danes. Five times the salary of *one of us* ordinary Arctic Eskimos' (197, emphasis added). Here, though, Smilla's hybridity is presented through her identification as an 'ordinary' member of *each* culture (her sense of belonging to *one and the other*), rather than for the newness of living on the borderline in an in-between Third Space. When an apparent understanding of such newness does emerge in the text, it is, however, linked with the need to define a *solid* identity: [36]

I've lost my cultural identity for good, I usually tell myself. And after I've said this enough times, I wake up one morning, like today, with a solid sense of identity. Smilla Jaspersen—Greenlander *de luxe*. (120)

Though Smilla is, then, sometimes presented (though not un-problematically) as inhabiting the in-betweenness of hybrid cultural space, her hybridity is treated throughout the text as an identity problem or the cause of a deep-seated and ultimately irresolvable identity crisis.

The urgency of Smilla's pursuit for a 'solid' identity and sense of belonging, is underscored not only by the repeated question 'Who am I?', but also by the steady accumulation of Smilla's child-hood reminiscences littering the text. These memories constitute a seeking back to roots, an attempt to rediscover 'home' (204), a place to which one belongs. But for all her efforts to rediscover her roots, Smilla does acknowledge the impossibility of returning to an original identity that 'has never been truly mine' (169). As a hybrid, the essence of identity, whether of Greenlandic-ness or Danish-ness (although she is only concerned with recovering the former) has been forever denied her. Whilst Smilla is granted the choice of *either one or the other*, neither alternative can ever finally be realised as her hybridity forces her to live out the miserable existence of eternal alienation from both, exiled into some sort of cultural vacuum.

This is a view of hybridity bearing more in common with the theories of degeneracy formulated by nineteenth century racist biology i.e., that hybridity constitutes a weakness, lack or de-ficiency, than with the notion of hybridity espoused by many postcolonial critics, which contests the traditional essentialist conceptions of identity and their affirmation of a sovereign, autonomous and self-sufficient subject.[37] The postcolonial conceptualisation of hybridity is based on an understanding that the Self is always discursively constructed through its relation to the Other, that there is always already a destabilising moment within any so-called 'unified' discourse. This splitting at the site of enunciation explains why hybridity is produced by the colonial power itself, and resistance is not necessarily just a 'simple negation or exclusion of the "content" of an other culture', but 'the effect of an ambivalence produced within the rules of recognition of dominating discourses as they articulate the signs of cultural difference and reimplicate them within the deferential relations of colonial power'.[38] Hybridity is that moment of subversion, of the emergence of other denied knowledges, in which the authority of colonial discourse is displaced by the ambivalence of its own constructions of difference.

Hybridity therefore becomes the liminal Third Space of negotiation, enabling the articulation of in-between identities and positions which are 'neither the one nor the Other', but something *new*:

The hither and thither of the stairwell, the temporal movement and passage that it allows, prevents identities at either end of it from settling into primordial polarities. This interstitial passage between fixed identifications opens up the possibility of a cultural hybridity that entertains difference without an assumed or imposed hierarchy.[39]

The irony here, then, is that whilst Bhabha's argument is based precisely on the realisation that hybridity resists and frustrates any attempt to restore the dangerous narratives of ethnic or cultural absolutism, Høeg's model of hybridity is steeped in an ambivalence which seems to miss this point. On the one hand, Smilla is represented as a hybrid figure who inhabits this Third Space and is thus enabled to challenge and subvert the authority of the dominant culture, but at the same time the traditional essentialist discourses that hybridity deconstructs are sustained. In short, Høeg's text cannot enact 'the performativity of translation as a staging of cultural difference'.[40]

The problem with *Smilla's* adherence to the notion of fixed and unchanging identity is not only that it undermines its own attack on, amongst other things, the fixing of Inuit identity and culture, but that it grounds a willingness to shoulder the weight of certain political baggage associated with essentialist discourses; the discriminatory politics of exclusion and assimilatory inclusion:

> There is one way to understand another culture. *Living* it. Move into it, ask to be tolerated as a guest, learn the language. At some point understanding may come. It will always be wordless. The moment you grasp what is foreign, you will lose the urge to explain it. To explain a phenomenon is to distance yourself from it. When I start talking about Qaanaaq, to myself or to others, I again start to lose what has never been truly mine. (169)

This passage clearly shows how the essentialist view of identity as a primordial totality (it can never be successfully articulated, let alone translated) provides the basic ingredients for the monocentric logic of assimilation.

It is in this sense that the hybrid members of the Greenlandic diaspora in the novel are perceived in terms of their success or failure. This is judged not only by the criteria of self-integrity and staying true to one's roots, but also by degree of assimilation: Juliane is an utterly broken outsider, Andreas Fine Licht is thoroughly assimilated but at the same time scorned for having deserted his original identity. Isaiah, on the other hand, 'was on the verge of success. He could have made it. He would have been able to absorb Denmark and transform it and become both' (68). What makes Isaiah a successful candidate according to this view is that Danish culture is absorbed without entailing the betrayal or abandonment of roots, and this harmonious and integral figure is held up as a beacon against Smilla's dissonant, fragmented self. Like the fabric and design of his coat (68), he will stitch together a 'harmonious patchwork of cultures'[41] rather than find a position from which to articulate 'the narrative of cultural difference which can never let the national history look at itself narcissistically in the eye'.[42] The immigrant's 'success' thus seems only to be achieved through assimilatory inclusion into Danish society: whilst retaining a certain *exotic* Greenlandic-ness, Isaiah, had he lived, would not have constituted a threat to the norms and values of the dominant national culture. What *Smilla* interrogates are the conditions and possibilities for such successful integration—the prospect of which appears, already in the opening pages of the novel, to be as dark and bleak as the December setting of Isaiah's funeral.

Constituting Denmark: 'ask to be tolerated as a guest ... '

Some Danes talk about a threat to national values ... But there is a national value which is very important for the future of our society—a value which really is threatened ... That value is tolerance. Tolerance doesn't mean a blue-eyed acceptance of all that is foreign ... [It] means that we should be open towards one another without too many prejudices.

Thorkild Simonsen, Minister of the Interior[43]

Nations, as the crude yet common nationalist ideology maintains, develop and evolve along some sort of single path or historical continuum of progress, nurturing an homogeneous people of one blood whose origin can be traced to an ancient national past. Rejecting all such essentialist, holistic or organic conceptions of society, Benedict Anderson's notion of 'imagined communities' conceptualises the nation as constructed, written or narrated. The nation, he argues, is the collective's narrative to itself as 'an imagined political community—and imagined as both inherently limited and sovereign'.[44] The nation theorises itself as homogeneous and homocentric, identical with itself in principle and indivisible in its totality. Its drive towards unity and consolidation frequently invokes the need to change its cultural configuration, to solidify cultural identity: in its most extreme forms it strives to purify the nation either by forcing emigration or by eradicating portions of the population through ethnic cleansing. National boundaries are constructed and policed to protect the integrity of those *inside* and to keep the threatening other *outside*.

However, the concept of national purity is highly problematic. An individual, like a nation, has no simple origin or inside, but is always already in the process of being written by an outside of language and law. The possibility of a pure inside of a nation is precluded by the notion, discussed earlier, of difference at the heart of identity. National boundaries are used to distinguish between an inside and an outside: the inside is the nation, the outside is everything that is not-the-nation. This boundary constitutes the identity of the nation, and yet, it depends not only on the inside but also on the outside—the other terms in the system of differences. Thus the nation's outside is constitutive of its inside: 'The frontier does not merely close the nation in on itself, but also, immediately, opens it to an outside, to other nations. Frontiers are articulations, boundaries are, constitutively, crossed or transgressed.'[45]

With the trope of hybridity, Bhabha deconstructs the notion of the border as a mechanism of exclusion and inclusion. Nations, he claims, are characterised by an *internal* ambivalence; the nation-space is the site of different temporalities, different histories, different ethnicities, different social practices, etc., and is the domain in which the negotiation of cultural values and priorities is constantly played out. Bhabha identifies this ambivalence of the nation as a tension between what he calls the pedagogical (the authoritative discourses of state ideology in which the 'nation as a people' is articulated), and the performative (the everyday 'details of life'),[46] which may reinforce or antagonise the pedagogical. In this way, by arguing against the notion of an originary, organic community, Bhabha claims an authority for cultural difference:

cultures are only constituted in relation to that otherness internal to their own symbol-forming activity which makes them decentred structures— through that displacement or liminality opens up the possibility of articulating different, even incommensurable cultural practices and priorities.[47]

In *Smilla*, there is a move, on one level, towards Bhabha's notion of cultural difference. The nationalist claim that Denmark is a homogeneous society, a nation of One People, is questioned, and the text points rather to the differences *within* the unity of the nation: *Smilla* is an attempt to re-write the nation from the perspective of the marginalised and exiled living *within* the nation-space. The main character, a self-empowered postcolonial hybrid living in the metropole, subverts the authority of the dominant culture from the *inside*. Furthermore, in the same way that Høeg objects to the fixing of Inuit culture and reminds us there are several different languages and cultures existing in Greenland, that not all Eskimos are the same, he also tries to show how Danish national identity has traditionally been conceived in ways that have denied or erased difference. Ice becomes a metaphor for modern social cohesion or national cultural identity:

I see Denmark before me like a spit of ice. It's drifting, but it holds us frozen solid in the ice masses, each in a fixed position in relation to everyone else.

Isaiah's death is an irregularity, an eruption that produced a fissure. That fissure has set me free. For a brief time, and I can't explain how, I have been set in motion, I have become a foreign body skating on top of the ice ...

... From this angle a new Denmark comes into view. A Denmark that consists of those who have partially wrested themselves free of the ice.

Loyen and Andreas Fine Licht, driven by different forms of greed.

Elsa Lübing, Lagermann, Ravn, bureaucrats whose strength and dilemma is their faith in a corporation, in the medical profession, in a government apparatus. But who, out of sympathy, eccentricity, or for some incomprehensible reason, have circumvented their loyalty to help me.

Lander, the rich businessman, driven for a desire for excitement and a mysterious sense of gratitude.

That is the beginning of a social cross-section of Denmark. The mechanic is the skilled worker, the labourer. Juliane is the dregs. And I— who am I? (204-05)

There is a certain ambiguity at play in this metaphor. On the one hand, because Smilla herself skates like 'a foreign body' she is thus frozen out of the imagined community which has iced itself in. On the other hand, those who have helped Smilla 'out of sympathy, eccentricity, or for some incomprehensible reason', have reached out towards the other, this 'foreign body', and 'have partially wrested themselves free of the ice'.

Furthermore, this passage can be seen to illustrate nicely the (sometimes slippery?) tension between what Bhabha calls the pedagogical and the performative. It suggests that people's identities are defined, overseen or under surveillance (ice can be transparent), and represented by the pedagogical—they are completely subjected to social institutions and literally 'fixed' in the homogeneous empty time of the ice. The view of 'a new Denmark' granted to Smilla is that of a diverse population who, with their different lifestyles, beliefs, interests, class and cultural backgrounds, have followed individual strategies and thus 'partially wrested themselves free' from the ice in their performative, everyday living—which, whether it reinforces or undermines the pedagogical, is always one dimension of the play of tension making up the ambivalence of the nation-space. Here, difference no longer belongs *outside*, out there on the other side of the national boundaries, but *within* the nation-space itself. Minorities or marginalised groups thus become 'the outside of the inside', the 'part-in-the-whole'.[48]

So, on the one hand, the text does recognise that difference exists *within* the nation-space, but at the same time it maintains an essentialist view of identity and thus promotes the ethnocentric discourses of exclusion and inclusion discussed earlier. The perception of national cultural identity as authentic and unique, something that is possessed or lost is visible in Høeg's treatment of both Inuit and Danish culture. In fact, these distinct and autonomous cultures are often contrasted in order to prove the authenticity of one (Inuit) above the other (Danish). Indigenous culture is awarded primacy by the text because the Inuit are represented as living closer to nature, and as possessing a somehow truer, more real community: 'People live so close together in Northern Greenland. Sleeping many to a room. Hearing and seeing everyone else at all times' (204). In the novel, the great advantage held by this organic community over modern Danish society appears to lie in the fact that it has not (yet) been ravaged by the corrupting forces of modernity, the social effects of which are, of course, exemplified by the agonisingly lonely and miserable existences assigned to the alienated inmates of the White Cells.[49] Although it is, of course, only immigrants and members of the working class ('The mechanic is the skilled worker, the labourer. Juliane is the dregs' [205]) who live in the White Cells.

This somewhat depressing view of Danish social cohesion is emphasised through the contrasting image of a Danish organic community, an idealised Denmark of the past which is ironically invoked through the figure of Sonne, the 'quintessential Dane'

(353), and the romantic myth of an originary, authentic Danish identity:

> He's a nice young Dane … He could have been sitting at home under the cuckoo clock with his mother and father in Ærøskøbing, eating meatballs and gravy, praising Mama's cooking, and basking in Papa's humble pride. Instead, he wound up here. In worse company than he could ever imagine. I feel sorry for him. He's a little piece of what's good about Denmark. The honesty, the integrity, the enterprise, the obedience, the crew cut, and money matters. (297)

This genuine boy scout and 'quintessential Dane' turns out to be not from Ærøskøbing (on the small island of Ærø) but from Svaneke (on the distant island of Bornholm). In this context, both places are interchangeable; both are charming little villages straight out of picture-postcard Denmark, and both could not be further away, culturally, geographically or temporally, from Copenhagen, Denmark's metropolitan centre. The implication is, of course, that true and honest Denmark is found on the periphery, in those areas less ravaged (or un-touched) by the forces of modernisation, and free from outside influence or foreign presence. In short, Sonne and his idyllic birthplace represent the virtues of an original and untarnished folk culture basking in the modest glory of a kind of innocent, primordial, and perhaps even prelapsarian, Danish national identity:

> He blushes. He wants to protest. Wants to be taken seriously. Wants to exert his authority. The way Denmark does. With blue eyes, pink cheeks, and honourable intentions. But all around him are powerful forces: money, development, abuse, the collision of the new world with the old. And he doesn't understand what's going on. (298)

Denmark is thus itself ironically presented as an unfortunate and unsuspecting victim of the dark side of modernity: brimming with modest virtue but imperilled by powerful *external* forces, which gradually eat away at the core of the nation, at its *internal* integrity. Here, the significance of Sonne's 'iron resolve to repress what's happening around him' (353) becomes clearer.

Furthermore, it could be argued that Sonne, as the true and honourable Dane with roots in folk culture (in contrast to the novel's main villains who belong to the social elite), represents the values implied by the Danish concept of *folkelighed*.[50] This concept was formulated by the theologian N. F. S Grundtvig (1783-1872) and has been defined as '[a] Danish word, normally applied to that which has a popular democratic unassuming quality or character'.[51] Inspired by the contemporary Romantic movement in Europe, Grundtvig sought the essence of Danish national identity in peasant culture and its origins in Norse mythology. He argued that the remnant of this original Danish/Nordic spirit could no longer be found amongst the elite and learned classes of Danish society, but lived on in traditional peasant culture, needing only to be re-awakened. Although Grundtvig attacked the elite's orientation towards other European cultures and their use of non-vernacular languages, considering this a betrayal of the Danish spirit, and awarded primacy to the *ordinary* people, his project was not to inspire revolutionary class struggle but to (re)create a harmonious national unity. On Grundtvig's view, national identity is not determined by race or ethnicity; rather, it is shared language and love of the fatherland that cements the people as one:

> People! what is a people? what does popular mean?
> Is it the nose or the mouth that gives it away?
> Is there a people hidden from the average eye in burial hills and
> behind bushes, in every body, big and boney?
> They belong to a people who think they do,
> those who can hear the Mother tongue,
> those who love the Fatherland
> The rest are separated from the people, expel themselves,
> do not belong.[52]

His long and eventually successful campaign to establish the *folkelig højskole* (Folk High School) in Denmark was part of this nationalist endeavour.[53] These schools were to provide the edification and enlightenment of the people and thereby raise their sense of national belonging; members of all classes would be admitted, the education was intended to further spiritual development rather than open up avenues of social mobility, and national history was prioritised on the syllabus.

The project of revitalising and nurturing the true Danish spirit through the establishment of *folkehøjskoler* and the co-operative movement concurred with the wide-scale movement to cultivate barren land following the substantial losses of Danish territory in the nineteenth century (first in the Napoleonic wars and then the 1848 and 1864 wars with Prussia). The phrase 'Outward loss, inward gain' ('Hvad udad tabes, skal indad vindes') that was adopted as the rallying cry for this new campaign to farm barren heath country shows clearly the relation between these geographical and spiritual projects.[54] This also gave rise to the popular perception that, seen retrospectively, the ceding of territories in the wars with Prussia (now mythologised in Danish national self-perception) was, in fact, loss turned into gain as it led to a much more homogeneous (that is, more harmonious) nation state. Danish nationalist discourse thus tends to proclaim modest forms of national greatness—the achievements of a small country, its homogeneous culture and the virtues of *folkelighed*.

This form of modesty ('Papa's humble pride') in Danish national self-perception is perhaps best understood in relation to the 'unassuming' character of *folkelighed*. Such humility should not be understood as a lack of national pride but, on the contrary, a manifestation of a deep-felt pride in Denmark precisely because of its modest size and appearance (hence the common and widespread phrase, 'this is a small country...').[55] The implication is, of course, that whilst it is easy to be enticed by the stunningly beautiful, there is something more virtuous and genuine in the love for 'flat and boring' Denmark, and consequently that the values of Danish-ness, epitomised by the concept of *folkelighed*, are not superficial but deeply embedded in the homogeneous national culture. The codification of this humbleness (based on the *folkelig* demand of equality) in national self-perception is *Janteloven*, which has been described as 'the "modernised" Ten Commandments of social morality—Danes are admonished to think nothing of themselves, not to set themselves above others, always to keep a low and humble profile. Today they apply this yardstick rigorously to the EC'[56]—in other words, *Janteloven* also implies the view inherent in nationalist discourse, that *others should not think they are better than us.*

Smilla takes issue with this type of narcissistic nationalism, not only through the use of irony (e.g. in the Sonne passages), but also by showing that such 'humble pride' in the supposed homogeneity of the nation, in the belief that the people are as one, is a disavowal of difference. In the scene in which Smilla is interrogated by representatives of the Danish bureaucratic machinery, the phrases 'In a little country like ours...' and 'Danish territory' (90) are contrasted. In this instance, the former indicates the nationalist belief in an homogeneous people living within the boundaries of the nation-space, whereas the latter is to be understood as the geographical regions that lie under Danish jurisdiction including, of course, Greenland. Here, the point being made is simply that, irrespective of whether or not she carries a Danish passport, Smilla will never be considered a full-blooded member of the imagined Danish community.

So although *Smilla* can be read as an attempt to battle against the narcissistic belief in Danish homogeneity (and its exclusionary impulse), the organic, organic, pre-modern societies of Greenland and Denmark are praised, albeit ironically in the case of the latter, for their autonomous and innocent condition—the condition prior to the experience of colonialism which left Greenland in a state of total dependence, performing a hazardous 'tightrope dance' on a line held up by its colonial benefactor (79). It is clear that the text presents *both* cultures—coloniser and colonised—as having fallen victim to the dark forces of modernity. Following this line of thought one could argue, and it seems to be intimated in the novel, that the return to a pre-colonial (and pre-modern) state of inno-cence would thus make possible the meeting of cultures on more equal terms. Of course, there's no going back to before the Fall, so to speak, but the claim that under certain circumstances it may be possible for different cultures to co-exist harmoniously needs further consideration.

Confronting the Danish reader with her colonial past and its present implications, Høeg hopes, perhaps, that she will not only acknowledge and repent the evils of colonialism, but also learn to respect Inuit culture as equal, albeit very different from Dan-ish/Western culture. On the one hand, through the text's ironic treatment of Sonne, this reader (who will certainly be familiar with, and perhaps even cemented into, the popular fictions of Danish national identity) is forced to re-think the myth of naïve innocence attached to the Danish colonial project, along with the dominant myth of an originary Danish identity. On the other hand, the reader is urged at the same time to recuperate those well-meaning, 'honourable intentions', represented by the figure of Sonne, that have been lost amid the sea of greed and corruption in the passage between Denmark and Greenland. Such 'honourable intentions' are, of course, sprung out of an essentially liberal ideal of respect and tolerance for cultural and ethnic diversity. In fact, the liberal position, which promotes cultural pluralism or cultural diversity, is one of the few relatively stable and constant view-points running through the novel. Not only is the argument made repeatedly against forms of discriminatory exclusion and for greater tolerance, but also against the total assimilation of minority cultures into the host society.

This is perhaps made most clear in the novel's repeated criticism of the Danish policies of the 1960s which, 'led to Green-land officially becoming 'Denmark's northernmost county', and the Inuit were officially supposed to be called 'Northern Danes' and 'be educated to the same rights as all other Danes', as the prime minister put it' (105). What is objected to here is not the egalitarian principle itself, but the fact that the Inuit were to be *'educated'* to equal rights—it is the project of assimilation, of Danification (illustrated by the character of Licht, the defector) which is so passionately condemned. As 'Northern Danes' the Inuit are discursively subsumed under the Danish nation[57] and denied a standpoint from which to articulate their difference—any potential threat to the dominant culture is remedied through methods of assimilatory inclusion. In *Smilla*, this ruthless eradica-tion of indigenous cultures by assimilatory practices is regarded as the inevitable result of the total absence of respect for other forms of life; the schoolteachers, we are told, 'didn't know one word of Greenlandic, nor did they have any plans to learn it' (105).

The critique of Danish imperialism in *Smilla* is, in fact, based on the liberal ideal of respect for the equality of cultures (which makes 'grading meaningless' [169]) that has been advocated by, amongst others, Charles Taylor. This liberal position, which provides the basis for the promotion of cultural diversity or pluralism, reifies the notion of monolithic cultures which have existed and will continue to exist over long periods of time,[58] and serves to retain the idea of solid pre-given ethnic identities which can be held on to or lost:

> Cultural diversity is the recognition of pre-given cultural contents and customs; held in a time-frame of relativism it gives rise to liberal notions of multiculturalism, cultural exchange or the culture of humanity. Cultural diversity is also the representation of a radical rhetoric of the separation of totalized cultures that live unsullied by the intertextuality of their historical locations, safe in the Utopianism of a mythic memory of a unique collective identity.[59]

It upholds, and not without a certain optimism, the idea that in any society it is possible, by promoting a model of political consensus based on cultural diversity, for two unified, homogeneous cultures to peacefully co-exist. That the text subscribes to this notion of the harmonious co-existence of different, self-generated cultures is perhaps most obvious if one considers the figure of Isaiah. But it also protests 'the classic Danish persecution of those who are different' (77), and demands 'tolerance' for the 'guests' who ask for it (169). In other words, the reader is urged to accept cultural diversity so that there will be no reason for Danes and Greenlanders to 'poorly…understand each other' (79), and consequently, so that any antagonisms can be resolved and everyone can live in peace and harmony in the pursuit of common goals.

However, the problem with the multiculturalist view is that in practice this consensus is based on the expectation that minorities should adjust to the norms of the dominant culture. As Bhabha states, 'although there is always an entertainment and encouragement of cultural diversity, there is always also a corresponding containment of it'.[60] In practice, cultural diversity is only accepted as long as it does not challenge the cultural and political priorities of the dominant group. The dominant ethnic group imposes its norms and values on minorities and thereby contains and regulates the articulation of cultural difference. Liberal pluralism thus becomes a model for assimilatory inclusion (cultural difference made safe for the dominant culture); the multicultural society allows ethnic minorities to retain certain cultural practices (but only in the private sphere—*let them wear their* kamiks *on Sundays*), whilst its rhetoric masks ideologies of racist supremacy.

Re-constituting Denmark: 'a small country ... '

The issues at stake in the analysis of *Smilla* offered here are perhaps best seen in connection with the prolific ongoing debate on immigration in Denmark—a debate which has intensified in the years following the publication of Høeg's novel.[61] This debate basically concerns the question of how to deal with the problem of the new and rapidly growing foreign element in the otherwise homogeneous and harmonious whole of Danish society.[62] As it is presented, in the mainstream media representation, largely as an issue of how to tackle the social problems that inevitably arise with a clash of incompatible cultures, the important factor of Danish nationalism in the debate is barely recognised. This lack of recognition (or disavowal) can also be seen as a function of the paradox lying within the nationalist discourse which upholds the belief in Denmark as an egalitarian and tolerant country, a model of democracy and social welfare. Pia Kjærsgaard, Leader of the far-right nationalist Danish People's Party (*Dansk Folkeparti*) has stated, 'The tendency towards the fanatical right-wing is un-Danish, and therefore I don't think we will have [such] problems'.[63] Similarly, that nationalist discourse operates as a mask for racist ideology is most often met with a flat denial from most sides of the political spectrum.[64]

The debate on the immigration problem, which dominated the agenda in both the local (November 1997) and general elections (March 1998), has generally been characterised by the articulation of two basic positions; the first demands the (preferably total) exclusion of immigrants from Denmark, and the second liberal view, supported by the majority, seeks a solution through the integration of minority groups into Danish society. The first position is based on the argument that refugees and immigrants should be expelled because they do not belong (and is often stated aggressively).[65] The scope of support given to this position is indicated by the rise of the recently instituted Danish People's Party which devoted its election campaigns almost entirely to this issue, and the adoption of a hard-line policy on immigration by the Social Democratic Party.[66]

The demand for the expulsion of refugees and immigrants is, of course, founded on a belief in the fragility or vulnerability of Danish culture, and is inextricably linked to the (Western) fear of colonisation by external forces: those advancing from the outside (the EU [particularly the Germans], the USA), and those exerting pressure internally (the outsiders living within the boundaries of the nation-space). This correlation is taken up by racist discourse which construes recent admissions of immigrants and refugees into Denmark as equivalent to an invasion by a foreign power.[67] Such concerns are not only aired by the far-right, but are often underwritten by views emanating from the broad political spectrum; for instance, in a televised electoral debate last year, the leader of the Socialist People's Party, Holger K. Nielsen's somewhat careless and hasty counter-argument to Kjærsgaard's contention that Denmark is turning into a multiethnic society, was that this is highly exaggerated because only 4-5% of the population are foreigners, and moreover, 'most of them look like you and I'.[68]

It is, of course, precisely the visibility of minority groups (racial, cultural, and political—i.e., their raising political demands) that disturbs the belief in Danish national homogeneity. Policy suggestions, therefore, typically address the question of how to decrease the visibility of minority groups; i.e., their number should be reduced (or checked), and/or they should be dispersed (spread out). Whereas right-wing nationalists tend to focus on the aggregate number of immigrants (each immigrant added makes matters worse),[69] those groups which take a more liberal stance are mostly concerned with the issue of integration—though still maintaining that Denmark is a small country and there is a limit to how many immigrants Danish society can absorb. The tightening of immigration laws has thus also been met with general approval from more moderate groups.

The second, and most popular position, the integrationist stance, is based on the liberal ideal of the equality of cultures discussed earlier: immigrants should be integrated into the labour market etc., on equal terms with Danes, but this is to be achieved on the terms of Danish society. Demands are thus frequently made of the minority groups themselves: i.e., that they must make a conscious effort to integrate themselves through learning Danish, taking various forms of education, and adapting or adjusting to certain norms and requirements of Danish society.[70] Thorkild Simonsen, Minister of the Interior, states: 'The new integration rules ... will reflect the expectations we have of the new arrivals. Efforts will be rewarded. On the other hand, there will be consequences [to face] if a foreigner does not to his ability work to become a well-functioning part of Danish society.'[71] The implication of this is that the cultural practices which are retained by minority groups will be relegated to the private sphere.

One of the major concerns for the integrationists has unsurprisingly been the importance of improving social interaction between the Danish population and immigrant groups. This generally takes the form of encouraging the admission of immigrants into existing social institutions (i.e., sports clubs, *folkehøjskoler* and other institutions of adult education). The improvement of social interaction is, of course, considered a necessary step in the absorption of minority groups into Danish society. Again, it is the question of visibility and the dispersion of number that is foregrounded here; recent discussions that have dominated the integration debate include the placement of refugees in the various *kommuner* (municipalities), the prevention of ghettoisation, and the uneven distribution in schools of children belonging to minority groups.

The integrationist demand that immigrants may retain certain cultural practices but must give up others and live by Danish norms is legitimised by two interconnected beliefs: the first relates to the notion of sovereignty and an essentialist, organic conception of the nation, and the second relates to notions of civilisation and progress and the perception that immigrants hail from 'backward' cultures. The belief that certain cultural practices are archaic is perhaps best illustrated by the discourses surrounding the scarf issue, the issue of arranged marriages, and gender roles in general.[72] In this sense, the integrationist stance takes the form of an internal benign colonisation, based on the logic of cultural supremacy: as an advanced culture, Danish society has the right (and even a duty) to educate immigrant groups who, in the long run, will be grateful for all the freedoms and opportunities that come with enlightenment and the shedding of outdated social norms— in other words, it maintains the ideal of assimilatory inclusion.

Whilst the liberal view encourages tolerance and promotes cultural diversity as a benefit to Danish society (though this usually takes the form of an appreciation of small pockets of cultural expression; i.e., music, ethnic restaurants, greengrocers), it also demands the containment of cultural difference—certain traits of cultural identity may be retained, but only as long as they do not challenge and disturb the harmonious equilibrium of Danish society. The limits of a multicultural society are made clear in the following statement by Uffe Ellemann-Jensen, former leader of the Liberal Party and Minister of Foreign Affairs:

Khomeini's death sentence over the author Salman Rushdie has made it clear to most people that there is a difference between Western and Islamic culture. We should not be afraid to say to those people from other cultures who wish to live in our country as new Danes: You can keep your own culture, but keep it to yourselves. Our society is and will continue to be built on our values. And you must respect this if you wish to live here...Our dilemma is that civilisation, human rights, freedom of speech—must be defended. But the more we entrench ourselves against barbarity, the more fragile the civilization we are trying to defend will become.[73]

It is precisely such self-complacency within Danish national identity that Høeg attempts to criticise in *Smilla*. His critique of the so-called 'benign' colonisation of Greenland attacks the belief that as a more progressed civilisation the colonising power has an historic obligation to raise peoples from 'backward' cultures to a higher level of modernity, and promotes an awareness of how Inuit culture was destroyed (though it could also be argued that as it enters the thriller genre, the novel exonerates the violence of the state by suggesting it is the activities of individuals [criminals, unscrupulous scientists, etc.] that are to be blamed). Moreover, this critique is furthered in the novel to the issue of how present-day Denmark deals with cultural difference. Here, Høeg's attention to the predicament of the postcolonial migrant should be considered alongside his ironic treatment of an originary Danish identity, and his attack on the notion of internal benign colonialism, i.e., that as a modern nation, Denmark has the right and duty to educate and assimilate immigrants from less developed societies.

In *Smilla*, the ethical stance on these issues, as we have argued, is clearly based on the tenets of Western liberalism: the demands for tolerance, equal rights, respect for cultural and ethnic diversity, etc. However, it should be remembered that it is precisely these ideals which provided a justification for colonialism (e.g., in the work of Mill and Locke), and which today form the basis for the notion of cultural diversity or pluralism. Certainly, the ambivalence in the text concerning the questions of identity and hybridity reveals a move towards an essentialism propagated by the multiculturalist view. Although Isaiah's is a story of heterogeneity which splits the Danish nation's essentialist identity and shows it—or rather, begins to attempt to show it—to be a liminal signifying space, a space marked with the discourses of minorities, the representation of hybridity in *Smilla* is one which reflects the liberal integrationist stance, which is, in practice, a model for assimilatory inclusion. Thus, whilst Høeg's narrative of post-colonial migrancy critiques the exclusionary impulse of Danish national identity, its representation of the hybrid cultural space of Copenhagen does not dismantle the fiction of nation. In the words of Spivak:

If it can be said that in cities is the sublation of the nomadic and communal living of forest and village, we have guarded that anthropological fiction in words like politics and citizenship... Yet Britain and India are still nations—a fragile rational fiction that serves well in wars, border disputes, daily suspicion, and prejudice. If in the urban public culture of the migrant these hostilities are provisionally suspended, should we declare the world in its model and predict a world-peace telos, banal as any other, in the utopian nonrecognition that the hybridization of 'national cultures'—through imperialism and development—does not resemble migrancy?[74]

Miss Smilla's Feeling for Snow touches the most sensitive chords in Danish society, and whilst most critics have tried to anaesthetise those sensitivities, our analysis has aimed to explore and interrogate the interrelated issues of colonialism, nation and migrancy that frame Høeg's novel.

Notes

All translations from Danish-language texts appearing in this paper are by the authors unless otherwise stated.

1. Peter Høeg, *Miss Smilla's Feeling For Snow*, trans. F. David (London: Harvill, 1997) 90. All further page references are to this edition and are given parenthetically.
2. V. S. Naipaul writing to Paul Theroux after a trip to Denmark in 1967.
3. For reviews which subsume the specificities of Danish colonialism under the banner of 'Western' or 'European' imperialism, see Søren Vinterberg, 'Peter Høeg's fornemmelse for kølig passion', *Politiken* 24 Apr. 1992, Liselotte Wiemer, 'Rejse på liv og død', *Det Fri Aktuelt* 24 Apr. 1992, Søren Schou, 'Spor i sneen', *Information* 24 Apr. 1992, Bjørn Bredal, 'Peter Høeg's fornemmelse for is', *Weekendavisen* 24 Apr. 1992. For those which consider Smilla's hybridity as an essentially psychological function, see Preben Meulengracht, 'En eminent spændingsroman', *Jyllands-Posten* 24 Apr. 1992. Lars Bukdal, in his review, 'Romanen med de rigtige meninger', *Kristeligt Dagblad* 24 Apr. 1992, complains that *Smilla's* critique of society is redundant or obsolete as it 'never gets a dynamic function in the novel when it all just fizzles out with a mad professor'. There is certainly a point to be made here—a great deal of Høeg's social criticism is abandoned in the later part of the novel where the thriller genre takes over. The ambitious project Høeg sets out with appears to falter half-way through the text when the focus turns away from a consideration of the violence of the nation-state and we are left with a portrayal of Smilla (as heroine) doing battle with a few greedy, self-serving individuals (the culprits). However, by no means does this render the critique of Danish imperialism and contemporary Danish society in the earlier sections of the novel irrelevant.
4. See Sara Danius's reviews, 'Fröken Smilla skakar om', *Dagens Nyheter* 18 June 1994, and 'Bortom Öresund: Peter Høeg följer en postkolonial karta', *Dagens Nyheter* 28 July 1994.
5. Bo Jansson, 'En postmoderne undergangsvision', *Spring* 7 (1994): 145.
6. Ola Larssmo quoted in Jansson, 'En postmoderne undergangsvision'.
7. In another review, Søren Schou writes '*Smilla* is an account of imperialism in the period that, with a comforting lie of necessity, we have christened the post-colonial', a novel 'about the present-day cultural conflicts between centre and periphery' ('Spor i sneen', *Information* 24 Apr. 1992).
8. Homi K. Bhabha, *The Location of Culture* (London: Routledge, 1994) 6.
9. Jan Kanstrup and Steen Ousager, 'Kolonihistoriens kilder', *Grønland* 36.2/3 (1988): 51.

10. Harry Haue, Jørgen Olsen and Jørn Aarup-Kristensen, *Det ny Danmark: 1890-1980* (Copenhagen: Munksgaard, 1983) 295.
11. See Lucien Febvre, 'Civilization: Evolution of a Word and a Group of Ideas', *A New Kind of History: From the Writings of Febvre*, ed. Peter Burke (London, 1973). For a critique of the discourse of development, see Arturo Escobar, *Encountering Development* (Princeton: Princeton UP, 1995).
12. W. Dreyer, *Den hvide races sejrsgang* (Copenhagen: Gyldendalske Boghandel, 1909) 492-93. Today, the most common Danish stereotype of Greenlanders is still that of the dependent alcoholic—and is represented in *Smilla* by the character Juliane.
13. Kaj Birket-Smith, *Eskimoerne* (Copenhagen: Gyldendalske Boghandel, 1927) 234. See also Birket-Smith, 'The Eskimos: Denmark's Formula for World's Northernmost Outpost', *Unesco Courier* 8-9 (1954): 19-21. Here, Birket-Smith praises the 'feeling of responsibility which has always characterised Denmark's attitude towards Greenland' and refers to the growth of the Eskimo population as evidence of the successes of Danish colonisation.
14. The Danish word *hvid* means 'white'.
15. Here we are drawing on Thomas Richards, *The Imperial Archive: Knowledge and the Fantasy of Empire* (London: Verso, 1993). See particularly his Introduction and Chapter 1.
16. This included, of course, the kidnapping of Eskimos. Jens Bielke offers an eye-witness description of the first Greenlanders' arrival in Denmark with the following description of their appearance:

De var grumme af natur,	They were ugly by nature,
små var de ud af statur,	they were small in stature,
ravsorte udaf skæg og hår,	raven-black of beard and hair,
dog de ganske lidet skæg får.	though they very little beard grow.
Deres hoved var stort og bredt,	Their heads were big and wide,
deres kindben glinsed' af fedt,	their cheekbones shone with grease,
deres ben var stakked' og små,	their legs were stocky and small,
et under, de på dem kan stå,	a miracle that on them they can stand,
men mange må forundres mere,	but many must wonder more,
hvor de ben det hoved kan bære?	at how those legs that head can carry?
Små var deres arme også,	Small were their arms as well,
deres hud brun og mørkegrå,	their skin brown and dark grey,
deres øjne syntes fast dumme,	their eyes appeared quite stupid,
iblandt os var de meget stumme	amongst us they were very silent

(Cited in J. Kisbye Møller, 'Jens Bielkes grønlandsberetning 1605', *Grønland* 33.5/6/7 [1985]: 131-32.)
17. For a history of the museum and the development of anthropology in Denmark see Ole Høiris, *Antropologien i Danmark: museal etnografi og etnologi 1860-1960* (Copenhagen: Nationalmuseet, 1986).
18. Following Home Rule in 1979, negotiations began concerning the return of archaeological, anthropological and historical materials collected in Greenland.
19. Birket-Smith, *Eskimoerne* 41. The last part of this citation has been omitted in a later edition of this book ([Copenhagen: Rhodos, 1971] 44). Further changes to this section of the book in the later edition include the omission of a

21. It may also be worth considering how in contemporary popular culture, Norse, Viking and Teutonic mythology has become an iconographic means establishing a 'lineage' for the beleaguered European diaspora (specifically non-native Americans) as in the case of motorcycle gangs and sections of heavy metal graphics which invoke horned helmets, broadswords and blond braids as an alternative 'history'.

23. See Høiris, *Antropologien*, and Bente Dam-Mikkelsen and Torben Lundbæk, eds, *Ethnographic Objects in The Royal Danish* Kunstkammer *1650-1800* (Copenhagen: Nationalmuseet, 1980). Following the loss of the 1864 war with Prussia and the promotion of an inward-looking gaze ('outward loss, inward gain'), the ethnographic section (which had developed from one of the world's earliest ethnographic museums established by C. J. Thomsen in 1841) lost its financial backing and was turned into a subdivision of the archaeological section.

29. However, it is important to note that colonial power is never entirely hegemonic, as some of the passages concerning surveillance in *Smilla* seem to imply. Such a monolithic view of power which supports the binaries coloniser/colonised, oppressor/oppressed should be reconceptualised, as Ranajit Guha argues in his work on colonial Indian history, *Dominance Without Hegemony: History and Power in Colonial India* (Cambridge, MA: Harvard UP, 1997). Within any power structure there is always space for resistance, just as in maps there are spaces or gaps between the tracks and boundaries in which the native/colonial subject may hide. Such spaces for resistance are made visible in the novel by its representation of the colonised subject as agent—i.e., in the actions of Smilla's mother and Smilla herself.

34. Benedict Anderson, *Imagined Communities: Reflections on the Origin and Spread of Nationalism* (London: Verso, 1991). Relating Anderson's work to this theme of the recognition of a fellow Greenlander raises interesting questions about the distinction between an ethnic group and a national group: does their

potential 'deep horizontal friendship' depend on whether Greenland is considered to be *de jure* a nation?

35. This should be considered in terms of the construction of woman as 'other', and polar opposites in phallogocentric Western discourse. Teresa de Lauretis writes: 'A feminist frame of reference ... it seems to me cannot be either "man" or "woman", for both of these are constructs of a male-centered discourse, both are the products of "the straight mind"... neither the Man with the capital M of humanism, or the lower case man of modernism: nor on the other hand, woman as the opposite or the complement of man...' ('Issues, Terms and Contexts', *Feminist Studies/Critical Studies*, ed. Teresa de Lauretis [Bloomington: Indiana UP, 1986] 13).

36. For a discussion of 'newness' and the hybrid cultural space see Bhabha, *Location* 7.

37. For a full discussion of hybridity and racial difference, see Robert J. C. Young, *Colonial Desire: Hybridity in Theory, Culture and Race* (London: Routledge, 1995).

38. Bhabha, *Location* 110.

39. Bhabha, *Location* 25, 4.

40. Bhabha, *Location* 227.

41. Homi K. Bhabha, 'DissemiNation: Time, Narrative, and the Margins of the Modern Nation', *Nation and Narration*, ed. Bhabha (London: Routledge, 1995) 318.

42. Bhabha, 'DissemiNation' 318.

43. Thorkild Simonsen, 'Tolerancens vilkår i Danmarks hyggekrog', *Ekstra-Bladet* 20 Feb. 1998.

44. Anderson 6.

45. Geoffrey Bennington, 'Postal Politics and the Institution of the Nation', *Nation and Narration*, ed. Bhabha, 121.

46. Bhabha, *Location* 15.

47. Homi K. Bhabha, 'The Third Space: Interview with Homi Bhabha', *Identity, Community, Culture, Difference*, ed. J. Rutherford (London: Lawrence and Winshart, 1990) 210-11.

48. Homi K. Bhabha, 'Culture's In-Between', *Questions of Cultural Identity*, ed. Stuart Hall and Paul du Gay (London: Sage, 1996) 57.

49. The White Cells is translated from the Danish 'Det hvide snit'. Translated directly, this means 'frontal lobotomy'. This metaphor appears to extend the theme of the colonialist probing of indigenous bodies, to that of the disciplining of the bodies of the marginalised in modern societies.

50. The irony at play here is further brought out in Sonne's name, which has certain connotations in Danish: he shares his name with the 'golden age' painter Jørgen V. Sonne (1801-90), and also with Christian Sonne, founder of the first *brugsforening* (co-operative) in Thisted, 1866.

51. Kaj Thaning quoted in Steven M. Borish, *The Land of the Living: The Danish Folk High Schools and Denmark's Non-Violent Path to Modernization* (Nevada City, CA: Blue Dolphin,1991) 306.

52. N. F. S. Grundtvig, *Folkelighed* (1848), cited in Uffe Østergård, 'Peasants and Danes: Danish National Identity and Political Culture', Interdisciplinary

Workshop on the National Experience, U of Lund, Dept of European Ethnology, 18-20 Oct. 1990: 32-33 (his translation).

53. That the establishment of the *folkelig højskole* in Denmark was as much about a battle over minds as the education of the common people is clear when one considers that the first *højskole* was opened in 1844 in Rødding, in the region of Slesvig. Throughout the nineteenth century this region was contested territory, marked by ethnic conflict and a strong secessionist movement. In 1864, Slesvig was lost to Prussia; the northern part of Slesvig was returned by referendum to Denmark in 1920. In 1865, the Rødding *højskole* was relocated in Askov, just north of the new border with Prussia (Borish 193).

54. This connection is made by Borish: 'The term "inward" is apparently used in a dual sense, meaning both internal to the country (within Danish borders) and internal to the heart and mind of the individual Dane' (14). In the light of the expansionist nationalisms of the nineteenth century, Borish regards this as a commendable trait of the Danish national character.

55. Østergård uses the term 'humble assertiveness' to describe such humility: 'We know we are the best, therefore we don't have to brag about it', and identifies 'a note of flat-hill self-satisfaction' in a song by Grundtvig:

> Far whiter mountains shine splendidly forth
> Than the hills of our native islands,
> But, we Danish rejoice in the quiet North
> For our lowlands and rolling highlands.
> No peaks towered over our birth:
> It suits us best to remain on earth.
> [...]
> Even more of the ore, so white and so red [the colours of the flag—*Østergård*]
> Others might have gotten mountains in exchange
> For the Dane, however, the daily bread is found
> no less in the hut of the poor man;
> when few have to much and fewer to little
> then truly we have become wealthy.

(Grundtvig, 'Langt højere Bjerge', 1820; Østergård, 'Peasants and Danes, 19 and 28, his translation.)

A more recent example can be seen in an article by Bertel Haarder, former Minister of Education; 'We can go to Norway and feel disappointed about being born in a flat and boring country. But if once, as a child, one has reclined behind a barn at sunset, with the scent of hay and peas and the singing of the lark, then one can understand the poet who wrote, "I think it is most beautiful in Denmark"' ('Hvad Truer Det Danske?', *Uddannelse* 24.8/9 [1991]: 483).

56. Ulf Hedetoft, *Euro-Nationalism: Or How the EC Affects the Nation-State as a Repository of Identity* (Aalborg: Aalborg U, 1990) 23.

57. It may be interesting to note that because Greenlanders today are registered by birthplace, rather than by ethnic group, there is a lack of precise statistical data on the cultural division of labour, inter-marriage, migration etc., as

indicators of the relations between the ethnic groups, thus obscuring social biases.

58. Bhabha, 'Culture's In-Between' 57.
59. Bhabha, *Location* 34.
60. Bhabha, 'Third Space' 208.
61. It should be pointed out that in the popular imagination Greenlanders are not considered to be 'immigrants' in the same sense as, e.g., Turks, Somalians and Bosnians. This is probably due less to any 'feelings of responsibility' Danes may hold towards Greenlanders, than to the fact that Greenlanders are not regarded as a 'threat' to Danish cultural norms and values because (a) they constitute a relatively small group (there is no fear of being 'swamped' by Greenlanders), (b) the longstanding relationship between Denmark and Greenland makes the presence of Greenlanders in Denmark expected, and (c) Greenlanders have already to a large degree been assimilated into Danish culture.
62. The confusion over what terms should be applied to minority groups is illuminating: *indvandrere/flygtninge* ('immigrants'/'refugees'), *de fremmede* ('aliens'/'foreigners'), *andengenerationsindvandrere* ('second-generation immigrants'), *danskere med en etnisk baggrund* ('Danes with an ethnic background'), *etniske danskere* ('ethnic Danes') and *nydanskere* ('new Danes'). Hyphenated terms have also come into usage, e.g., *dansk-tyrkere*, *dansk-tamiler*.
63. Cited in 'Gud, Konge og Kjærsgaard' *Børsens Nyhedsmagasin* 7 Mar. 1997: 40.
64. The idea that racism is not a widespread problem in Denmark, but is limited to the behaviour of a few individuals is common. See, for instance, Borish's treatment of racism in Denmark in *The Land of the Living*.
65. Tom Behnke, MP, *Fremskridtspartiet* ('The Progress Party') infamously suggested on television news that if Somalia continued to deny access to refugees who were not granted asylum by Denmark, they could be equipped with parachutes and dropped over their homeland. For a repetition of his statement, see Ole Birk Olesen, 'Smid dem ud med faldskærm' ['Throw them out with parachutes'], *Ekstra-Bladet* 30 Aug. 1997.
66. This led to the sacking of Birte Weiss as Minister of the Interior. Her replacement, Thorkild Simonsen, was believed to be tougher on immigration.
67. This view is stated clearly, for example, in the full-page manifesto entitled 'Warning!' in which the anonymous authors state: 'There is no difference between the consequences of a military invasion and ensuing massive civil takeover, and the massive civil takeover which is currently taking place through the de facto immigration of foreigners' (*Danskeren* 8.1 [1994]: 13).
68. 'Partilederrunde', DR 1, 19 Feb. 1998. Thorkild Simonsen makes a similar statement: 'In the statistics, the—perhaps—anonymous Swiss counts as much as the—perhaps—colourful Somalian.' ('Tolerancens vilkår').
69. See, for instance, *Ekstra-Bladet*'s free special issue 'De fremmede', June 1997. This was launched with a TV advertising campaign that featured a queue of immigrants, the sound of a cash till ringing, and the newspaper's logo written in Arabic script. Such paranoia is fuelled by almost daily reports in the press about how many *grænseoverløbere* (illegal immigrants) have been caught attempting to cross the Danish border.

70. The Jews are generally considered as a success story of integration into Danish society. However, their integration was essentially effected by the Jewish community's decision to adopt Danish norms. Those cultural practices that were not sanctioned by Danish society were relegated to the private sphere. A law adopted in 1814 laid the foundation for the integration of the Jewish community: 'The law...amongst other things, demanded that the Jews follow the country's laws on inheritance, social security and education. Legal documents of marriage and testaments should be written in Danish or German and without the use of the Jewish calendar. Furthermore, as a precondition for achieving civil rights, it was demanded that young people would take an examination in Jewish faith comparable to confirmation in the Christian church' (Benito Scocozza and Grethe Jensen, *Danmarks Historiens Hvem, Hvad og Hvornår* [Copenhagen: Politiken, 1994] 204.)

71. Simonsen, 'Tolerancens vilkår'.

72. One striking example of the belief in archaic cultural practices is a statement by Frode Muldkjær, Chairman of the Children's Council: 'A special target campaign is necessary because a proportion of ethnic families live in a culture of violence and beating. Not that we should necessarily point fingers at it. We did it that way too only 60 or 70 years ago, we've just reached further in the humane development that started when men stopped hitting women with clubs' (*Politiken* 29 Mar. 1997).

73. Uffe Ellemann-Jensen, 'Vor tids største problem: vores forhold til "fremmede"', *Liberal* 1 (1994) 14.

74. Gayatri C. Spivak, *Outside in the Teaching Machine* (New York: Routledge, 1993) 252.

Jati: Translating India

Mahesh Daga

[T]he surest sign that a group or society has entered into the self-conscious possession of a new concept is … that a corresponding vocabulary will be developed, a vocabulary which can then be used to pick out and discuss the concept with consistency … The possession of a concept will at least standardly be signalled by the employment of a corresponding term.[1]

Each concept is associated with a word, but not every word is a social and political concept … A concept is … more than a word: a word becomes a concept when the plenitude of a politicosocial context of meaning and the experience in and for which a word is used can be condensed into one word.[2]

Introduction: The Language of *Jatiyata*

It is a safe bet that a present-day (literate) inhabitant of India will experience little difficulty or hesitation, either linguistic or conceptual, in naming her national identity. If Hindi-speaking, she will describe herself as *Bharatiya*, it being understood that the term simply refers to a citizen of India,[3] an Indian national *simpliciter*, irrespective of her religion, language, caste or any other, more particular, allegiances. It may be difficult to imagine, therefore, that barely a century ago this secular term of seeming antiquity did not appear as self-evident and natural a way of self-description as it does today—not even to the 'advanced' nationalists of the time. In the last quarter of the late 19th century, most Hindi publicists did not see, much less describe, themselves as *Bharatiya*. In its contemporary noun-form, the term *Bharatiya* very rarely received a mention in their language of public communication.[4] Indeed, at the turn of the last century, there was no popular linguistic equivalent

Translating Nations, ed. Prem Poddar, *The Dolphin* 30, pp. 203-47.
© 1999 by Aarhus University Press, Denmark.
ISBN 87 7288 381 2; ISSN 0106 4487.

for the conceptual term *Bharatiya* in the socio-political language of the Hindi-speaking world.[5]

Parallel to this, there was a yet more significant omission. In contemporary discourse, the concept of nation is popularly glossed by the term *rashtra*. In the last quarter of the 19th century this term was very seldom invoked in Hindi-language public discourse.[6] The most frequently used term that denoted the idea of nation was the generic term *jati*. This novel usage of the term existed, quite unproblematically, alongside its other older existing usages, the most important of which continued to be that of referring to a specific caste group.

Defining a nation, one assumes these days, presupposes the idea of a people. In the current vocabulary, one speaks of *janata*—a term of sufficient generality that embraces the people of the entire Indian nation. This term too entered the lexicon of Hindi public discourse relatively recently. Although I cannot claim to put a precise date on its first usage, it was definitely not part of the public vocabulary in the closing decades of the 19th century. At that time, the term which came closest to signifying the concept of a people was *prajah*. Unlike *janata*, the meaning of the term *prajah* was conceptually linked to the idea of *raja* or 'king'. And despite the change of political system in colonial times, it continued to remain conceptually tied to the idea of subjecthood to a king. In other words, it could not allow one to speak of a people in its contemporary meaning—as an entity in its own right, distinct from a political and state system.

This paper is devoted to a discussion of what has been thought to be one of the central categories of public discourse in late-19th-century colonial India, that of *jati* or nation. The questions I shall raise are: did 19th-century Hindi publicists operate with a determinate, coherent conception of nation, and if so, what was the conceptual basis for the construction of this community? What principles of inclusion and exclusion were at work, and how did this conception of a nation reconcile and accommodate the claims of the different groups and communities?

It will be evident from what I have said so far that in contrast to other historical studies on the question of nationalist discourse in India the methodological approach I follow focuses a great deal on the language and conceptual vocabulary of public discourse. I will seek to demonstrate that the ambiguities and confusions surrounding the question of *jati*-as-nation in the earlier period, i.e. the late 19th century, far from being any sign of arbitrariness, derive as much from the linguistic–conceptual vocabulary available to the Hindi publicists as any other external determinants, and, importantly, that the changes that take place in this vocabulary of public discourse, in a long and slow historical process that begins in the early years of the present century and spans the next couple of decades, is symptomatic of crucial changes in the conception of the nation itself.

Translating Communities: *Jati* as 'Nation'

Recent historical inquiries into the conceptual contours of Indian nationalism in the late 19th century have concurred on two basic points: first, that in defining the boundaries of the nation, there was a considerable uncertainty or, to put it more positively, 'provisionality' in earlier public discourse.[7] Evidence of this, it has been remarked, can often be found in the writings of the same individual. Thus, to take a much-rehearsed example from 19th-century colonial Bengal, the *littérateur* Bankimchandra variously defined his nation as Bengali, Aryan, Hindu and so on.[8] Since historians have, almost as a rule, omitted to consider the conceptual implications of this, it is more or less implied that this evident *tentativeness*, inconsistent and contradictory as it may seem to a modern observer, need cause us no special difficulty of interpretation. It appears to be generally assumed that the task of defining a nation in a society as diverse, complex and vast as India should be attended with so much initial hesitation or confusion.[9]

The second point, alluded to earlier, is that the term that was used to express the idea of the nation—*jati*—was a generic one. Historians have noted the widely different senses in which this term was used in the 19th century: the same term could in different contexts and uses refer to a caste, a race, a religion, a linguistic community, not to speak of the whole of humanity (*manushya jati*).[10] Does this diversity of usage complicate or inflect, or even compromise, the emerging identity of the nation? This question, too, has not been seen to be particularly interesting or relevant.

What has engaged the interest of historians is the question of what this diversity and fluidity of usage might reveal about pre-modern social vocabularies. In this context, it has been remarked that this 'polyphony' in the uses of *jati* is emblematic of the 'richness' of pre-modern social vocabularies and, by implication, pre-modern notions of community. The argument is that the modern notion of enumerated community—a result of colonial (modern) classificatory and enumerative procedures, an aspect of modern technologies of governance—led to an 'impoverishment' of the earlier supple sense of community reflected in the plural denotations of the term *jati*.[11] Partha Chatterjee has summed up the argument in his usual succinct manner:

One could, obviously and without any contradiction, belong to several *jati*, not simultaneously, but contextually, *invoking* in each context a collectivity in which membership is *not* a matter of self-interested individual *choice* or contractual agreement but an immediate inclusion, originary, as it is by birth.[12]

Whether or not one agrees with Chatterjee's argument that there was little logical contradiction in extending the use of the term *jati* to include the community called 'nation',[13] it is certain that this community was very unlike any pre-modern forms of community hitherto denoted by the term, including the community of caste. The questions, therefore, are: How is one to make sense of the Hindi publicists' attempt to generate a wholly new kind of meaning for an older term? Does it mean that they did not think the nation was in principle any different from other existing or older forms of community? Or were they forced to take recourse to this term only because their socio-political language did not provide them with a credible alternative? Or, finally, was it a self-conscious conceptual innovation that invited a future in which other senses of the term would become more marginal or subordinate to its new meaning—or was the whole process more or less methodologically unselfconscious?

I think any conceptual understanding or history of the term *jati* (as 'nation') must address itself to these questions. Yet these questions have not been raised, much less answered. Whatever the reasons for this silence, it has resulted in important methodological elisions, the most significant of which, from the point of view of this study, is the failure to take into account the methodological point that the language or concepts of public discourse are neither a simple embodiment of the users' intentions, consciousness, etc., nor do they reflect, in any straightforward manner, (changing) social and political worlds. They are ontologically prior to and constitutive of both.

Before moving on to a more substantive consideration of the idea of *jati*, let me dwell a little on some of the problems that must be acknowledged in trying to interpret 19th-century public discourse on *jati* from the standpoint of conceptual history. First, there is the problem of a bilingual (colonial) context. Terms used in non-English languages are often implicated in two very different, but not disjointed, semantic and conceptual structures. This dual context of signification implies that terms like *jati, desh* or *samaj*, to cite random examples, derive their meanings not only from their location within the conceptual structure of Hindi but also partly from their role as stand-in terms for concepts that originated in the English language. Something of this semantic and conceptual duality is indicated in the following remarks of a 19th-century Hindi publicist:

Jatiya gaurav—this is an expression which is now frequently used in the speech and writings of those who are conversant with both English and Sanskrit but if you ask some one who is proficient in Sanskrit alone he will tell you that what this phrase refers to is the pride or greatness of one's own caste. But amongst the English-educated or those amongst whom thoughts characteristic of that language have been familiar this phrase is used in a wholly unique way. By jatiya gaurav they do not mean the pride of any one particular caste amongst the Hindus but the honour and prestige of the entire Hindu samaj *community*, or, even, the whole prajah [*subject-population*] of India.[14]

This passage gives an idea, albeit in a very preliminary way, of the difficulties that attend the task of rigorously defining the distinction between word and concept in a colonial context. From a methodological point of view, an historical concept cannot be said to have emerged in a language unless the latter incorporates within it what historian Richard Koselleck describes as 'a sufficient generality and plenitude of meaning'. How then is one to regard a word like *jati* in its new linguistic role of connoting a nation? Does the mere fact of this use grant it the status of a historical concept or does it remain a mere word in its new incarnation?[15] The problem is particularly acute in 19th-century Hindi discourse, as, driven by the need to create a socio-political language suitable for the quick-changing social and political conditions, this was a time of constant experimentation with new and existing terms.

Koselleck's caveat about concepts being a 'concentrate of several substantial meanings' is rephrased, in slightly different terms, in Quentin Skinner's claim that the self-conscious presence of a new concept in historical discourse is 'standardly' signified by the emergence of a corresponding vocabulary. It is therefore possible to ask if there is a minimal vocabulary in whose absence it is theoretically difficult, if not logically impossible, to speak of the concept of nation in a self-conscious way. Applied to the modern concept of nation, this plenitude of meaning (Koselleck) or new vocabulary (Skinner) would probably have to include the following elements: the idea of a people, territory, a common past or history, some form of shared culture, and, not least, political power.

At the very minimum, the conceptual premise of an *Indian* nation presupposes the logically prior idea of an Indian people. However, as I said earlier, in the socio-political lexicon of the late-19th-century Hindi-speaking world, there exists no linguistic (or conceptual) equivalent for the term 'Indian'. [16] Nor is there a term of a sufficient generality that corresponds to the notion of people in its modern, plebeian sense. To reiterate: the difficulty with the term *prajah* is that it can be used only in relation to that of the ruler.[17] The idea of a people, on the contrary, denotes precisely that conceptual separation characteristic of modern politics, between the realm of the state and civil society. It is only in the 20th century that a term which translates the idea of people in the non-statist sense, *Janata*, has come into currency.[18]

The failure to distinguish between community and nation (or the frequent slippage from one to the other) has in some measure to do with the fact that the conceptual vocabulary of the Hindi publicists did not allow for this distinction. But even this somewhat overstates the case, for it is far from clear that they consistently intended to separate the two conceptually in the first place. In the absence of a notion that corresponded to the idea of the nation as distinct from community, the only linguistic possibility was to use the same term *jati* in more inclusive and exclusive senses. The problem with this was that it could only be done contextually and not always in a less than ambiguous manner. Trying to give a new meaning to the term *jati* was not successful since it carried with it a diachronic structure of meanings.[19]

In one sense the vicissitudes surrounding the concept of *jati* as 'nation' are paralleled in the prevailing terms of discourse in the English language. There was both a considerable fluidity and a studied casualness in the usage of the term *nation* in the discourse of 19th-century colonial administrators. On the one hand, terms such as *race, people* and *nation*—often in their plural forms—were quite indiscriminately and interchangeably used to refer to a wide variety of groups, 'native' or otherwise. On the other hand, in concomitance with the rise of an Indian élite putatively seeking to speak on behalf of an entire nation, there was an increasing tendency throughout the late 19th century to deny the existence of even a prospective or potential Indian nation. It must be made clear that even in the language of the colonial administrators the term *nation* itself did not have the kind of conceptual precision and fixity that has come to be associated with it in this century. To cite just one example, whilst the title of the notorious 1871 tract, *The Indian Musalman*, written by W. W. Hunter, assumes an identity based on religion, Hunter variously refers to Muslims, among other things, as a 'race', a 'class', a 'community', a 'people' and a 'nationality'.[20]

Speaking of the rhetoric of constitutional discourse in Victorian England, historian James Vernon makes the observation that because this discourse 'was used strategically as a language of legitimation, it was continually reproduced in different and contrasting ways'. Interpreted this way, he goes on to add, 'it becomes difficult to conceive of the language of the constitution as a unitary discursive system, for it always intersected with other discourses, its boundaries continually shifting as it was used for different strategic purposes'. His final point is that by recognising the 'fluidity, fragility and discordances of constitutionalist discourses' the historian can avoid the teleology that creeps into studies which focus on particular subjects such as the 'working class' or 'radicalism', as there is an inherent tendency in such approaches 'to exaggerate the coherence and development of these discourses which helped construct or activate that object'.[21]

What Vernon says about the rhetoric of constitutional discourses is highly pertinent to the discourses on *jati* (as 'nation'). As with the constitutional discourse of Victorian England, the rhetoric of *jati*, or more precisely, of *jatiya unnati* (the improvement/betterment of one's *jati*),[22] provided the key language of legitimation for the Hindi publicists. Indeed, if one were forced to pick out just one crucial phrase from the discourse of Hindi publicists of that time, it must certainly be *jatiya unnati* and its cognates such as *jatiya uththan* ('upliftment') and *jatiya ekta* ('solidarity' or 'unity')—phrases that recur obsessively throughout the 19th century. What is important to note is that the complex of ideas and practices that went with *jatiya uththan* or *unnati* were highly variegated: from the question of gender and religious reform within the community to the development and propagation of a common *jatiya* language, from the issue of the ritual sacrifice of cows to inter- and intra-regional disparities between communities.

Each of these issues involved a different polemical and strategic application of the idea of *jati*,[23] and the discourse of *jati* was therefore continually reproduced in different and contrasting ways, precluding the emergence of a unitary discursive system. Not surprisingly, each different use introduced a very different definition of *jati*. Thus in the context of community reforms, it was *jati*-as-caste that was foregrounded;[24] in the movement for the propagation of Hindi, it was the community of north Indian Hindus that was the principal addressee; the question of the protection of cows rhetorically included a much wider Hindu community where inter-provincial frictions could underscore the regional basis of *jati*.[25] It was only in matters involving a greater political representation of the non-white 'natives' that the idea of *jati* tended to encompass the whole of the *prajah* or subject-population of India.

It is impossible for me to provide here a full panoply of examples to illustrate all the different ways in which the discourse of *jati unnati* was invoked and consequently the varied forms of *jatiya* identity that were put forward. Nor is it necessary to do so. Notwithstanding the proliferating uses of *jatiya* discourse throughout the 19th century, from the perspective of *jati*-as-nation not all of these diverse uses are equally significant. Some were contained within the pre-existing rubric of meanings associated with *jati*, e.g. *jati* in the sense of caste in the context of social reforms, and certain other senses which proved fairly evanescent, soon to be overwhelmed by the more dominant strains of *jatiya* discourse that were beginning to emerge. In the specific context of the Hindi-speaking world, the promotion of Hindi or Devnagari[26] and the protection of cows (as a matter of utmost religious importance) from ritual sacrifice by Muslims came to acquire the most sustained prominence.[27] To keep my task within manageable proportions, I will focus briefly on the discourse associated with one of these movements, the movement for the promotion of Devnagari or Hindi, which will allow me to isolate some of the conceptual assumptions underlying the 19th-century discourse of *jati*-as-nation. Interestingly, it will also highlight how the idea of *jati*-as-nation, for all its ambivalence, was inherently conflictual.

The promotion of Hindi script and, over time, a more substantive conception of a Hindi language that was purged of all Urdu and Persian influences was an avowed concern of almost all Hindi language papers.[28] Writers and publicists routinely expressed their anger and disappointment at the lack of official recognition given to the Hindi language: i.e., its failure to be accepted as a medium of communication in colonial administration and courts. There were periodic exhortations to 'Hindus' to promote their own language. If there was a lesson to be learnt from world history, as the papers would reiterate, it was that no community in the world had ever made progress without the prior development of its own distinctive language and literature. In the words, for example, of *Bharat Jiwan*: 'the *unnati* [development] of mother-tongue is the main cause of *jatiya* pride. It is a first step in *deshiya unnati*';[29] or 'the *unnati* of the *desh* and the *unnati* of mother-tongue are as inseparable as fire and smoke.[30] As one of *Bharat Jiwan*'s correspondents rhetorically asked: 'Readers! ... can there can any *unnati* in a *desh* where [its] own language is not respected and revered ... *unnati* of a *desh* has always been preceded by the *unnati* of [its] language!'[31]

In other words, Hindi was not simply the mother-tongue of a section of people, however large, but the language of the *desh* itself—indeed its very own language. In point of fact, the question was not at all one of numbers—of how many spoke the Hindi language. This much is implicitly indicated even in the above. The correspondent was not in any doubt that here was a *desh* whose own putative language was 'not respected and revered'. In less rhetorical moments, there were more explicit admissions from the Hindi publicists, both angry and humble, that the beloved language of their *jatiya* pride was not spoken, much less understood, by a large number of them.[32] These were, of course, not just the illiterate, untutored common folk (the *sarva sadharan*), but some of the most literate of Hindu castes. But why then could Urdu, spoken by a substantial number of elite Muslims and literate castes within the putative Hindu community, not be regarded as a *deshiya* language?

In the minds of the Hindi publicists, the answer to this was simple. Urdu and the Persian from which it derived were languages that did not belong to the *desh*. They had been brought to India by the Muslim kings who had invaded centuries earlier. The case of Urdu was akin to that of Norman French in England:

When the French conquered England, the language there too was corrupted. People considered the French language as superior. It even became popular in high-class households. The affairs of the state too were conducted in this language. At that time, the *jatiya* language English, which was the language of the *sarva sadharan* (the ordinary or common people), was given no respect at all ... but soon as the English ... began to acquire the good sense to affirm [recognise] their own identity, their *jatiya* language began to prosper and the *videshi* (foreign) language—called Norman French—was completely uprooted. Even today, there are a lot of words in English which are borrowed from foreign languages like Latin and Greek but only that English is considered good which has more indigenous (*deshi*) words than foreign (*videshi*) ones ... the case of Urdu is exactly the same as that of Norman French.[33]

Hindi language was not simply linked to some abstract notion of *unnati*: it was the very stuff of Hindu identity. The moral of this piece of comparative history for the 'Hindus' could not be more emphatic. As *Hindi Pradip* reminded the 'Hindus': 'Although long contact with people from Persian, Arabic and Turki countries has forced you to learn a lot of words from these languages, your real [lit., main] language is Hindi.' It was time to

[c]ome to your senses! Open your eyes! Know who you are! [G]et hold of your sense of identity [lit., *apnapan* or 'ownness'] ... Remember! You do not belong to the Persian *desh*, why then call the Persian alphabet your own! Why regard Turki, Persian or Arabic as your own ... Let those words [from these languages] which have got assimilated [into Hindi] remain, but from now on, as far as possible, reject words from these languages.

As *Brahmin* put it more succinctly on another occasion: 'The alphabet of Hindi is more pure and *sahaj* (natural) than all other alphabets. The Hindi language is superior to all other languages. For the Hindus especially ... their pride, fate and fortune—in this world and the next—depends on it ... What use is Persian and Arabic to Hindus?'[34] Hindi was the most superior language of all because it alone could express the most intimate inner feelings— 'nij man ki bahu bat', 'the many great matters of the heart', according to Harishchandra[35]—of the Hindus. In this respect, it was no different from the characteristic call of even the most humble of creatures in the world—the lowly sparrow:

The smallest of child knows that even birds and animals—not to speak of humans—not only possess their own unique language but also have the deepest sense of attachment [*mamatav*] to it. For the sake of food, a parrot ... may learn to speak like humans but in communicating its own innermost feelings both within its own *jati* (*sajatiyon*) and outside—

amongst other communities (of birds)—it will follow its own language. Regrettably, the Hindus are even worse than the lowly sparrows (*chidiyas*) in this respect.[36]

For all the intimations of timelessness and innermost feelings of the heart, even the strongest of advocates of the Hindi language acknowledged that, in the time-scale of history, Hindi was but a relatively recent language. However stretched, its antiquity in its earliest, most rudimentary, form could not be dated prior to the arrival of the very Muslim invaders whose language(s) they dismissed so summarily as *videshi*.[37] The crucial argument was therefore not about the actual antiquity but the *potential* antiquity of the Hindi language. By purging itself of all alien and foreign influences and drinking deeply at the well of the ancient Sanskrit language, Hindi could recreate itself in the present and lay claim to being the only deserving inheritor of the ancient Vedic/Aryan legacy of Bharatvarsha. In other words, it was *logically* necessary that the Hindi language that the publicists sought to propagate could not be the mongrel, impure dialects that were strewn all around them. No Hindi that was tainted by the historical process of contact with other languages could qualify as the *shuddh* (pure) language of Hindu *jatiyata*.[38]

There are a number of important themes that emerge from this discourse on *jatiyata*. First, at the conceptual level, the imagined community of *jati* came to be viewed more and more through a dominant prism whose three faces were constituted by language, religion and antiquity. For all the immense empirical and historical differences that obtained within the so-called Hindu *jati*, their inclusion in this *jati* was still originary. Empirical issues were important only in a practical context, on the conceptual plane they were of no consequence. A concentrated expression of this conception of *jatiyata* was immortalised in the slogan 'Hindi, Hindu, Hindustan' by Pratap Narain Mishra in 1890. As another leading Hindi publicist argued in one of his most self-reflective pieces on the issue of *jatiyata* in the closing years of the 19th century:

The reason why there is little jatiyata or mutual empathy in Hindustan is because there are such great differences of language and (religious) belief … When ancient Bharat was in a state of *unnati* and the feeling of jatiyata was present in all its fullness, Sanskrit was the sole language of the entire *desh* ... [and the Vedic *dharma* was the sole religion] ... unless Bharat regains those qualities of unity, mutual empathy, one common language for the whole *desh*, and one system of (religious) belief its renaissance (*punar-uththan*) is forever impossible.[39]

The second point is that this conception of *jatiyata* is primarily cultural. The idea of political (state) power, itself an essential element in a self-conscious vocabulary of nationhood, is as yet absent or very weakly articulated. This is not to say that this conception of *jatiya* identity did not have political implications. Indeed that is my third point. The process of imagining the community of *jatiyata* by Hindi publicists was both hegemonic and inherently conflictual, not just vis-à-vis other communities (e.g. the Muslims) but also within the Hindu population.[40] As a well-known political theorist has recently reminded us:

An identity is established in relation to a series of differences ... These differences are essential to its being ... Identity requires difference in order to be, and it converts difference into otherness in order to secure its own self-certainty. Identity is thus a slippery, insecure experience, dependent on its ability to define difference and vulnerable to the tendency of entities it would so define to counter, resist, overturn or subvert definitions applied to them. Identity stands in a complex, political relation to the differences it seeks to fix.[41]

I will consider the full implications of this later; for the moment it should suffice to note that in defining the cultural basis of *jatiyata*, Hindi publicists had in principle and in concept excluded all those who fell outside the purview of that definition. The question that logically arises therefore is, who are the Hindus? It is to this question that I turn in the following section.

Who are the Hindus?

For all its ambivalence, dissonance and contradiction, if there is a dominant and recurring leitmotiv in the *jatiya* discourse of late-19th-century Hindi publicists, it is the cultural conception of a Hindu *jatiyata*. The questions I address in this section are: Who are the Hindus? Who is included and who is omitted from its imagined purview,[12] and on what conceptual basis? Before I proceed, however, I need to take issue with a line of historical interpretation that has, in the recent past, acquired some prominence.

Attempts have recently been made by some historians to establish the idea that in the minds of the Hindi publicists of the 19th century, the term *Hindu* had both a generic and a specific meaning. In its generic usage, it has been argued, the term had an inclusive and extended sense, referring not just to a specific religious community but to the entire subject population of India.[43] Much effort and ingenuity has been expended to bolster the claim. Yet considered in the light of the ostensible historical 'evidence' which has been adduced in its favour, it seems to me to be no more than a figment of the historians' imagination.

There is essentially one tiny piece of historical evidence that has been presented in favour of this claim.[44] It comes from a public lecture given by Bharatendu Harishchandra in Ballia in 1884.[45] Throughout the address, Harishchandra employs the term Hindu in a straightforward, tautological manner. At one point, however, he makes the following assertion:

Brother Hindus! You too should give up the insistence on sectarian differences. Increase mutual affection. Chant this *mahamantra* (grand slogan): whoever lives in Hindustan, whatever colour or *jati* he may belong to, is a Hindu. Whoever lives in Hindustan, whatever colour or *jati* he may be, is Hindu. Help the Hindu. Bengali, Maratha, Punjabi, Madrasi, Jain, Brahmo, Musalman should all hold one another's hand.[46]

Now I do not want to enter into a detailed argument about what the correct textual interpretation of this passage should be. I just want to suggest that it is *at least* doubtful if Harishchandra actually meant to include the Muslims in his catch-all, expansive definition of Hindus. I believe the passage in question actually ends with the words, 'Help the Hindus'. It is useful to remember that in the paragraph immediately preceding this, Harishchandra presents a long list of advice to 'Muslim-brothers' on how to improve their current depressed lot; what they should or should not do. In the beginning of this one, he turns his attention to Hindu-brothers, exhorting them to overcome their sectarian differences and to increase mutual affection. The advice concludes with the words, 'Help the Hindu', meaning any Hindu living in Hindustan, irrespective of his *jati*, religious sect or colour. This is also supported by grammatical evidence in the passage: in the next sentence Harishchandra, instead of addressing the self-same 'Hindu-Brothers', turns to a different category of subjects, 'Bengalis, Marathas, Madrasis, Vedic, Jain, Brahmos, Musalman ...'.[47]

Happily for us, notwithstanding the ambiguity about the precise scope of the category of Hindus in this passage, the issue of a 'correct' interpretation in this instance is, at best, an academic one. The more significant question is whether this particular definition of Hindu, even if it were to include the Muslims, is at all representative—either of Harishchandra's own views, or those of other Hindi publicists of the time. I believe that the answer to both these questions is an unqualified no. Its status is that of a singular anomaly even within Harishchandra's own oeuvre, not to speak of any other Hindi publicist. The best that can be said about Harishchandra's use of this sense of the term on this particular occasion is that it is a one-time idiosyncrasy. I am yet to come across a second instance in his large corpus of writings where he can even remotely be said to have used the term in this inclusive, extended sense. Besides, no other Hindi publicist of the time, to the best of my knowledge, *ever* used the term with this meaning. If they ever equated *Hindi* with Hindustan, that was meant to emphasise the cultural primacy of the Hindus in India. There simply was no 'semantic circle' like that to which historian Sudhir Chandra refers with such eloquence:

'Hindustan is ours because we are Hindus' and 'he who inhabits Hindustan is a Hindu' were two ways in which Hindu and India(n) were made synonymous. Moving one way, Harishchandra used the term Hindu and insisted that it meant all Indians. Moving another way, Pratapnarayan argued that Hindus constituted the real India, and clearly stated that it was by virtue of their association with Hindus that non-Hindus qualified as Indians. Whichever way one moved along his semantic circle—and the same person could move both ways—at its centre lay an implicit communal assumption.[48]

Before I close this subject, let me briefly refer to an editorial that appeared in *Bharat Jiwan* in 1889. The purpose of this editorial was to express the paper's growing consternation at the rather unconsidered and thoughtless manner in which Indians continued to use the term *native* to identify themselves, particularly on official occasions.[49] Unlike peoples of Europe and America, even China and Afghanistan, who referred to themselves as 'French, English, American, Russian, Chinese, Afghani, etc.', the paper remarked, people in India did not identify themselves as Indians. 'It is commonly seen that when our country brothers, whether they belong to the general class [of commoners] or they are rajas-maharajas (chiefs), write or speak in English they describe and identify themselves as *Natives* or *Natives of India*.' Those who describe themselves in these terms, admonished *Bharat Jivan*, forget that 'another gloss of the term is Natal, a name which was coined to describe a South African province inhabited by a people who are regarded in the whole world as uncivilised and devilish'.[50] The problem was, however, to suggest an alternative self-description which could encompass the *entire* population of India. 'Someone might say that we should call ourselves Hindus. But the term Hindu cannot be applied to include everyone living in Bharatvarsha since there are [amongst Indians] some Muslims, some Parsis, some Christians, some Jains, etc. ... But is there no other alternative [term]? Surely there is one ... and that term is *Indian* ... You should call yourself *Indian* since this term can be used by everyone who lives in India.'

What better occasion than this, one might have thought, to apply the term *Hindu* in the expansive way used by Harishchandra in his Ballia lecture! Note that *Bharat Jiwan* does not reject the term *native* on the ground that it denies to those who live in Bharatvarsha the putative status of nationhood which is so readily assumed by the French, the English, the Chinese, the Afghans and so on. What it condemns is the fact that those living in India are equated with African peoples, and thereby condemned to an unfair level of 'bestiality'. The other point, implicitly stated, is that even those who 'spoke and wrote in English' found it difficult to describe themselves simply as Indians. Being a native of India simply suggested the fact of domicile and had little to do with one's nationality. The difficulty of conceptualising the idea of an Indian, as opposed to a Hindu, *jatiyata* will be taken up in the conclusion of this paper.

Hindus or Aryans?

There is a systematic ambiguity in the use of the term *Hindu* in the late 19th century. This ambiguity is rooted in the fact that Hindi publicists employ the term in two very different, although mutually implicatory, ways. This gives rise to a good deal of empirical and contextual imprecision in the use of the term. In the first substantive sense, it is used synonymously with the term *Aryan*. In the second, it refers not simply to the Aryans but to a much wider (residual) category of Hindus. This latter use mimics the way the term was employed by colonial authorities in census classification.

But who are the Aryans?[51] Again, in the public discourse of the late 19th century there is no unambiguous, universally accepted answer to this. But in those cases where the term Aryans is used in a more *self-conscious* way, it is usually said to be co-extensive with the four *varnas* of the Hindu *jati*—the *aryavratavasi chaturvarna*. In other, more rhetorical moments, however, the last of the four *varnas*—the so-called *shudras* or lower castes—is very often left out. Aryanness then becomes restricted to the so-called twice-born upper castes. It is not my purpose to pursue this point in any great detail here, but one implication of this must be noted: the cultural identity of Hindu *jatiyata* was overwhelmingly Brahminical and upper-caste in its orientation.

The cultural identification of Hindu identity with an Aryan one is so extensive that it does not need any detailed cataloguing. What I very briefly wish to indicate here is the metaphor of fraternal kinship—rooted in a supposed common ancestry over many millennia—that powerfully animates the idea of Aryanness. Consider the following two examples—both addressed to Hindus:

Crave [*moh*] your *desh*, your language and your *apnapan* [ownness or identity]. Don't let go of them even if death is the alternative. Take the most profound pride in the glory of you ancestors, your *Aryanness*. Think nothing of the whole world in comparison, regard even their best qualities as inconsequential ... [52]

[H]ave the Hindus of different provinces forgotten that they are the children of *the same Aryans* ... Would the children of [ancient] sages like Vashist, Shandilya, Garg, Gautam, etc. forego their eternal kinship because they now live in distant lands? [T]he differences of language, dress, and customs and behaviours ... are not allowed to hinder unity amongst Hindus. All Hindus should strive single-mindedly towards the progress of their *jati*. [53]

The last example is particularly interesting because it points to the tensions that exist between the idea of Aryanness and the notion of a wider Hindu community which includes 'all Hindus'. The lower castes amongst the Hindus could not easily claim their ancestry amongst the ancient sages who fathered the Aryans of the current time. Their inclusion among the Aryan-brothers was more uncertain.

Hindus as a Statistical Artefact

Alongside the Hindu-Aryan identity, there is another use of the term *Hindu* in the late 19th century, which is essentially numerical. Soon after the first systematic country-wide census was carried out in 1881,[54] Hindi publicists would often speak in the name of a statistical entity which was numerically quite precise—200 million, give or take a few. This entity created through the classificatory procedures of colonial censuses was actually based on a residual category of Hindus. For the purposes of colonial census, the term *Hindu* was not identified with any particular set of religious beliefs. Hindus were simply those who could not be enumerated under any other identifiable major religion in India. As one of the regional censuses in 1881 put it: 'Every native who was unable to define his creed or who described it by any other name than that of some recognised religion or of a sect of some such religion, was held to be and classed as a Hindu.'[55]

It is difficult to exaggerate the importance of this statistical notion of Hindus (an 'artefact of census categorisation',[56] as some have recently called it) for the discourse of 19th-century Hindi publicists. It did, after all, give their assertion of the cultural pre-eminence of Hindu *jatiyata* in India the stamp of moral and demographic authority. In other words, when they spoke of Hindu *jatiyata* they were not merely propounding a minority view but speaking for what was easily the largest section of people in India. In both the cow-protection movement and the movement for the promotion of Hindi or *Devnagari*, for instance, there was a frequent conflation of these senses of the term *Hindu*. The claim that Hindi was the language of Hindus, and the cultural conception of Hindus as Aryans with Sanskritised Hindi, far removed from the coarse, impure dialects of the majority of the common people, was fused with the statistical notion of Hindus as the most numerous community in India.

It is also possible to see this constant play between the cultural and the numerical in more structural terms. Thus in the domain of state and political rhetoric generally—in cases where numbers had an important role to play—it was the term *Hindu* in its numerical sense which was foregrounded, whereas in the cultural domain, the term was used to indicate the Aryan identity of Hindus.

The Place of the Outcastes in *Jatiya* Discourse

Before I move on, one final point remains to be made. This concerns the status of those so-called Hindus who fell outside the bounds of even the last of the four *varnas* of the Hindu fold. In other words, those who were considered to be outside the pale of caste society altogether: the untouchables and the so-called indigenous peoples. It is no exaggeration to say that as far as the Hindi publicists were concerned they only existed in a limited, virtual presence within the 200-million-strong Hindu community.

On the conceptual plane, *Hindu samaj* in its widest scope referred to the domain of four-fold *varna* community.[57] No attempt was made to even conceptually include the outcastes and other indigenous peoples within the fold of this Hindu *samaj*. There was occasional concern about the conversion of some lower caste Hindus, to Christianity in particular. There were occasional appeals, as well, about the need to promote a sense of unity amongst the Hindus as a whole—although other than as an expression of a pious wish, it was difficult to see what it might entail since few concrete proposals were ever mentioned. In any case, none of these appeals ever specifically mentioned the 'ati-shudras' or the 'vanvasis' (the untouchables or the so-called indigenous people). The only conclusion that can be drawn from this is that the moral sensibility of the Hindi publicists was not sufficiently offended by the enormous discrimination which was the lot of an important section of its own putative community.

The issue of untouchability, for instance, never once came up for serious discussion in the discourse of Hindi publicists during the entire 19th century.[58] So even as the idea of Hindu *jatiyata* was vigorously argued and the Hindus were regarded as forming the overwhelming part of the Indian population, subordinate groups within the *jati* were hardly worth a consideration. Their main function was to swell the ranks of the Hindus: to allow for the claim of Hindus being the pre-eminent cultural entity in Bharat-varsha. The idea of Hindi *jatiyata* was not, even potentially, that of a horizontal community. There was little questioning of caste privileges and hierarchy, much less the oppressions of the caste order.

It was only at the end of the first decade of the present century, when the very status of the untouchables as part of the Hindu community was questioned (e.g., in census enumeration),[59] that the issue of untouchability began to attract the widespread notice of Hindi publicists. It would, however, still take a decade or more before the *shuddhi* movement would regard the task of reclaiming the 'untouchables' back to the Hindu fold as especially urgent— driven as much by a humanistic concern for their welfare as by the fear of their being converted by the proselytising religions of Christianity and Islam.

The Place of Muslims in Hindi *Jatiya* Discourse

There is a curious paradox at the core of late-19th-century Hindi discourse concerning the Muslim community. On the one hand, one finds impassioned appeals, often directly addressed to Muslims themselves, about the imperative of improving mutual co-operation between Hindus and Muslims, and ending their perceived mutual antagonisms. On the other hand, these reasonably-worded appeals are counterbalanced by many more statements that refer to Muslims in extremely unkind ways. Viewed from our contemporary standpoint, even some of the more restrained of these later statements can appear offensive.

How can one make sense of this contradiction? It is no exaggeration to say that even the more recent historiography of the period, while acknowledging this paradox,[60] has sought to soft-pedal the issue. There are two steps to this strategy. The first is to abstract the fact of the contradiction from the tone and tenor of its expression. The second is to privilege the statements that speak of the need for unity and co-operation among the two communities as being on the whole more representative of the discourse. This has had the consequence of treating the offending statements as no more than temporary lapses from the norm—occasioned by 'some immediate issue' the passion of which 'passed as the issue that had aroused it subsided'. Such immediate issues include recent sectarian violence, official decisions that are seen to favour the Muslim community, and the like. This flies in the face of the fact that not only do these hostile statements not follow any discernible politico-temporal rhythm, but they also grossly outnumber the pleas that aim to elicit the co-operation of the Muslims and speak to them in more polite ways.[61]

Whatever the merits or compulsions of such selective interpretation of historical evidence, it is not particularly convincing. In any event, the principal issue, to my mind, is not whether one condones or condemns the attitude of the Hindi publicists.[62] The problem is: how do we understand this dichotomy of sentiments? Now I think that there is a more credible way of making conceptual sense of the Janus-faced nature of Hindi discourse about the Muslim community. A closer look at the diverse and conflicting pronouncements of the Hindi publicists reveals a broad pattern. The attitude of the Hindi publicists towards the Muslims may be, as a first approximation, summed up in the formula: *cultural* exclusion and *political* inclusion. The basis for the inclusion of Muslims in the *jatiya* discourse of Hindi publicists is not originary:

the basis for their inclusion is on the grounds of politics rather than being culturally-motivated.

The cultural exclusion of Muslims

The problem is as much conceptual as it has to do with empirical history. But since the focus of this paper is primarily the former, I will not deal with the latter dimension. From a conceptual point of view the question is: is there is plausible way in which Hindi publicists *can* include the Muslims in their cultural definition of *jatiyata*. If *jatiya* identity was to be defined, as it certainly was, primarily around religion, language and history, and often against the Muslim as the Other, on what bases could Muslims be *culturally* included? I think in the *cultural* domain of *jatiyata*, there is just one possible ground in the discourse of Hindi publicists on which Muslims can be included, namely the idea of sharing a common 'homeland'. The fact that even though Muslims had come to Bharat or 'Aryavrata' as invaders, they had, unlike the later British colonialists, settled down and made it their home for many centuries. This argument is occasionally made by Hindi publicists, yet the accompanying premise that goes with it questions and subverts the very possibility of it being taken seriously.

To make my argument more convincing, I will attempt a logical reconstruction of the common premises that form the discursive and narrative space in which the individual assertions of Hindi publicists, made in widely different contexts and with varying degrees of force, meaning and clarity, are located.

The logical starting point of the Hindi discourse about the Muslim 'other' is a contingent historical fact: the assumption of power by the British, and the consequent loss of *status* for the Muslims as the former rulers of the land. In their capacity as rulers in a none-too-distant past, Muslims had commanded a dominant status vis-à-vis the subject Hindu *samaj*. They generally abused the power that their superior position afforded them—the degree of abuse obviously varied, one or two were even benevolent, notably, Akbar[63]—to oppress the Hindus, to defile their religion and culture, to molest their women and plunder their wealth. As a result of this oppression over centuries, the glorious ancient civilisation of the Aryans, their language and learning, their wealth and social harmony, their morality and *dharma*, even the condition of their women, went into a precipitous decline. But thanks to the arrival of the British, according to some a case of divine intervention (at least at the level of rhetoric, perhaps even belief), the long night of terror had passed. The excesses of Muslim domination, the anarchy and lawlessness had been curbed. And, importantly, Muslims had been put in their rightful place.

This was the story of the past. To move to the present: Despite being vanquished, Muslims continue to revel in the memory of the past. Unlike the Hindus, they quite unreasonably believe that they must be accorded a special status even in the vastly altered circumstances of British rule. Some even harbour visions of a future rebellion in which they would turn the clock back, seize power from the British and revert to the (in)glorious days of their past rule.[64]

It requires no great imagination to figure out the implications that followed from this for Muslims: to begin with, they had to stop living in the past; to erase the memory of their earlier exalted status as rulers of the land. Additionally, they had to recognise that they were now, in common with Hindus and others, no more than ordinary subjects of the colonial regime. Having lived in the country for so long, they had now to make common cause with its Hindu inhabitants and not see themselves as a species apart. To quote Harishchandra's Ballia lecture again:

It is right for Muslim brothers, too, who have now settled in Hindustan, that they should thinking of the Hindus as inferior, and instead relate to them exactly as brothers do. They should give up all practices that hurt the feelings of the Hindus ... Many of them think that the thrones of Delhi and Lucknow continue to exist. Friends! Those days are gone ... [65]

The same sentiments could of course be expressed with greater rhetorical (and historical) flourish:

Mussalmans should remember that the hierarchy and difference which existed between them and Hindus at one time can no longer be maintained. It is appropriate that [they] regard their superior status and

dominance in the past as a mere dream. They ought to realise that even
though the country remains the same, and even the Hindus remain the
same, they are no longer what they were at the time of (the glories!) of
Allaudin Khilji and Mohammed Tughlak. Whereas earlier the Mussalmans [were free] ... to [commit] what atrocities they liked and whatever
depravity they fancied, now it's the ... justice-loving English government
that [rules us]. Even though the sun which illumines this land every day
is the same as the one that lit up the eyes during the days of Aurangzeb;
[even though] the lamps ... that shine in the theatres remain the same, the
theatre itself has undergone complete transformation. Muslims should no
longer expect to see the same scenes which they had grown accustomed
to watching during the days of Mogul theatre.[66]

However black their depiction of the Muslim-ruled past might
have been, there appears to be a hint here that things might just
improve if only the Muslims could forget the past hierarchy and
accept the Hindus as equals. But unfortunately, things were not
quite so simple. What remains unarticulated in these arguments so
far is the precisely that accompanying premise of the common
homeland argument that I mentioned earlier.

It wasn't just a case of Muslims forgetting their past. They also
had to learn something quite new apart from unlearning the past
hierarchies. What they had to learn was the fact that the Hindus
were the ancient inhabitants of India and constituted the greater
majority of the population. Thus it was to be their language and
their culture, which would have to be accorded primacy. Let's look
at the 'logical' steps in this argument:

Musalmans here consider Musalmans from other countries such as
Turkey and Iran as their brothers and have a great deal of affection for
them because they belong to the same *jati*. [On the other hand] they
regard the Hindus of their own motherland as their worst enemies [*dili
dushman*] ... notwithstanding the fact that they have been living here for
twenty generations or more, they have no feeling for people of other *jatis*
who live here ... [67]

The demand that the Muslims show some affection for the *jatis*
living in India, as opposed to their co-religionists elsewhere, could
easily mutate into the demand that they show greater affection for
the Hindu (Aryan) culture than their own:

There are Musalmans in other countries too but they speak the language of whichever country they live in. They read only their religious treatises in Arabic. [Therefore] their contention that they need (should) only study Urdu is useless obstinacy (vyarath ka hath). Ordinary Musalmans may even agree [to give up Urdu] but their leaders such as the Syed [Ahmed Khan] stoke the fire of enmity in them. We (people) want Hindi so that...the common people (sarva sadharan) might receive education and the state of the country improves. But they [Muslim leaders such as Syed Ahmed, etc.] are devoted to Urdu because they are only concerned about their own welfare and not whether the condition of the country improves or declines. Everywhere [in the world] there is the same story: those [outsiders] who come to settle down in a country, their lifestyle, language, etc. changes in keeping with those of the people who live there. They are seen as foreigners unless they adopt the language, lifestyle, etc. of the [original] inhabitants. Instead of this assimilation, the Syed argues that the Hindus should keep their Hindi to themselves and the Musalmans need only learn their own crooked [sic]. Persian alphabet. Is this advice calculated to increase mutual affection and goodwill? ... The Syed should pay a little heed to where this division might lead to.[68]

[W]hen the Turks, Arabs, Moguls and Iranians newly arrived in India, they lived like foreigners. And—of course—they ruled the country. At that time, they mostly spoke their own language(s). But now they have become the same [as us]. Why do our Musalman-brothers [continue to] behave like foreigners. They ought to now reduce [the use of] foreign alphabet and foreign words and enhance the real *jatiya* language Hindi. Musalman-brothers! Why cling to [this] pointless fanaticism [*ta-assuva*], now that you are residents of Bharat ... improve and enhance the language of this country! As we said before, your Urdu is exactly like Norman French.[69]

I am aware that there is a danger here of reading too much into statements that were obviously made in a polemical context. And, as befits polemics generally, there is here an inescapable element of exaggeration—an extra edge of passion. The reason why I have still chosen to cite them is, first, that they appear in a journal which was among the most 'reasonable' in its style of argument and modes of expression throughout the 19th century. Second, and most importantly, regardless of their polemical content, there is no questioning their *conceptual* premise: for Muslims to be included in the imaginary homeland of *jatiyata*, they had to accept the cultural primacy of the Hindus. To sum up this part of the argument: in the conceptual vocabulary available to the Hindi publicists of the 19th century, there is no credible way in which the Muslims could be included in the cultural definition of *jatiyata*.

Before I proceed further, there is one last point that I want to deal with. This concerns the statements of Hindi publicists in which they talk of Hindus and Muslims as the 'two arms or two eyes of Mother-India',[70] or 'two sisters-in-law in a joint family'[71] and so on. Historians have often read these statements as indicative of a *composite* conception of Indian nationality in the minds of Hindi publicists. I believe that this interpretation is deeply flawed. While these fleeting *metaphors* may—and usually do—say something about the intentions of an individual publicist on a particular occasion, they give no clue whatever about the conceptual basis of how these two arms, eyes, brothers, or even sisters-in-law might be *culturally* reconciled in the composite nation. Second, these statements are, by and large, made in a *political* context. When it comes to defining the cultural basis of *jatiyata*, Hindi publicists do not, indeed cannot, in the interest of Mussalmans, but exclude the Muslims.

It would require a sophisticated new gloss on historical interpretation, indeed a wholly new conception of Indian history, to create the *cultural* basis for the inclusion of Muslims in the imagined *jatiyata* of India. This new history, some of whose premises first arise in the early part of the present century, would take almost a period of twenty years to be rewritten in its new 'nationalist' mode. I will touch upon this point in the conclusion to this paper.

I have so far argued that there is no cultural basis on which Hindi publicists can include the Muslims in their definition of *jatiyata* in the 19th century. Culturally, Bharatvarsha is primarily and pre-eminently Hindu (Aryan). At the cultural plane therefore, on issues of language, history and religious practice, there is a pronounced lack of any sense of inclusiveness and accommodation. I now move from the cultural domain to the political one.

Very briefly, my argument is that the periodic pleas for co-operation between Hindus and Muslims that are advanced throughout the 19th century are primarily made in a political context and are based not on cultural but pragmatic grounds. The simple truth was that the non-white population could demand a measure of political representation from the colonial state only by coming together, by making a common *political* cause. In other words, it is only at a political plane that the notion of a composite *jatiyata* comes into being. Its basis is not cultural but the fact of common political subjecthood.[72] The essential point that I am trying to make is admirably brought out in an editorial that appeared in *Bharat Jiwan* in 1885. It will therefore help to reproduce it some detail:

Without unity amongst Hindus and Musalmans, there can be no *unnati* in India. Unless the two groups co-operate, no remedy can be found for the general suffering ... Hindus and Musalmans are like the two hands or the two eyes of one body ... These days, however, whatever little goodwill and unity existed amongst the two [earlier] has disappeared because of many causes ... Religious enmity and arguments have always been there and have been a source of *fasad* (friction or conflict) every year on the occasion [for example] of Muharram but there have now arisen *political* differences between the two as well. But this is undoubtedly a huge mistake.

... Hindus and Musalmans are subjects of the same king, are governed by the same laws and rules; [they] even live in the same country. [They] can make [joint] submissions about their [common] woes to the government ... why is it then that there are differences [amongst them] in such an important area as this? [T]he consequences of this disunity are terrible— those instigating disunity have nothing to lose! ... Therefore, this appeal [to Musalmans] to renounce this *jatiya* enmity so that people from other countries do not laugh at us!

Even though (we) Hindus and Musalmans have great many differences in matters of *dharma*,[73] in political matters we must be one. [T]hose who want to break this [political] unity are committing a great sin and are the enemies of India; even though they disguise [lit., 'dress up'] themselves outwardly as its friends.[74]

Bharat Jiwan talks here of a *political* unity between Hindus and Muslims which could exist, indeed which had to exist, in spite of religious differences. In the non-state domain, one could continue to fight and argue. But one could still unite politically. The implication was quite stark: this conception of politics excluded any religious or cultural content at all. As *Bharat Jiwan* argued on another occasion in a reply to the oft-repeated allegation by Syed Ahmed Khan, the prominent Muslim leader from NWP, who dismissed the Congress as a Hindu, more precisely, Bengali, body:

How wonderful! ... Has Syed saheb not seen that last year our Madrasi brothers helped the Congress more than the Bengalis. And how enthusiastic were our brothers from Bombay! In any case, *what has the National Congress got to do with the behaviour, conduct and riti-rasm of anyone! The subjects that are raised in the Congress do not favour any particular jati but are government-related submissions; they are not about any cultural rituals* [*riti-rasm*].[75]

At the political plane, there was no question of any substantive (cultural) *jatiya* identity. Indeed, questions of cultural identity—of 'behaviour, conduct and *riti-rasm*'—were excluded from the domain of the Congress from its very inception.[76] Here *jatiyata* signified no more than a condition of common political subjecthood. As *Hindi Pradip* often reminded the Muslims: 'one country, one sovereign, does it not follow that the *prajah* too should live as one'.[77] But could they live as one, purely on a political plane? It is this question that the *jatiya* discourse of 19th-century Hindi publicists failed to resolve conceptually. Nor was there, in the interest of Mussalmans, an answer to it in the realm of empirical history of the time.

The Discourse of Jatiyata: Conclusion

I begin this concluding section by questioning a highly influential historical account of the nature of nationalist discourse in colonial north India. The central argument of this account—pioneered by Gyan Pandey in his highly acclaimed book *The Construction of Communalism in Colonial North India*—has since been repeated by a number of other historians working in the same field.[78] It would not be too much of an exaggeration to suggest that it has emerged as something of a new orthodoxy in historical interpretations of nationalist discourse in the Hindi-speaking areas of colonial India.

Pandey's central contention is that in the 'earlier stages of the national movement' (i.e., prior to the 1920s), the 'nation of Indians was visualised as a composite body, consisting of several communities, each with its own history and culture and its own special contribution to make to the common nationality'. The emerging Indian nation, he goes on to argue, 'was conceived of as a collection of communities: Hindu + Muslim + Christian + Parsi + Sikh, and so on'.[79] Further, he argues that 'sometime around the 1920s' this view of the nation undergoes a fundamental change and the Indian nation comes to be regarded as 'much more a collection of individuals, of Indian citizens'. It is in the context of this change, according to him, that the concepts of 'communalism and nationalism as we know them today come to acquire their present signification ... to a large extent in opposition to each other.' And, finally:

The cry of Hindu nationalism ... of India as essentially the land of the Hindus— is part of the discourse of communalism that came to the fore in the 1920s. Before that, Indian nationalists had sought to emphasise the fact that India was more than only, or primarily, Hindu'.[80]

From what I have said so far, it must be plain as daylight as to where I stand in relation to Pandey's historical account. Let me reiterate it nonetheless. I believe that Pandey's interpretation of the nature of nationalist discourse is *fundamentally* erroneous except on two points. Although even these two points have to qualified and understood differently from the way Pandey seems to suggest. First, it is true that the identity of the nation was composite in the earlier period—i.e., prior to the 1920s. But it was composite not in the sense that Pandey implies. The notion of compositeness has to be substantially qualified.

As I argued in the previous section, the idea of composite *jatiyata* of the earlier period was primarily articulated in a political context. That is to say in the institutional domain of the colonial state. In the *cultural* domain, there was *never* any question in the minds of the Hindi publicists, the principal subjects in relation to whom Pandey makes the claim, as to who constituted the *jatiya* identity of Bharat or India—it was the Hindus (more precisely, Aryans) who were the primary *jati* of India.

The problem arises because Pandey does not think seriously enough about the implications of his own argument that, prior to 1920, 'the several communities' who were supposed to make up the composite entity called the Indian nation could have their 'own history and culture' and their 'own specific contribution'; in other words, their own distinctive cultural identities. The major problem here is that this distinctive 'history and culture' of each different community was not historically pre-given. It was being constructed, imagined, invented, created from the bottom-up. And this process of identity-creation was both *political* and inherently conflictual. In the case of the Hindi publicists of late-19th-century colonial India, the *jatiya* identity was not being constructed in a power-vacuum: it was being constructed against the Muslim other. What the Hindi publicists were asserting, sometimes implicitly, often very explicitly—and in opposition to the Muslims—was that they were the primary community in India. As Pratap Narain Mishra put it: 'Hindi, Hindu, Hindustan'.

The second point about which Pandey is partially right is that there *does* take place a fundamental change in the discourse of nationalism in the 1920s. He is also right in claiming that the categories 'communalism' and 'nationalism' as we know them today acquire their signification in this period of Indian history. But this fundamental change takes places precisely because of the realisation, particularly on the part of Hindi nationalists, that they could not claim a *primacy* for their exclusivist, indeed exclusionary, cultural identity outside the domain of the colonial state and still expect that this assertion would have no implications for how power was to be shared at the political plane. In other words—to invoke the earlier formula—it was impossible to culturally exclude the Muslims from the definition of the nation and yet be able to convince them that they should extend political co-operation in the domain of the colonial state institutions: cultural exclusion had political implications. And not just in the realm of the state institutions but also in social life: the increasing sectarian violence of the 1920s, for instance, which Pandey rightly focuses on as one of the primary impulses for this change. The cry of Hindu na-

tionalism—of India as essentially being the land of the Hindus—
which Pandey locates as first arising in the 1920s—had existed for
nearly four decades prior to that. What changes in the 1920s is the
fact that this cry is now regarded, from the point of view of the
new 'secular nationalism', as 'communal' and unacceptable. This is
not to say that the late-19th-century Hindi discourse was communal because that would an anachronism, since what seems to be
implied in such an interpretation is that if only Hindi publicists
had more good will for the Muslims, they might have chosen to be
good nationalists rather than narrow-minded, sectarian commu-
nalists. The point is that in the conceptual vocabulary available to
Hindi publicists it was impossible to even make sense of the latter
historical dichotomy of communalism vs. Nationalism.[81]

To recall Koselleck and Skinner: what the period of the 1920s
signifies is that the nationalists 'have entered into the possession of
a [new and] self-conscious vocabulary of nationhood'. It is now
possible for them to conceptually distinguish not just between
what is nationalism and what is not (i.e., communalism). But , also,
for the first time, there is a new term that is being consistently used
to refer to this nation—*rashtra*. The more self-aware of the nationalists now renounce the earlier *jatiyata* for the latter *rashtriyata*. The
rashtra is over and above any individual *jati*, however important.
To assert the claim of any particular *jati* over the *rashtra* is now to
be denounced as narrow-minded *sampradayikta* (communalism). Of
course, these are not the only changes. Whereas earlier Hindi
publicists hardly ever used the term *Bharatiya*—not to speak of
using it in the sense of the new secular nation of the 1920s, it is
now difficult to find a self-aware secular nationalist who referred
to himself simply as Hindu or Aryan to signify his nationality.
There are equally important changes in the conception of the
people itself, from being *prajah* (subjects) and *sarva sadharan*
(common folk). It is now possible to talk of *Janata*, a term free of
any connotations of subjecthood (*prajah*). Of course, linguistic
changes are not adopted universally overnight—so the older
terminology still exists, and is even used—but their conceptual
meanings have altered.

A New Vision of History

As I argued earlier, the exclusion of Muslims from the imagined community, the *jatiya* identity, of the Hindi publicists was not arbitrary. The manner in which this exclusion was expressed, its tone and tenor, may have differed from one individual to another, even the same individual on different occasions and contexts—but its conceptual premises were remarkably constant. Whichever way the Hindi publicists looked at it—religion, language, history, or common residence—the inclusion of Muslims could not but pose insoluble problems. (Unless of course they questioned the very premises on which, in their view, the modern idea of *jatiyata* was conceptualised.) No such fundamental critique ever emerged in the late 19th century.[82]

On what basis then were the Muslims included in the conception of the Indian nation in the 1920s? I suggest that this new inclusion was primarily based on a sophisticated new gloss on the idea of Indian history. This new history—which found admirable expression in Nehru's *Discovery of India*—is what allowed the concept of a composite Indian nation, comprising its enormous diversity of peoples, languages, religions, to emerge. Nehru of course did not create this new view of history *ex-nihilo*. It had been in the making for more than a couple of decades.

I cannot discuss the issue in great detail here. But I will suggest an acceptable outline. The first move in this innovative rewriting of the past, was a redefinition of the status of the Muslims as a community. The tricky question had been: Were the Muslims *as a whole* to be regarded as outsiders or foreigners? Invaders who had not only conquered, by force of violence, the land of the Aryans some six centuries before the arrival of the British but also committed unspeakable atrocities? It was important to distinguish, in other words, between the Muslim *rulers* and the larger Muslim *community*. Already by the first decade of the present century the Hindi publicists' view of the Indian past saw a new-found appreciation for the old 'fact'—that a majority of Muslims living in India were not foreigners but indigenous Hindus who—under duress or otherwise—had embraced Islam. In other words, the defining feature of the Muslim community was not the fact of their past rulership but the fact that a large number of them were 'indigenous' converts from Hinduism. The second step was to take a less aggregated look at the period of Muslim rule. There were *individual* rulers who were certainly intolerant but, equally, there were others who were the very model of a secular, non-discriminatory, non-partisan kingship—notably Akbar. In any case, even the cruelties of the *individual* Muslim kings could, in some cases, be better explained not as acts borne of religious bigotry but motivated by considerations of power and *realpolitik*.

The third step was to locate the subjugation of India not to some hoary past of seven or eight centuries ago, but to the more recent time of 1757 when the last independent ruler of Bengal, Sirajudaullah, was removed by the forces of the East India Company led by Robert Clive. This was very different from earlier versions where the Indian nation (or, more precisely, the Hindu *jati*) was presumed to have lost its sovereignty at the hands of the Muslim conquerors in the middle of the 12th century.

However important this shift in historical chronology, and of dating India's loss of independence, might have been, the really crucial move was a redefinition of India not as a Hindu or Muslim nation but as a people-nation—indeed a civilizational entity—that always had the idea of assimilation and mutual co-existence at its very heart. Thus, even as there was constant influx of new peoples, religions and beliefs throughout its history, this assimilationist tendency—of incorporating what was best in the new and peacefully co-existing—with it always won the day.

Notes

1. Quentin Skinner, 'Language and Political Change', *Political Innovation and Conceptual Change*, ed. Terence Ball, et al. (Cambridge: Cambridge UP, 1988) 8. See also, more generally, Quentin Skinner, 'Some Problems in the Analysis of Political Thought and Action', *Meaning and Context: Quentin Skinner and His Critics*, ed. J. Tully (Oxford: Polity, 1988).
2. Richard Koselleck, *Futures Past: On the Semantics of Historical Time*, trans. Keith Tribe (Cambridge, MA: MIT P, 1985) 83-84.
3. Even those groups and peoples who might otherwise deny the very premise of a single nation called India would most certainly understand, as long as they know Hindi, what the term denotes.

4. About the only instance of this that I have found in the public discourse of late 19th century is an article by Pratap Narain Mishra. Ironically, this particular use of the term *Bharatiya* was meant to emphasise the exclusive Hindu identity of Bharat or Hindustan. See 'Shri Bharat Dharma Mahamandal', *Brahman* 15 Nov. 1889. I should also point out that the term *Hindustani* which has in recent times been eschewed by many secular Indians for its seeming conflation of Indian (national) with Hindu identity was very rarely used in a similar vein in the 19th century. By and large, the term *Hindustani* was used in a geographical or enumerative sense, either to refer to the inhabitants of a particular region—often the Hindi-speaking northern parts, sometimes the whole of India under British rule—or the region itself. (Cf. Chris Bayly, *Rulers, Townsmen and Bazars: North Indian Society in the Age of British Expansion, 1770-1860* [Cambridge: Cambridge UP, 1983] Ch. 1.) Having said that, in the same article in which Mishra invokes the term *Bharatiya*—he also uses the term *Hindustani* to signify the same meaning: 'Although Mussalmans, Christians and Parsis, all live here, they are called Hindustanis, and that is an appellation which is derived from our name. [W]e are Hindus and this country is our land.'

5. I should emphasise here that my principal concern is not whether a particular word or term was popularly used in the language of public discourse in the late 19th century. What I am interested in is whether a certain *concept* or *range of meanings*, now inextricably linked with the term *Indian*, is invoked. In general, it is neither a necessary or a sufficient condition of possessing a concept that one ought to have a corresponding term for its embodiment. It has been argued by historians of western political discourse that the concept of rights, for instance, predated the emergence of the term. See, for example, Richard Dagger, 'Rights', *Political Innovation and Conceptual Change*, ed. Terence Ball (Cambridge: Cambridge UP, 1988). For further examples of this kind, see Ball, *Political Innovation* 14-15. On the distinction between word and concept generally, cf. Skinner, 'Language'.

6. In July 1896, *Chaturvedi Patrika*, a caste journal published from Agra, carried an article titled, 'Samajik Vishaya' ('Community Matters') which made use of the term twice: in the first instance, as a synonym of *jati* and in the second parenthetical usage as *rajya*—a kingly state or geopolitical territory. Similarly, in 1899, for instance there was a Hindi translation of a Marathi text (written by one Kesav Vaman Pethe) carrying the title Rashtra Bhasha which was published from Banaras. By the close of the first decade of the present century—in the columns of *Abhyudaya* for example—the term begins to be used more often (although still far less than the older term *Jati*). But almost all of these usages of *rashtra* can be glossed—without any significant loss of meaning—by the term *jati*. A concept of *rashtra*, which approximates more closely to its meaning in contemporary terms emerges over a period of about two decades. It is only by the middle of the 1920s that the use of the term becomes rather more distinctive although it still does not completely substitute the use of *jati*-as-nation. The essential point anyway is not so much the use of the term *rashtra* as about the changing conception of the nation. I

should also clarify that the term *rashtra* is not an invention of the late19th century but a Sanskrit term of much earlier provenance.

7. Sudipta Kaviraj, 'Imaginary History', Nehru Memorial Museum and Library Occasional Papers, 2nd ser. 7 (1988) 14.

8. Cf. Partha Chatterjee, *Nationalist Thought and the Colonial World: A Derivative Discourse?* (London: Zed, 1986) Ch. 3 and *passim*; also Chatterjee, *Nation and Its Fragments: Colonial and Post-Colonial Histories* (1993; Delhi: Oxford UP, 1995) and Sudipta Kaviraj, 'The Imaginary Institution of India', *Subaltern Studies*, ed. Partha Chatterjee, et al., Vol. 7 (Delhi: Oxford UP, 1993). It hardly needs pointing out that the three 'nations' differ very widely in their referentiality. Indeed they are mutually contradictory.

9. See, for instance, Gyanendra Pandey, *The Construction of Communalism in Colonial North India* (1990; Delhi: Oxford UP, 1992) 209-10.

10. This was not formally inconsistent with the etymology of the term, one of the original meanings of the term being simply that of a logical class. See Ranajit Guha, *Dominance Without Hegemony: History and Power in Colonial India* (Cambridge, MA: Harvard UP, 1997). My concern, however, is not with the entire exhaustive range of meanings associated with the term *jati* but only with its usage as a category of social and political classification.

11. The *locus classicus* for this view is Kaviraj, 'Imaginary History'. Kaviraj's view has been more or less uncritically reproduced by a number of historians. See for instance Pandey, *Construction*, Arjun Appadurai, 'Number in the Colonial Imagination', *Orientalism and the Postcolonial Predicament*, ed. P. V. der Veer and C. Brackenridge (Princeton: Princeton UP, 1993), Chatterjee, *Nation*, and, more recently, Inderjit Grewal, *Home and Harem* (1996). Yet while the logical merit of Kaviraj's argument is undeniable—given that the census is a relatively modern instrument of governance, enumerated communities could not possibly have existed earlier—the overall conclusion that he derives from this is certainly more defeasible. His argument that the enumeration of communities was *conceptually* central to the emergence of a nationalist imagination remains open to question as well. See below.

12. Chatterjee, *Nation* 221-22.

13. Regardless of the literary elegance of Chatterjee's formulation, there are two serious problems he appears to gloss over: one logical, the other substantive. The logical difficulty is that, on the one hand, Chatterjee holds that the pre-modern individual community was not a matter of *interested* choice. In other words, communities were non-contractual or involuntary in nature. On the other, he also appears to claim that individuals could invoke (presumably with some element of autonomy or freedom) a variety of identities in different contexts. The substantive historical problem which follows is that this logical contradiction must have led, at least on some occasions, to a conflict between these various pre-modern identities. As an illustration, consider the choices that were available to a pre-modern individual who happened to, let's say, fall in love with someone who did not belong to his or her *jati*. Could it be plausibly argued that the individual could, in such an instance, disregard the primacy of his or her *jati* affiliation? Not just that, but

also evade the possible sanctions of both her own *jati* and the wider community? In short, it seems to me that the idea of multiple identities, however fluid, remains inherently conflictual. This is not to deny that some modern identities—particularly nationalist ones—are more exhaustive in their claim on an individual's identity and have caused more harm and spilt more blood than was ever possible in earlier times.

14. Laxmi Dutt Tripathi, 'The *Jatiya Bhasha* of Bharatvarsha', *Hindi Pradip* Feb. 1886 (emphasis added). I will consider the non-methodological implications of this passage in a later section of this paper.

15. An example that might illustrate Koselleck's point is provided by the modern concept of state which, according to him, combines a 'variety of objects' such as 'domination, bourgeoisie, legislation, jurisdiction, administration, taxation, and army, to invoke only present-day terms' in order that it emerges as a substantive concept (Koselleck, *Futures Past* 83-84).

16. The Indian National Congress, for instance, was referred to as *Jatiya Sabha* or *Mahasabha*. The appellation 'Indian' was, almost as a rule, left untranslated. It is a safe bet that barring historians of the 19th century, few users of the Hindi language today would be able to read the phrase as a rendering of the original Indian national congress. For *jatiya mahasabha* literally translates as the 'great council of *jati*s'.

17. It would be possible to make a case that my interpretation of the Hindi publicists' vocabulary is insensitive to the changing context in which it is being used. Surely an instance such as the above is a clear case of a linguistic innovation being made to signify a conceptual change. The problem, however, is that the use of the term is also implicated in its older usages which are also invoked by the Hindi publicists. It would be difficult to count the number of instances where the term *prajah* is glossed, both self-consciously and otherwise, in its older, almost literal, meaning to make political arguments. In other words, although the change of context does impart the term with new shades of meaning, the continued use of the older term also operates back on its linguistic context to influence and modify it.

18. Not unexpectedly, with the rise of the term *janata*, the term *prajah* has fallen into disuse. The anachronism of using a term such as *prajah* with its connotations of subjecthood to a king can longer be maintained. Although *prajah* does survive partially in the locution *prajatantra*, meaning 'democracy', this indicates a significant mutation of its original meaning.

19. Richard Koselleck, 'Linguistic Change and the History of Events', *Journal of Modern History* 61 (1989): 657-59. In the specific historical context of the political debates on the question of democratisation in Europe in three different languages—French, German and English—Koselleck makes the point that the conceptual vocabularies available in each of the three languages determined the distinctive trajectories that the debates followed. The reason for this was that 'the arsenal of terms utilised within any synchronously employed language contained givens that were diachronically stratified in different ways and that served both to develop and limit the stock of arguments. The terms employed had a diachronic thrust that could not be fully or freely controlled by the speakers' (657).

20. Soon after the publication of the book Hunter was appointed the Director-General of Census operations in India. The object of the book was to examine the question of the loyalty of the Indian Muslims in the aftermath of the 1857 rebellion. The subtitle to the book asked: 'Are They Bound in Conscience to Rebel Against the Queen?' Cf. David Lelyveld, *Aligarh's First Generation: Muslim Solidarity in British India* (Princeton: Princeton UP, 1978) 14-15. Historian Gyan Pandey makes the point that right up to the last decade of the 19th century, before 'nationalism had emerged as the discourse of the age and strong nationalist stirrings against colonialism were beginning to be felt in India', terms such as *race, nation, class*, etc. were used quite indiscriminately to describe very diverse groups of people. Unfortunately, though, he seems to ignore the moral contained in these cautionary remarks in the latter part of the book. In reading the discourse of late-19th-century publicists, he seems to erase this fluidity to emphasise how 'the language of nationhood was the common language of the times' (Pandey, *Construction* 1-2 and 209-10).

21. James Vernon, 'Notes towards an Introduction', *Rethinking the Constitution*, ed. James Vernon (Oxford UP, 1995) 9 and *passim*.

22. The term *unnati* has been translated by historians, almost as a rule, as 'progress'. The problem is that it is far from certain whether 19th-century Hindi publicists were fully sensitive to—not to speak of their acceptance of—the teleological, post-Enlightenment assumptions about the meaning and purpose of history which underpinned the modern liberal notion(s) of progress. Consider, for example, the following aphorism by Harishchandra, from 1884: 'sab unnatiyon ka mul dharma hai' ('the root of all *unnati* [plural] is religion') (Bharatendu Harishchandra, *Bharatendu Samagra*, ed. Hemant Sharma [Varanasi: Pracharak Granthavali Pariyojana, 1987] 1011). This is repeated in almost identical terms by others in the 19th century. See, for example, *Bharat Jivan* (1884-94, 1902-03), *Brahman* (1883-90) and *Chaturvedi Patrika* (1895-99). However one tries to make sense of this, the notion of *unnati* that it invoked cannot be semantically or conceptually reconciled with the idea of progress—neither in its theory nor certainly in its practice.

23. The use of the phrase 'strategic application' should not taken to imply that it necessarily involved conscious calculation on the part of the of Hindi publicists. On the contrary, it was precisely because the discourses on *jatiya unnati* remained insufficiently self-reflective that it could carry such a wide range of meanings.

24. The reform of religious, ritual and gender practices was a central preoccupation of a whole host of caste journals that were published in the late 19th century. Among those that were published in Hindi, see for example, *Kshatriya Patrika* (Bankipur, 1881-90), *Chaturvedi Patrika* (Agra, 1895-99), *Pandit Patrika* (Banara, 1899-1900) and *Dwija Patrika* (Patna, 1889-92). In addition, there were a large number of pamphlets dealing with a similar set of issues. The entire body of this literature is replete with discourses on *jatiya unnati* in the specific context of particular caste groups. What is remarkable is the isomorphism which exists between these discourses of *jatiya unnati* and those others (in journals that are ostensibly not caste-based, such as *Anand*

Kadambini, Harishchandra Chandrika, Brahmin, Hindi Pradip, etc.) which spoke of *jatiya unnati* in much wider terms, referring not specifically to castes but to a larger Hindu community, occasionally even the non-Hindu communities. Very often, unless one is aware beforehand of the title of the journal in question, it is impossible to tell whether a particular discourse on *jatiya unnati* is addressed to a specific caste group or to much larger community.

25. The term *Hindu* here primarily (but not always) refers to upper-caste Hindus or 'Aryans' as north Indian Hindi publicists often liked to call themselves. I will discuss this point in greater detail below.

26. A detailed account of the movement and its role in the construction of a Hindu identity in north India is available in Christopher King, *One Language, Two Scripts: The Hindi Movement in Nineteenth-Century North India* (Delhi: Oxford UP, 1994). Earlier works include J. Lutt, *Hindu Nationalismus in Uttar Prades 1867-1900* (Stuttgart: Klett, 1970) and Paul Brass, *Language, Religion and Politics in North India* (Cambridge: Cambridge UP, 1974).

27. The cow-protection movement has received extensive historical attention. Historians have studied in great depth the social history of the movement, its organisational structure and geographical reach, the extent of its mobilisation of a Hindu community, the pattern of violence that it generated, and so on. See, for instance, Anand Yang, 'Sacred Symbol and Sacred Space in Rural India', *Comparative Studies in Society and History* 22.4 (1980); S. Freitag, 'Sacred Symbol as Mobilising Ideology: The North Indian Search for a "Hindu" Community', *Comparative Studies in Society and History* 22.4 (1980); Peter G. Robb, 'The Challenge of Gau Mata: British Policy and Religious Change in India', *Modern Asian Studies* 20.2 (1986); Gyanendra Pandey, 'Rallying Round the Cow: Sectarian Strife in the Bhojpuri Region, c. 1888-1917', *Subaltern Studies*, vol. 2, ed. R. Guha (Delhi: Oxford UP, 1983); and Pandey, *Construction.* Earlier studies include Lutt, *Hindu Nationalismus*, Chris Bayly, *Local Roots of Indian Politics: Allahabad 1880-1920* (Oxford: Clarendon, 1975) and Brass, *Language.*

28. Even caste journals, primarily concerned with social and religious reforms within particular caste groups, would occasionally focus on the issue of the promotion of Hindi language. See, for example, *Kshatriya Patrika.*

29. In contemporary Hindi, *desh* is usually meant to refer to a politically independent country as opposed to any of its provinces (*pradesh*). In the late 19th century, the boundaries of a *desh* seemed far from certain. It could refer to a cultural or geographical region, an administrative province, or even a city; and occasionally the whole country—*Bharat desh.* Conversely, the term *videshi*, which is now used for a non-Indian or foreigner, could be applied to an outsider to a city, a province, a particular region and so on.

30. *Bharat Jivan* 29 July 1889 and 16 June 1890. This sentiment was expressed so widely in the writings of Hindi publicists that it is unnecessary to document it exhaustively. Harishchandra's epigram of 1877: 'nij bhasha unnati ahai sab unnati ko mul'—'the *unnati* of one's own language is the root of all *unnati*'—is an early example. (Bharatendu Harischandra, 'Hindi ki unnati par Vyakhan', reproduced in the first four issues of *Hindi Pradip*, Sept.-Dec. 1877.)

31. The letter was written by one Gopal Ram, *Bharat Jivan* 5 Oct. 1889.

32. See, for instance, the testimony in 1882 of Harishchandra before the Hunter Commission, which was set up to decide the question of the language of instruction in schools administered by the colonial authorities. As Harishchandra admitted: 'It is rather difficult to answer the question, what is our vernacular language? In India it is a saying—nay, an established fact— that language varies every *yojana* (eight miles). In the North Western Province alone there are several dialects ... The vernacular of this province ... varies according to the caste, birthplace and attainments of the speaker' (Harishchandra, *Bharatendu Samagra* 1055-6). In a report written in 1876, J. C. Nesterfield, Director of Public Instruction, in Oudh, aptly remarked of the Sanskritised Hindi that was being propagated by Hindi publicists as 'a language, no one speaks, and which no one, unless he has been specially educated, can interpret' (quoted in King 103).
33. . 'What is Our Language', *Hindi Pradip* June 1882.
34. Pratap Narain Mishra, 'Yeh Samay Vyarath Batoan ka nahin Hei' ['This is no time for useless chatter'], *Brahmin* May 1891.
35. Harischandra, 'Hindi ki Unnati Par Vyakhan'.
36. Mishra, 'Yeh Samay Vyarath Batoan ka nahin Hei'. This is no rhetorical flourish. Hindi publicists occasionally produced analogies from the animal world to emphasise that *jatiyata* was an existential condition of life itself, in all its forms. Consider, for example, the following: 'Remember! ... even birds and animals do not let go of their sense of community. However hard you may try to teach a parrot your own tongue, when it comes to communicating amongst its own and sharing its joys and sorrows, it will speak its own language. You may paint a crow a million times, but it will soon acquire its original black colour. However hungry a lion may be it will not touch the hundred different kinds of vegetation that are offered to it nor will a deer a thousand different kinds of meats. But we are so devoid of any sense of ownness (*nijatva*) that we are totally indifferent to anything that is our own ... that is the reason why while every other *jati* is racing along towards *unnati*, our wealth, strength, pride is even now depleting every moment ... God forbid! If this state persists even for a hundred years, it would not be surprising if terms such as *Hindu*, *Hindustani* and *Hindi*, etc., will become mere words.'
37. Court-poet Chand Bardai's *Prithvi-Raya-Raso*, written during the reign of the Rajput king Prithviraj in the 12th century, was widely regarded by publicists as the first extant work in the Hindi language. See Vasudha Dalmia, *The Nationalization of Hindu Traditions: Bharatendu Harischandra and Nineteenth-Century Banaras* (Delhi: Oxford UP, 1995).
38. King gives an extensive account of the kind of moral-aesthetic qualities that Hindi publicists tended to associate with Hindi and Urdu respectively (184). The former was supposed to embody the virtues, among others, of being 'indigenous, pure [and linked to] a golden past'. Urdu, on the other hand, 'was foreign, impure [and indicative of] a decadent present'.
39. Balkrishna Bhatt, 'Jatiyata ke gun', *Hindi Pradip* Feb. 1897. Lest this should give the impression that this discourse of *jatiyata* had acquired a seamless self-certainty, let's just remind ourselves that the self-same Mishra who produced

the slogan 'Hindi, Hindu, Hindustan' in the year 1890 also said the following in the previous year: '[T]he knowledgeable believe in the principle that each *jati* is known by its language, dress (outward appearance), food and *dharma*. Accordingly, it is imperative for man to protect these four elements. To look to others in these matters, to hope that they will help, or to be plagued by uncertainty [literally, *dar* or fear] or (self-)doubt, all these are destructive of the essence of one's community. There is no country on ... earth where each of its constituent groups (*samudaya*) does not maintain its own style in these four respects. Not to speak of Europe, America, etc., where God has been kind in every way. In our country, the Bengalis, the Madrasis, the Gujaratis, the Marwaris, each [community] has complete attachment (*mamatav*) to its own language, dress, food, etc. Wherever they go, whatever state they find themselves in, they do not leave behind their sense of ownness (*apnapan*). But [one feels] sad for our Hindu-slaves of NWP since in their case nothing is as it should be. Their wax-noses are malleable in every respect. Because of these attributes, there is neither peace for them at home nor respect outside' (*Brahman* 15 Oct. 1889). This formula about the essential elements of *jatiya* identity is repeated in 1892 when Mishra speaks of *jatiyata* as being constituted by a common 'bhasha, bhojan, bhes, bhav [emotions] and bhratatva [brotherly feeling]' (*Brahman* 9.5 [1892] and *passim*). Similar examples can be cited from later writings of Bhatt as well.

40. I will consider the case of Muslims in a separate section. As for conflicts among Hindus in the specific context of the *Devnagari* movement, the 'kayasths and kashmiris', for instance, were repeatedly condemned for their continued use of Urdu. On several occasions they would be disparagingly referred to as 'ardh-Muslim' (half-Muslims). See, e.g., *Hindi Pradip* June 1882. The tone of condemnation may have varied from one occasion to another, but there was no questioning the moral righteousness of the cause. Being Hindus, Kayasths and Kashmiri could not turn their back on their very own mother-tongue. The Kayasths, in particular, were a favourite target of Hindi publicists' wrath as they were believed to place their own selfish material interests above those of the community. Kayasths enjoyed a large share in government jobs because of their knowledge of Urdu and Persian. Cf. *Bharat Jivan* 20 Oct.1884. The fact that a number of Kayastha journals were published in Urdu was the icing on the cake. On one occasion, *Bharat Jivan* asked the Kayasths if 'you know of any Musalman who has got marriage invitations printed in Hindi or Sanskrit' and went on to plead that at least in such sacred matters as marriage they should desist from adopting Islamic practices (17 May 1886).

41. William E. Connolly, *Identity/Difference: Democratic Negotiations of Political Paradox* (Ithaca, NY: Cornell UP, 1991) 64.

42. The way in which Hindi publicists resolved what Partha Chatterjee has called the 'women's question' is not my concern here. The question I consider here is which communities or *jatis* were included in the *jatiya* identity conceived by Hindi publicists. The women's question plainly is not primarily about *whether* they were included but about *how* they were included.

43. The argument is first made, rather fleetingly in a footnote, in Pandey, *Construction*; this is followed by Sudhir Chandra, who elevates it to the main body of his text and makes considerable rhetorical use of it (*The Oppressive Present: Literature and Social Consciousness in Colonial India* [Delhi: Oxford UP, 1992]). But the credit for the most recent and also the most elaborate of such attempts must belong to Dalmia (32-37). Her thesis, argued none-too-clearly over half-a-dozen pages, is basically that the term *Hindu* historically combined three different but overlapping usages. In the first usage, which she calls 'pre-colonial', Hindus referred to all the inhabitants of India. In the second, it referred to a religious denomination of 'closely inter-related faiths'. And finally the term also had a nationalist usage, referring, in other words, to the Indian nation. Her claim is that these diverse meanings of the term— which she describes as 'territorial', 'religious' and 'nationalist'—were often simultaneously invoked in the late 19th century by Hindi publicists. I consider the validity of this claim in the following paragraphs.

44. The only other bit of evidence that has been provided is a lecture that the Muslim leader Syed Ahmed delivered in Lahore in 1884, in which he is said to have used the term *Hindu* for the 'inhabitants of Hindustan' (Pandey, *Construction* 216). Dalmia bases her claim about the pre-colonial meaning of the term *Hindu* principally on Mukherjee, who treats of the 'geopolitical' connotations of the term in the middle ages. The crucial question that she fails to raise, much less answer, is whether this pre-colonial meaning of the term continued to be invoked well into colonial times. She simply assumes it is.

45. The lecture was titled 'Bharatvarsha ki unnati kaise ho sakti hei' ('How can India Improve?'). Neglected by his contemporaries and by future historians for many generations, this lecture has enjoyed a spate of attention in recent times, acquiring in the process the status of a *locus classicus*. Part of the appeal of this lecture lies in its condensed brevity: synoptic in nature, vast in scope. Historians have usually read it as a representative early statement of 19th-century Hindi nationalist consciousness.

46. Harischandra, *Bharatendu Samagra* 1013.

47. It must be remembered that this was an oral lecture, later committed to writing. The change of grammatical mood from one sentence to another is a far safer indication of where one line of argument ends and another begins than its written form.

48. Chandra 125. It should be reiterated that one half of this supposed 'semantic circle' is constructed on the basis of the single passage from Harishchandra that I quoted earlier. There were no two ways along which the same person could move. Not surprisingly, Chandra is forced to conclude: 'Thus, despite his well-intentioned expansion of the term Hindu, Harishchandra continued to think of Indians as Hindus, to the exclusion of Muslims.' It is not difficult to see why, despite the lack of any credible evidence, secular historians have felt compelled to suggest an interpretation of this kind. It does seem positively embarrassing, if not scandalous, that the discourse of 19th-century Hindi publicists should be so exclusivist. That their cultural definition of *jatiyata* should begin and end with the Hindus. This exclusivism is rendered

even less agreeable in the light of the fact that this is not just a matter of academic interest or historical curiosity. A long-standing variant on that exclusivism of 19th-century discourse continues to exist in a virulent form in contemporary Indian politics. Faced with the difficult choice of how their history might feed into present-day political discourse, therefore, secular historians have chosen what seems to me to be the easier way of denial. Indeed the whole of the Ballia lecture of Harishchandra's has become so important lately partly because it can pass off as a more tolerant form of Hindu *jatiyata*.

49. The italicised terms appear in English in the original. So does the title of the editorial, 'Natives and Indians'. There is no small irony in the fact that a term such as *native* or *native of India* could not easily be glossed in Hindi. Nor could the term *Indian* in the sense of nationality ('Natives and Indians', *Bharat Jiwan* 9 Sept. 1889).

50. The contemptuous tone which *Bharat Jiwan* adopted vis-à-vis the 'people of Africa and countless islands of the Pacific Ocean' was hardly uncommon among the Hindi publicists of the 19th century. (Indeed, it would not be erroneous to suggest that something of this attitude exists among a section of the Indian middle classes even to this day.) At one level, it was more or less an extension of the same contempt with which Hindi publicists would often speak about the lower-castes and other socially oppressed groups.

51. For a useful summary of the Aryan theory of race—developed by German comparative philologists in the 1840s and 1850s, notably Max Mueller, and its application in the Indian context, see Joan Leopold, 'The Aryan Theory of Race', *Indian Economic and Social History Review* 7.2 (1970), and 'British Applications of the Aryan Theory of Race to India, 1850-1879', *English Historical Review* 89 (1974).

52. Pratap Narain Mishra, 'Apnapan' (1886).

53. Laxmi Narain Vyas, 'An Appeal by Prayag Hindu Samaj', *Hindi Pradip* Nov. 1882. Emphasis mine.

54. Bernard Cohn, 'Census, Social Structure and Objectification', *'An Anthropologist among the Historians' and Other Essays* (1968; Delhi Oxford UP, 1987) is the classic study of the development of the institution of census in colonial India. As Cohn points out, although the first country-wide census was carried out in 1871-72, it was replete with 'such imperfections' that not 'much reliance was put in the census in the time'. See also N. G. Barrier, *The Census in British India: New Perspectives* (Delhi: Manohar, 1981). Census 'data' acquired importance in the eyes of Hindi publicists only by the mid-1880s.

55. Quoted in K. W. Jones, 'Religious Identity and the Indian Census', *The Census in British India*, ed. Barrier, 92.

56. S. and L. Rudolph, *In Pursuit of Laxmi* (Chicago: U of Chicago P, 1987) 37.

57. The term *samaj* in its nineteenth-century usage referred not to society but to different forms of communities—*brahmin samaj, kayastha samaj, Hindu samaj* but not *Bharatiya samaj*—although it has frequently been rendered as such. Occasionally, there appears the term *sabhya samaj* but this seems to imply a civilised community, as opposed to the *sarva sadharan* or common people, rather than civil society. Indeed, there is still no linguistic or conceptual

equivalent for the term 'civil society' in the Hindi language right down to the present day.

58. One of the few instances where the question of the lower-caste Hindus is acknowledged, however briefly, though the untouchables remain unnamed, is the following passage in Harishchandra's lecture 'How can India Improve?': 'Vaishnavas, Shakta and other groups and sects should end their mutual bickering. This is not the time for such quarrels. Hindus, Jains, Mussalmans must all get together. Respect everyone, whether of high caste or low, and treat people according to their abilities. Do not look down upon and demoralise people of low caste. Everyone must unite' (Trans. Pandey, *Construction of Communalism* 276). Apart from expressing a pious wish for unity, Harishchandra gives no clue as to how the mutual antagonisms between the various castes within Hinduism might be overcome.

59. K. W. Jones provides an acute analysis of this process in the context particularly of Punjab. For instance, the prominent nationalist leader of Punjab, Lala Lajpat Rai remarked in 1915 that the so-called 'Gait circular' of 1910, a circular in which the commissioner of census had suggested that the 1911 census should contain 'a separate set of tables' to list what he called 'debatable Hindus', has had 'a quite unexpected effect and galvanised the dying body of orthodox Hinduism into sympathy with its untouchable population, because that was so necessary to avert its downfall. The possibility of *losing* the untouchables has shaken the intelligent section of the Hindu community to its very depths, and were it not for long established prejudices and deep-rooted habits, the untouchableness would soon be a thing of the past' (quoted in Jones, 'Religious Identity' 93).

60. Thus Pandey: 'even as they ['Hindu nationalist intelligentsia'] argued for Hindu-Muslim unity [there was] a distinctly anti-Muslim tone in the writings of some even of the most supposedly advanced and secular sections of [them] in the last quarter of the nineteenth century' (*Construction* 218). Also Chandra: 'Even as Harishchandra, Bhatt, Radhacharan and Pratapnarayan [i.e., early Hindi littérateurs and publicists] clearly grasped the correlation between Hindu-Muslim unity and the country's destiny, they could be perfectly venomous against Muslims, cutting at the root of their own efforts' (*Oppressive Present* 119).

61. So unless one believes in the absurd suggestion that Hindus and Muslims were engaged in perennial civil war through out the nineteenth century— with a few days of truce thrown in—it is difficult to sustain this argument! It has been said that however offensive such anti-Muslim statements might seem to us, they should not be take at their face-value since 'we are likely to hear more in [them] than was heard by ... contemporaries or intended by the writer[s]' in view of our changed moral sensibilities (Chandra 136). Chandra also makes the claim that in India 'sectarian antagonism and polemics' were traditionally 'articulated in rabidly offensive language'. In support of this large thesis, he reproduces excerpts from a solitary 11th-century Sanskrit play which attacks the religious ideas of non-Vedic sects! And, finally, Chandra asserts that 'exaggeration and fantasy were characteristic features of the

popular Indian mode of perception and articulation'. Even if one were to disregard the glaring fact that Chandra's historical material comes almost wholly from 'high' literary (and literate) discourse, one cannot but be struck by the orientalist flavour of his description! It should be noted that only a couple of paragraphs earlier Chandra talks of how 'Hindu feelings against Muslims' were sometimes so *subtly* expressed that they were almost 'elusive'! (135-36).

62. Chandra seems to think so. But the point surely is this: however uncomfortable it might be for a well-meaning secular Indian historian to *accept* this as an important aspect of inter-community relations in late 19th-century north India, it does not help matters to try and make the past more palatable either by downplaying the significance of particular 'facts' or by the use of comfortable anachronistic labels—such as 'communalism' or 'communal attitude'. Particularly if the purpose of the latter is not so much to help understanding as to stand testimony to the historian's condemnation.

63. As one would expect, there are frequent 'local' disagreements about the extent of the abuse, sometimes within the utterances of the same person at different points of time, but the larger picture remains remarkably constant.

64. As befits all large historical narratives, this one too is not without its local disagreements. Thus an individual Hindi publicist could, on occasions, deny, qualify, add or subtract from one or more aspects of it. Thus while talking about the atrocities of the Muslim period, to take just one example that occasionally came up, one could commend it for the fact that—whatever its other faults—at least the wealth of the country was not being drained or 'looted' in the way in which it was by the British rulers.

65. Harishchandra, *'How can India improve?'* (1884).

66. 'Musalmanoan ke hit me' ('In the interest of Muslims') *Hindi Pradip* Nov. 1885.

67. 'Jatibhed Janit Durgati', *Hindi Pradip* May 1881.

68. 'The statement of Syed Mohammed', by 'An Arya', *Hindi Pradip* Sept. 1882.

69. 'Hamari Bhasha Kya Hai' ('What is our language?' *Hindi Pradip* June 1882.

70. See, e.g., Pratap Narain Mishra: 'Hindus and Muslims are the two arms of Mother India. Neither of them can exist without the other. They should, therefore, help each other as a matter of social duty. In this lies the welfare of both. No person can be happy by chopping the left arm with the right or the right arm with the left' (trans. in Chandra 119). *Bharat Jiwan* combines the eye-and hands metaphor: 'Without unity amongst Hindus and Musalmans, there can be no unnati in India. Unless the two groups co-operate, no remedy can be found for the general suffering ... Hindus and Musalmans are like the two hands or the two eyes of one body' ('National Congress' *Bharat Jiwan* 23 Jan. 1888).

71. Harishchandra, 'How can India be Reformed', *Bharatendu Samagra* 1013.

72. Chandra, for all his ingenuous arguments about composite nationhood, has to acknowledge that *'normally*, it was with reference to specific issues that demanded unity ... that a larger conception of national unity was explicitly articulated' (126). What he fails to remark on is that these specific issues demanding unity are primarily political in nature.

73. The general difficulty of translating *dharma* as religion should be noted—although in this instance it more or less captures the meaning.
74. 'National Congress', *Bharat Jiwan* 23 Jan. 1888.
75. 'Jatiya Mahasabha' *Bharat Jiwan* 7 May 1988. Emphasis added. The terms *National* and *Congress* appear in English in the original.
76. *Bharat Jiwan* and others were echoing here what was repeated every year at the formal annual sessions of the Indian National Congress right up to the end of the century and beyond. Cultural questions first began to occupy the Congress well into the present century.
77. 'Mussalmanoan ke hit me' *Hindi Pradip* Nov. 1885.
78. See, e.g., Chandra and Dalmia.
79. Pandey, *Construction* 210.
80. Pandey, *Construction* 260.
81. Other than conceptual reasons, the most important change that takes place in the 1920s and which, in a way, necessitates the emergence of the communalism-nationalism dichotomy is the emergence of nationalism as a mass *political* movement, on a country-wide scale, rather than a sporadic élite activity. In other words, as the domain of politics begins to displace the domain of culture (which had hitherto been the primary focus of nationalist discourse). It is now the imperative of politics and political activity, rather than culture, that shapes the newly emerging contours of a secular Indian nation. This change obviously does not take place overnight. It happens over a period of almost two decades, starting from the so-called constitutional (Morley-Minto) reforms which take place in 1909 and institutionalise separate electorates for the Muslims—and thus pose the first of many problems for the earlier formula of cultural exclusion, political inclusion.
82. Gandhi was possibly the only major Indian leader who ever questioned these fundamental premises. See Chatterjee, *Nationalist Thought*.

Performing Writing at the Crossroads of Languages

Caroline Bergvall

In this essay I will argue, mainly through the work of three writers, that the development of what one could call plurilingual writing—writing that takes place across and between languages—highlights the impact which varying forms of plurilingualism (including second- or third-language writing) can have on our understanding of socio-linguistic frames and the performativity of cultural identities. I will try to show how, by critiquing the binary enclosure (Same pitted against Other) of monolingual identity (paired as it unfailingly is with national identity), plurilingual writing can be seen to be setting up the conditions through which to operate against the grain of conventionalised notions of translatability and intelligibility.

Indeed, as we shall see, these textual activations of different linguistic environments do not feed into the humanist universalism and its assumptions of transparent translatability which the banners of 'global culture' and 'multiculturalism' have come to signify. Rather, they are used to articulate and revalorise sites of untranslatability. As Nikos Papastergiadis usefully suggests, 'interaction between two cultures proceeds with the illusion of transferable forms and transparent knowledge but leads increasingly into resistant, opaque and dissonant exchanges'.[1] As such, issues of displacement, dislocation and plurilingualism become here positively envisaged as an investigation of the particularities of cultural localisation and linguistic cross-fertilisation. Sometimes subterraneanly, sometimes overtly, it is of course the question of origins, the myth of origins, as much as that of the Eternal Return (or homecoming) which this work critiques. Using as my main

Translating Nations, ed. Prem Poddar, *The Dolphin* 30, pp. 248-67.
© 1999 by Aarhus University Press, Denmark.
ISBN 87 7288 381 2; ISSN 0106 4487.

examples a piece by Joan Retallack, Rosmarie Waldrop's *Key to the Language of America* and the Korean-American writer and artist Theresa Hak Kyung Cha's *Dictee*, it is by analysing some of the textual forms their investigations take that I will be making my points.

Unmastery

Charles Bernstein has argued in relation to Gertrude Stein that 'unmastering language is not a position of inadequacy; on the contrary, mastery requires repression and is the mark of an almost unrecoverable lack'.[2] A similar point is made by Blanchot in his discussion of Walter Benjamin's influential 'Task of the Translator' when he states that '[the translator] is always in more difficulty as he [sic] translates with the language to which he belongs than at a loss with the one he doesn't possess'.[3]

In both quotations, what seems to be at stake is a reevaluation of the notion of the inherent exile, which, following Mallarmé and a proto-Modernist Messianism, a writer would be facing in relation to their own language, and which writing, or 'le vers', would be called upon to transcend.[4] Mallarmé here famously pits what he considers to be the incompleteness, the imperfection of languages and of language ('le défaut des langues') against the motivated aspect of the poetic line. In sharp contradistinction to this over-valorisation of a transcendentalist poetic, both Blanchot and Bernstein suggest that it is by pulling out of their own linguistic community or by exercising a pulling out from conventionalised syntax, that the writer or the translator ground themselves in (rather than beyond) language and, more significantly, as language. Not by way of sublimating the language (*langue*) into the perfected *parole* of writing. But rather, by developing, through a sense of 'unmastery', and that of a language not 'possessed', writerly strategies which forward a position of linguistic and cultural displacement. Displacement is here envisaged, not as exile, but as the very condition for a positive understanding of relocation across and against the unificatory principles of national language and national culture. Paradoxically, this also frees the writing up from the ideated constraints which the utopian longing for the one unalterable Language, hidden behind the imperfections of all languages, irremediably sets into place. It is as such telling that the nostalgic view of language as Babelian loss has historically frequently guaranteed the deployment of exclusionary and nationalistic approaches to writing and hermeticism.[5]

Holes

Taking Blanchot's argument for unmastery and dis-possession one step further, Deleuze talks of this 'unmastery' as an act of stuttering. One which enables the manifestation of the inherent pluri-lingualism contained within any live language and one which seeks to inscribe the complex vitality of 'reterritorialization': 'Il ne s'agit pas de parler une langue comme si l'on était un étranger, il s'agit d'être un étranger dans sa propre langue.'[6] For Deleuze, the point would be to write 'like a dog digging a hole' in order to find what he calls the writer's 'own point of under-development'.[7] The poetic and cultural significance of thinking about language in the Deleuzean 'minor' scale, as a pooling of culturally buried or under-developed fields, is that it seeks to establish the activity of writing as an ongoing composite which must make itself open to the particulars of space and place, while remaining forever suspicious of any kind of national literature:

Only the possibility of setting up a minor practice of major language from within allows one to define popular literature, marginal literature and so on. Only in this way can literature really become a collective machine of expression and really be able to develop its contents.[8]

Deleuze's insistence on a positive 'stuttering in one's own language' inscribes in this respect a relation to language and languages which refutes their illusory homogeneity, and valorises them, in their changing contemporaneity, as shot through by the particulars of their multifarious historicity. This also has major consequences on the way one might come to view the operations of translation and the notion of translatability.

A thing Das Ding a ling

Joan Retallack's work as a whole, and her latest pieces even more pointedly, provides a challenging reflection on the demands of translation as seen from the point of view of writerly practice. In fact, one of her latest pieces, 'Scenes of Translation', sub-titled ironically 'from the Translation', uses the translative activity as its explicit motif and motivation. The text is also, perhaps inevitably, one of Retallack's most cross-lingual so far.

'Scenes of translation'[9] presents itself as written in three languages (American, Cuban, German) which are organised across three distinct columns, headed: 'LOCAL TRAVELLING—EXCURSIONS—SIGHT-SEEING'. Hence, at entry, and with an eye on the heritage of translated literature, Retallack makes a point of assimilating the activities of the poet-translator as that of a tourist who absorbs and appropriates by snapshotting their way in and out of languages and literatures. Allusions to the writing of postcards, to being photographed, to carrying a (misleading) phrase-book, to deciphering phonetic transcriptions of some of the Cuban segments are scattered across the text and act as a reminder that no amount of factual and associative investigations into the landscape, or environment, of the text can ever piece together a full, complete, settled and settling picture of what is taking place. No package-tour to 'the woodland'. If the poet as tourist had intended to translate, to superimpose, from German to American, the work of Georg Trakl ('Trakl, I don't speak' being the very first words of the text in the left column, and excerpts of his poems being dispersed throughout the text), the setting into play, in the second line, of Cuban poet Jorge Guitart's own text entitled *Trakl, Yo No Se Aleman* immediately disturbs the dual traffic of conventional translation by introducing a third term (Spanish). Translation becomes instead explored, teased out, as an operation of dispersion, collation and assemblage through a range of visual, phonic, linguistic and trans-linguistic games. Here 'all der Fall ist/inflatable, growing' from the strains of Retallack's prosthetic reading and writing of Trakl. And if the writer is, at one point, sarcastically tempted to call up the 'untransvest' of writing and translating, unswayingly she sets up 'a sort of/unc conditional hypothermal/of accident untransflatable'.

Retallack's 'untransflatability', which one could take to mean both conflation and dispersion, points here to a network of fielded navigations between German, Spanish and English, between sonic games which extort lost familiarities out of cross-lingual rapprochements 'a thing das Ding a ling/pebbles fall-ing l'ink Kieselstein', and between sections of syllabic splittings: '...LOSS/NINOS MO URNING BECAUSE EL ECTRICK CIT YO AS PERGES NACHT AS PERITE(Y)/LOSSNINOS MOURN IN GBE CAUSEEL LECT RICK CITY O...'. Through its insisting syllabic variations, the sample above inevitably reminds that to leave blanks between words can be traced historically as a phenomenon whose aim has always been to reduce, disable ambiguities and control the dissemination of sense. It is then telling that Retallack should choose to close, rather than end, her text by opening it up to a beyond of our present literacy and translative awareness: '[the rest of this poem is (also) (too) in tatters]'.

No whole

In many ways one could see in this piece a writerly and highly problematised application of Benjamin's claim that translation should be envisaged as a process which needs to address the foreignness of languages and which inevitably needs to *take place at the site* of the language-text being translated, and not *take its place* by appropriating it into the language and culture of arrival. By turning translation into an unpacking of various sources, and allowing for these sources to be relayed to the reader without being churned into an intelligibly smooth, 'translated', ultimately ideologically obscuring, textmass, Retallack attempts to broaden that site, those sites.

Here, translation is made to function as a reflection on writing. As such no original text, but its own slow forming and interpretation of reading, leads it on. The Trakl sections act as a prompt, one motif amongst others. 'There is no unity to be recovered, no task of thinking of the origin as such, since the origin, now the anorigin, is already that on which rests the move to a synthetic unity. Any unity will be an after-effect.'[10] Or as the critic Rosie Braidotti, quoting the artist Martha Roszler, succinctly puts it in her essay on the polyglot, 'there cannot be fragments where there is no whole'.[11] Rather than talking of a prosthetic writing/reading (which implies the restitution of an original), perhaps one should therefore talk of Retallack's work as an approach to cultural and linguistic material which provides a cybernetic understanding of writing, one which constructs interpretative, located and reconstructed environments for reading.

The practice of translation as a writerly form, can, as seen above, strain readers' understanding of the relation they entertain with their own and with other linguistic cultures. By 'unmastering' the principles of translation and 'stuttering' through its utilisation of materials, such a practice problematises the viability of monolingualism and critiques the colonialist and nationalistic strands which still underlie more conventional views on translation. It also sets up a bridge between process-based procedural work (which much of Retallack's work rests on) and the issues of social and personal relocation which much cross-lingual and experimental translation work comes out of.

By contrast, Robert Kelly's homophonic rewriting of Hölderlin, 'Path Moss', pulls at the English to the point of making it 'sound' (and 'look') German, 'So sprocket though unfeared it / Mix, kneller then is far-mooded'. Homophonic translations, what the French call 'traducson', enable games of correspondence between texts and languages. But by decontextualising, or indeed evading, some of the more internal layers of the first text, they can also replicate, rather than question, issues of absorption and appropriation in translation. Kelly's comments on his text are quite revealing of this: 'Working with Holderlin's text, trying to hear it in English. As English. The point of the homoeophonic: to hear the other as own.'[12] That the sole phonic aspect of the entry-text should be made to carry the definition of it being 'other' (on what grounds?) at the exclusion of the wider semiotic systems which structure the text and its language and for the purpose of subsuming it into an 'own' (definition?) is in itself quite remarkable.

That a procedure of this kind can be applied at a formalistic level while showing a casual disregard for the kind of cultural under-pinnings such a procedure *could* unpack is furthermore nothing if not troubling. The wider issues of linguistic and literary relocation are here kept firmly within the bounds of a process-based activity which maintains, textually as well as critically, the status quo of a universalist stance: 'You are studying a text that no-one wrote.'

Make notice me

For writers like Theresa Hak Kyung Cha, Rosmary Waldrop, Anne Tardos, Guillermo Gomez Pena and others who resort to using translation procedures or multiple languages in their work, formalistic devices cannot be divorced from an awareness of issues of locatedness, paired as it is for them with experiences of immi-grancy and migrancy. Rather, they form part and parcel of the conceptualisations of their writing: what does it mean to 'be' and 'be seen to be' a foreigner. In effect, the issue here will often be that of finding a way to textually grapple with the dictates of social relocation and the making of new linguistic identities.

For cross-lingual, as well as for second or third language writers, it is the unmastering, rather than the unmastery, of language which is from the onset embedded in the textual project itself. From the onset, it cannot but articulate itself at a cultural and linguistic slant from the linguistic cultures they are writing in. This underlying 'unmastering' may in turn choose to apply itself to master, to reabsorb, to neutralise this gap, as in the case of Joseph Conrad's English.[13] It may also, as in the case of Beckett or Stein, be explored to highlight and forward rhetorics of unmastery within the second language. Forever navigating between the givens of their own cultural language and the acquired familiarities of the adopted tongue, one could ask oneself what kind of articulacies can arise from such a project and what kind of formal and ideo-logical strategies, what kind of cultural placing it does enable (and disable).

Writing out of these premises, writers cannot fully mirror themselves into, or for that matter internally divorce themselves from, the larger agencies of the language they write themselves into, one could speculate that the parallelism between the construction of identity and the coming to language is here reactivated by this move into another socio-linguistic environment. 'You have the feeling that the new language is a resurrection: new skin, new sex', writes Kristeva in her book *Strangers to Ourselves*.[14] Beckett's well-known explanation of his switching to French as 'pour faire remarquer moi' (literally and in 'estranged' French: to make notice me)[15] is in this respect telling of the potential for diverting and rethinking the performance of identity which the second language may provoke.

This cannot, of course, be separated from an acknowledgement of the silencing mechanisms which the native tongue may have established, at a personal as well as trans-personal level. In the case of Beckett, whose French textuality never fails to call into question the making and unmaking of language, as much as for Joyce, who did intralingually 'invent a new language within English' (Bernstein), it is difficult to ignore that their work would one way or another have been articulated in response to the collective exile set into motion by the British attempts at eradicating Irish culture and language. Writing oneself out of one's language while recirculating it textually could hence be seen, not as a way of mourning the language left behind, but rather as a way of unmasking the role any dominant linguistic culture plays in guaranteeing the authentication of its memory and the univocality of its identity. As we shall see, for both Theresa Hak Kyung Cha and Rosmarie Waldrop, to write in a number of languages and registers enables them to question not only the performativity of identity but also that of their relation to the performativity of history.

Simulated pasts

For the Korean-American writer Theresa Hak Kyung Cha, writing constructs its own particularised environment by problematising the lessons of history and language. More specifically, writing will seek to deconstruct her status of naturalised exile by refusing to master it as a social and writerly identity. In her book *Dictee*, the issue is one which announces 'a second coming' out of the 'simulated pasts resurrected in memoriam'.[16] The emphasis is on simulation, the artificiality of memory, the construction of the past.

The title of her cross-genre, cross-lingual book, first published in 1982 in the States, and recently reprinted, is in itself immediately indicative of her textual strategies. Indeed, the title means 'dictation' in French but it has tellingly lost its required French accent (*dictée*). Losing the conventional accent announces thus another kind of accentuation. One which acknowledges her past as it now stands, recollection only feasible if montaged in-between cultures and languages. It is by losing one accent at entry that Cha signals the multiple accents of her polyglot identity and the activities of translation it implicitly demands.

The first few pages, a prologue to the book, are a jumbled-up attempt at fixing school-days experiences in a French Catholic school. Grammar lessons, 'Complétez les phrases suivantes', coexist with English learning sections—

1. I want you to speak
2. I wanted him to speak
3. I shall want him to speak

—and religious imageries and scansions. All of which provides Cha with the opportunity to set the wider scene for the tellings of the book, 'Tell me the story / Of all these things / Beginning wherever you wish, tell even us', in the languages which make her up: 'From A Far / What nationality / or what kindred and relation / … Tertium Quid neither one thing nor the other / Tombe des nues de naturalized / what transplant to dispel upon'.[17]

The opening theme of dictation is of course also telling of the more deep-rooted cultural and historical dictations which form the main motifs and questions of Cha's book: how does one manage one's languages in relation to history, memory, identity, gender. What barbarisms assists language's and identity's foundational plots.

En suivant la vue absente

The textual work of *Dictee* consists of an amalgam of stylistic devices and of fact-finding props, such as photographic 'evidence', hand-written 'documents', official administrative letters, Western and Eastern anatomical maps, French-English translations, dual-language poems, Chinese calligraphic texts. Calling herself ironically a teller of good fortunes—'Let the one who is diseuse. Diseuse de bonne aventure. Let her call forth'[18]—it is to recover only to simultaneously destabilise the viability of the traces she draws out around her personal experiences as well as the ways in which she handles iconic female figures of recent Korean history, that she commits her exploration of cross-lingualism.

Cha's frequent use of unclaimed personal pronouns (the narratives are full of loosely attributed 'I' and mutable 'she', 'we'), embedded as they are in a number of incomplete proper-name narratives which criss-cross between the 'personal' and the 'historical', renders the material all-in-all elusive, frequently ambiguous and drawing a tenuous line between activating and creating memory. In this she seems to be problematising the tenability of taking refuge in exile-narratives for the construction of her naturalised Asian-American identity. The inscription of loss is not here integrated to the promises held by redemptive and/or confessional narratives. Indeed, this dark, harrowing book, constantly critiques and resists, rather than affirms as 'proofs', the material assembled and deployed. All are but aspects of a 'sequence, narrative, variation/on make believe'.[19]

Cha's dotted accounts of her family history against the backdrop of the violent colonisations of Korea are pitted against any temptation to add her voice to the often nostalgic and reconciliatory project of much post-colonial writing. I would argue that it is precisely because Cha cannot dissociate her narrative treatments from the impulse to manifest, rather than describe, her cross-lingualism that it makes for such uncomfortable, uncompromising read. There is nothing stable, no 'return' envisageable behind the constructions of her textualised languages: 'Conséquemment / en suivant la vue absente / which had ceased to appear / already it has been / has been / has been without ever / occurring to itself that it should remember / Sustain a view. Upon / itself.'[20]

Although there is a pull in the entire book towards 'Uttering again to re-vive. The forgotten',[21] the collaging of *Dictee's* many textual voices, and her cross-fertilisation of languages as well as cultural heritages, do not serve to reify the experience of the exile, that ultimate Other, but rather to engage in a series of profound, restless meditations on the ways in which to document 'the map of her journey', that 'extended journey, horizontal in form, in concept'—the journey of her writing and its unvarying displacements of any constitutive myth of origins.

Homi Bhabha, following in this the terminology set up by Chicano writers, defines the space such writing occupies as 'borderline': 'Borderline artists may have fragmented narratives, archives that are empty, memories that are potent yet powerless, but their experience of survival gives them a special insight into the constructed, artefactual, strategic nature of those events that are memorialised, by the powerful, as being the 'facts' of life, or the reportage of historical record.'[22] Borderline writing is here seen to mean not only a pushing at the boundaries between languages but, more precisely, a localised carving out of these boundaries into zones of activity and experientiality which empty out the assumptions on which monolingual cultures rest. As such, the borderline as zone is unstable and changeable. It is also highly specific of the particulars of each writer or writing community. It functions by making inroads into the different linguistic communities the writer is, one way or another, associated with, and demonstrates a critical and poetic withdrawal from belonging to 'either side' of borders. It invariably strains conventions of intelligibility, both linguistically and at a wider cultural frame.

The role of the reader in such an environment is immediately questioned and contextualised. Indeed, the allusive syntax and photographed material with which Cha taps into events and signs of resonance to readers familiar to Korean culture, establishes, for a reader unfamiliar with that culture, or with the experience of 'naturalisation' (such as myself), an uncomfortable rift between what it is that I know that I'm reading (hence recognizing: the form used, the languages used, the nine Greek Muses which structure the book's nine chapters, my own incomprehension when faced with Eastern calligraphy) and what it is I think I am reading (hence presume to be reading: the form used, the languages, the nine Greek Muses which structure the book's nine chapters, my own incomprehension when faced with Eastern calligraphy). The question of the reader's role in a book of this kind calls up again and again the question of cultural locatedness. That of the writer as well as that of the reader. It forces a process of slowing down which pushes up against the bounds of one's cultural intelligibilities. One which demands of readers that they take into account and as an indissociable part of reading, their own cultural and linguistic background.

Stubborn chunks

This experience of being prompted to recognize one's own cultural specificities when presented with the 'unreadable' specificities of a writer's cultural foreground is also what forms the very basis of the Mexican writer and performance artist, Guillermo Gomez-Pena. Most of his projects are written in several languages, usually a mix of American-English, inner-city slang, Mexican and Chicano idioms. Pena is also one of the first to have termed this multi-lingual approach to writing: *borderlanguage* . From the point of view of text-based performance, it constitutes one of the better-known examples of a writing strategy which uses linguistic differences to locate and problematise issues of cultural dominance, linguistic supremacy, marginalisation and the universal Other. It is the conflictual divisiness of locatable linguistic and cultural differences that his work seeks to display and play with. In the same way as for Cha, it rests not so much on the creation of one ideal reader as on the fruitful resistance to writing-in the one reader. It is, for instance, telling that during the time of his collaborations with Cuban writer Coco Fusco, they would change the leading language according to where they were performing, to the one or ones that the specific audience was most likely not to be fully or at all familiar with.[23]

To establish points, blocks of incomprehension in the audi-
ence/reader is here far from a hermetic device in the proto-
Modernist sense. Rather it is one which reclaims and repositions
the locatedness and fluctualities of languages. For if one could
superficially say that Pena's projects determine to a large extent a
pointed, locatable community of readers or audiences (the Chicano
population of New Mexico), the sheer juxtaposition and range of
idioms and languages he uses, strains even this particular reader-
ship/audience and highlights instead the unstable plurilingualism
of the multiple and multiplied subject position. Reterritorialisation
does not in this sense so much attempt to actualise an eternal
return to a mythified Mexico, does not so much essentialize the
otherness of the foreigner, or the stranger, as inscribe the validity
of linguistic *mestizaje*[24] in the constitution of contemporary
identities.

Similarly, by working out of and showing up the split language
base from which she originates, Cha locates herself precisely and
culturally at the junction between specific linguistic communities
and histories. Thus she also explicitly questions the linguistic
grounds which determine the negative construction of difference
and which displace her work and identity as other. It is by accu-
mulating linguistic locales, English-American among them, rather
than developing a textual identity which subsumes itself to
monolingual identity, that Cha seeks to articulate and reinscribe
our understanding of national language and culture. Her textuality
functions as a space of intervention which syncretises and juxtaposes linguistic systems and revels in the heterogeneity of inter-
locked cultural differences. As Rosie Braidotti summarises it,
'Writing is for the polyglot a process of undoing the illusory
stability of fixed identities, bursting open the bubble of ontological
security that comes from familiarity with one linguistic site.'[25].

The fact that writers such as Cha and Pena would not only
critique monolingualism, their nationalist and exclusionary
implications, but ultimately revel in the potentialities which the
destabilisations of heterogeneous writerly and linguistic practice
contain, is one clear sign that the very notion of socio-cultural
displacement can no longer be sustained by the parameters of exile

literature or for that matter, by the oft uncritical and unspecific valorisation of hybridity as a third, compensatory and translative term.

Jarrings, interruptions, the assumptions of incomprehension in the reader, all point to a positive re-evaluation of untranslatability against a discrepantly universalist translatability. Bhabha tellingly speaks of this as 'the stubborn chunks', the opaque, resistant detail in the traffic between cultures which signals contextual differences against a totalizing project: 'Hybrid hyphenations emphasise the incommensurable elements—the stubborn chunks—as the basis of cultural identifications.'[26] In such a context, it is untranslatability, not translatability, which favours a recognition of the particularities of personal and collective experience.

Except for

For Rosmary Waldrop, both a poet and a noted translator from both German and French, the project of her *A key to the Language of America* does not so much rest on being from the onset 'seen to be' a foreigner to America, but rather on the ways in which it is her process of reading and writing which brings home and clarifies her own condition as an immigrant to America: a 'white, educated European who did not find it difficult to get jobs'.[27] The title of her book is the same as that of the book which supports her exploration. Written by the missionary Roger Williams and published in 1634, *A Key into the Language of America* was, when it was first published, also subtitled: 'or an Help to the Language of the Natives of that Part of America called New England'. Being the first systematic and sympathetic study of a native American language, Narrangasett, and its customs, the original book took a critical view of the colonialist attitudes of the burgeoning Christian settler communities of the region and led to Williams being exiled from his community. That Waldrop should decide to use the same title as his, for her rewriting of Williams' work, is of interest in relation to the activity of superimposition this seems to imply. As if her personal experience could only but graft itself, critically and poetically, onto an American landmark piece to render itself visible: 'All in all, my book could be called an immigrant's take on the heritage and complex early history of my adopted country' she writes in her preface.

By seemingly taking over the material of this book, seemingly colonialising it with her own late-twentieth century readings, Waldrop shows for the ambiguous complexities inscribed in attempting to enter into and relate to the underlying, sometimes buried or evacuated material of her adopted country. Indeed, if she states quite clearly that 'like the first settlers, I came from Europe. I came, expecting strangeness, expecting to be disoriented, but was shocked, rather, by my lack of culture shock', she also immediately acknowledges as part of her own Eurocentric heritage, the colonialist attitude and blind spots that enabled the making of white, Christian Europeanist early America: 'Nothing seemed different from my native Germany—except for the Indian place-names.' For Waldrop then, the gesture of superimposition enables a reflection on the ways in which tracing up linguistic histories can favour a critical and personal reassessment of one's cultural givens and assumptions. Waldrop's 'except for' and 'like the first settlers' is revealing of the historical identification she first applied in order to settle in America. This is in stark contrast to the destabilised and decentred manner in which she comes to handle her material and question her own identity sites in relation to it: '*Year of parades. Celebrating exploits unsuited to my constitution. As if every move had to be named expansion, conquest, trinity, and with American intonation.*'[28]

Placing her text within Williams's overall structure, Waldrop chooses to set up a collage which encompasses Narrangasett vocabulary, passages from Williams's seventeenth-century English text and her own poetic interventions. Digging into the book in order to excavate her own experiences as a contemporary Americanised poet—'an eye devouring its native region must devote special attention to its dialect'[29]—Waldrop highlights the inevitable clashes and discontinuities which inform, at any stage of its development, the violently recuperative nature of early Americanisation. By maintaining different typestyles and lay-outs as well as a range of idioms, she highlights some of these clashes in the context of her own writing: 'Prefer the movement of planets or buffalo to European coat-men, identifiable strains to city planning even when applied to lexical items. Wetomémese. A Little House. Which women live apart in, the time of their exhaustive volume.'[30]

Her writing of reading tends towards a process of non-absorption which acts throughout as a reminder of the disparate and differential sources which form her project. By implication, it also calls up the disparate and differential sources on which any monolingual community rests but neutralises by recirculating and translating them back into itself: Deleuze's take on the social evacuation of languages' inherent plurilingualism.

Thematic of the body, 'flesh, considered a cognitive region', and issues of gender—'is called woman or wife'—are furthermore used throughout as one of Waldrop's observational vantage-points. The way she locates in Williams's text the cultural burying and reorganisation of the female gender, seems in fact to be a prime factor in informing Waldrop's linguistic reterritorialisation. By applying personal commentary to historical source material, she identifies the points of cultural closure which define her as female: 'I was stuck in a periodicity I supposedly share with Nature, but tired of making concessions to dogs after bones.'[31] Waldrop's book provides in this sense a stimulating example of the ways in which cross-lingual experience not only calls up internal sites of cultural appropriation, but also and more pressingly, extricates some of the foundational narratives which add a strain on the processing of identity and the acquisition of the second or third linguistic environment. For Waldrop, the activation of her cross-lingualism heightens, rather then minimises, problematics of gender embedded as they are in historical and linguistic structures: 'I must explain my sex / for all its stubbornness / is female / and was long haunted, diligently / by confusions of habit / and home, time and / the Western world.'[32] The critical activity of reading and the collages she develops to locate her personal experience act here as a 'borderline' process between contemporaneity and historical material, between gender and desire. The intertexual and stylistically dispersed manner in which Waldrop proposes to assimilate this borderline provides her with a means to examining linguistic relocation not only as inescapably articulated by the pervasiveness of gender performativity but also as a way of pushing against the limits of the differential signs of gender, '*I knew getting rid of prejudices would make me fall into some other puddle*'. The other puddle. This is the pervasiveness of sexuality and the questioning of sexual desire which, in her text, both denies and allows the key to her incorporated hyphenisation: 'If the dark quarries inner caves / the sexual act takes on / a sheen of purchase / the difference of invasion / and exodus obscured by labor'.[33]

It is on an opening, an open question, looking neither 'forward' nor 'backward' but somewhere along the maps of a performative present that she concludes her text.

Else-here

As I hope to have shown, the premise which could be seen to underlie and underline the cross-lingual work discussed here is that of decentring monolingualism and problematising the contemporaneity of hyphenated identities. Being situated neither 'here' nor 'there', neither in 'the past' nor in an unconditional present, but else-here, the question of contemporaneity, as addressed by these poets and many others with them, rests on the evaluation of historical and personal material from the point of view of a particularised and complex socio-spatial locatedness.

In all the pieces discussed, the writers indicate structurally the connection between the form taken by their textual material and the subjective experience of relocation and untranslatability which informs this material. Methodologies deployed are invariably brought to light as part of the text. In this one could read, not only a refusal to obscure in the reader the various tools which construct the text and the performativity of identity but more importantly, an approach to writing which demands of readers that they address their own locatedness in the reading of the work. It is then to the loosening up of the boundaries between private and public, to the opening up of personal experience as irremediably playing on and played by wider social frames, that much of this work finds its motivation.

Placed neither at a transcendental degree zero, nor at a nostalgic point of longing for one cohesive language, the dispersed textualities staged here highlight some of the implications of the pluri-lingual experience which is increasingly straining the social fabric of contemporary societies. This dynamic and pragmatic approach to textual experimentation as an open and running commentary on the tenuous monolingualism of our socio-cultural spheres strikes me as one of the more optimistic, responsive and exciting aspects of this kind of work. Indeed, and by way of conclusion, Anne Tardos's *Cat licked the Garlic* shows quite humorously how removed from the anxieties surrounding the myth of Babel, cross-lingual textuality envisages itself to be:

> Some of them restent en anglais.
> Some of them then die wenigen
> petit pois go jouer. Them then die
> vielen grossen állati nagy Imre.
> Sway this way, petit pois des bois.

> Then je partition my own (mon)
> petit cheval, c'est égal, go. Play
> Go. Go and play Noh. Playdough.
> Woa.

> This way and ainsi our ancestors
> formed ce qu'on appelle die
> Sprache.[34]

Notes

1. Nikos Papastergiadis, 'Restless Hybrids', *Third Text* 32 (1995): 18.
2. Charles Bernstein, *A Poetics* (Cambridge, MA: Harvard UP, 1992) 146-47.
3. Quoted by Peggy Kamuf in *The Ear of the Other: Otobiography, Transference, Translation*, ed. Christie McDonald (Lincoln, NE: U of Nebraska P, 1985) 155.
4. 'Seulement, sachons n'existerait pas le vers: lui, philosophiquement rémunère le défaut des langues, complètement supérieur' (Stephane Mallarmé, 'Crise de Vers', *Oeuvres Complètes*, Bibliothèque de la Pléiade [Paris: Gallimard, 1945] 364).
5. See A. Berman *L'épreuve de l'étranger* (Paris: Gallimard, 1984), Gérard Genette *Mimologics* (Lincoln, NE: U of Nebraska P, 1995), Sanford Budick and

Wolfgang Iser, ed., *The Translatability of Cultures: Figurations of the Space Between* (Stanford, CA: Stanford UP, 1996).

6. Gilles Deleuze and Claire Parnet, *Dialogues* (Paris: Flammarion, 1977; 1996) 73.
7. Gilles Deleuze and Felix Guattari, *Kafka: Toward a Minor Literature*, trans. Dana Polan (Minneapolis: U of Minnesota P, 1986) 17.
8. Deleuze and Guattari 18.
9. Sections of this work have appeared in *Arras* 2. The text in its entirety is to be published as part of Joan Retallack's *How to do Things with Words* collection for Sun and Moon. This commentary is based on a Xeroxed MS, with thanks to J. R.
10. A. Benjamin, 'Translating Origins: Psychoanalysis and Philosophy', *Rethinking Translation: Discourse, Subjectivity, Ideology*, ed. Lawrence Venuti (London: Routledge, 1992).
11. Rosie Braidotti, 'Nomads in a Transformed Europe: Figurations for an Alternative Consciousness', *Cultural Diversity in the Arts: Art, Art Policies and the Facelift of Europe*, ed. Ria Lavrijsen (Amsterdam: KIT, 1993) 44.
12. Robert Kelly '[working from Friedrich Hölderlin's 'Patmos'] Path Moss', *Chain* 4 (1997): 109-16.
13. Still, it is ironic how the thematics of novels such as *Nostromo* or *Heart of Darkness* betray Conrad's preoccupation with cultural dislocation.
14. Julia Kristeva, *Strangers to Ourselves* (New York: Harvester, 1991) 15.
15. Enoch Brater, *Why Beckett* (London: Thames and Hudson, 1989) 47.
16. Theresa Hak Kyung Cha, *Dictee* (Berkeley, CA: Third Woman, 1995) 150.
17. Cha 150.
18. Cha 123.
19. Cha 129.
20. Cha 125.
21. Cha 150. '[T]o re-vive' here plays on both the English 'revive' as a calling up of the past and the French 'revivre' to live again, to be (a)live again, as a shedding from the past. There is also a French play on the female adjective 'vive'.
22. Homi Bhabha, 'Beyond the Pale: Art in Multicultural Translation', *Cultural Diversity in the Arts: Art, Art Policies and the Facelift of Europe*, ed. Ria Lavrijsen (Amsterdam: KIT, 1993) 23.
23. For discussions between Coco Fusco and G. Gomez-Pena see Coco Fusco, *English is Broken Here: Notes on Cultural Fusion in the Americas* (New York: New P, 1995).
24. *Mestizaje* is defined by Rafael Pérez-Torres as 'the manifestation of the multiplicitous discourses from which Chicanos create a sense of identity. Mestizaje becomes a racial/radical marker of self-determination ... a cultural strategy [which relies] on the mixing and medling of cultures that defines the contemporary condition of world culture' (*Movements in Chicano Poetry: Against Myths, against Margins* [Cambridge: Cambridge UP, 1995] 210).
25. Braidotti 34.
26. Homi Bhabha, *The Location of Culture* (London: Routledge, 1994) 219.

27. Rosmary Waldrop, *A Key to the Language of America* (New York: New Directions, 1994) xix.

28. Waldrop 60.

29. Waldrop 5.

30. Waldrop 13.

31. Waldrop 54.

32. Waldrop 56.

33. Waldrop 52.

34. Anne Tardos, *Cat Licked the Garlic* (Vancouver: Tsunami, 1992) unnumbered pages.

Notes on Contributors

Meena Alexander is the author of *Nampally Road, Manhattan Music, Shock of Arrival, Faultlines* and numerous other books. She is a Professor of English at the City University of New York.

Caroline Bergvall is Director of Performance Writing, Darlington College of Arts, England. A writer and critic, her recent work includes a collaborative text performance *Eclat*, a walkman tour of domestic space in North London. Her forthcoming publications include *The Bride* and *Jets-Poupée*.

Mahesh Daga is presently at the University of Sussex completing a project on the genealogy of secularism in India.

Hans Hauge teaches at the Department of English, Aarhus University.

Lars Jensen teaches at Roskilde University and has a PhD from the University of Leeds. He is currently working on a book under the title *Reconfiguring Australian Identities.*

David Johnson is with the Open University, Milton Keynes, having previously taught at the University of Natal. He is the author of *Shakespeare and South Africa* (Clarendon Press) and co-author of *Democracy, Ethics and the Law* (Juta).

Graham MacPhee teaches English and Cultural studies at the University of Portsmouth. His forthcoming book is entitled *Afterlife of the Avant-Garde.*

Cheralyn Mealor is a postgraduate student at the Department of English, Aarhus University, writing a dissertation on the Millennium Dome.

Prem Poddar teaches Postcolonial Studies at the Department of English, Aarhus University.

Neluka Silva is a Senior Lecturer in English at the University of Colombo. Her research interests include South Asian writing, gender, nationalism and theatre. She has been involved in the Sri Lankan theatre for the last ten years.